T0334651

As the line between content producers and consumers increasingly blurs, this book takes an important step forward in bringing theory to bear on the way we proceed as communicators. The editors of this volume have brought together a varied and intrinsically interesting set of essays on topics that illuminate this new frontier, helping light the way forward while staying grounded in the wisdom of the past.

Jessalynn Strauss, *Assistant Professor, Elon University, USA*

This is an important and very timely collection. It expertly and engagingly fuses together the fields of public relations and fan studies, resulting in, not only a much-needed interjection into current scholarship, but also, an impressive and compelling read.

Lucy Bennett, *Research Assistant, Cardiff University, UK*

Today, public relations professionals and their publics are engaged in a dance of ideas that shapes and re-imagines interaction with organizations, services, products, and causes. Hutchins and Tindall's book focuses attention on the steps of this dance and shows us how the participatory space surrounding PR is fertile ground for authentic community engagement.

Jennifer Jacobs Henderson, *Chair and Professor of Communication, Trinity University, USA*

The field of public relations benefits in a number of ways from the insights within the new book *Public Relations and Participatory Culture*. Not only do the authors embrace fan studies literature, a field that has much to contribute to PR theory development, they also examine the interaction between these engaged publics and the growing importance of online communication and online communities. I strongly recommend you read this!

Sarah H. VanSlette, *Assistant Professor, Southern Illinois University Edwardsville, USA*

Public Relations and Participatory Culture

While public relations practitioners have long focused on the relationship between organizations and their stakeholders, there has never been a time when that relationship was so dominated by public participation. The new model of multiple messages originating from multiple publics at varying levels of engagement is widely acknowledged, but not widely explored in scholarly texts.

The established model of one-way communication and message control no longer exists. Social media and an increasingly participatory culture means that fans are taking a more active role in the production and co-creation of messages, communication, and meaning. These fans have significant power in the relationship dynamic between the message, the communicator, and the larger audience, yet they have not been defined using current theory and discourse. Our existing conceptions fail to identify these active and engaged publics, let alone understand virtual communities who are highly motivated to communicate with organizations and brands.

This innovative and original research collection attempts to address this deficit by exploring these interactive, engaged publics, and open up the complexities of establishing and maintaining relationships in fan-created communities.

Amber L. Hutchins is the Robert D. Fowler Endowed Chair in Communication, Kennesaw State University, USA.

Natalie T. J. Tindall is Associate Professor, Georgia State University, USA.

Routledge New Directions in Public Relations and Communication Research
Edited by Kevin Moloney

Routledge New Directions in Public Relations and Communication Research is a new forum for the publication of books of original research in PR and related types of communication. Its remit is to publish critical and challenging responses to continuities and fractures in contemporary PR thinking and practice, and its essential yet contested role in market-orientated, capitalist, liberal democracies around the world. The series reflects the multiple and inter-disciplinary forms PR takes in a post-Grunigian world; the expanding roles which it performs, and the increasing number of countries in which it is practised.

The series will examine current trends and explore new thinking on the key questions which impact upon PR and communications including:

- Is the evolution of persuasive communications in Central and Eastern Europe, China, Latin America, Japan, the Middle East and South East Asia developing new forms or following Western models?
- What has been the impact of postmodern sociologies, cultural studies and methodologies which are often critical of the traditional, conservative role of PR in capitalist political economies, and in patriarchy, gender and ethnic roles?
- What is the impact of digital social media on politics, individual privacy and PR practice? Is new technology changing the nature of content communicated, or simply reaching bigger audiences faster? Is digital PR a cause or a consequence of political and cultural change?

Books in this series will be of interest to academics and researchers involved in these expanding fields of study, as well as students undertaking advanced studies in this area.

Public Relations and Nation Building
Influencing Israel
Margalit Toledano and David McKie

Gender and Public Relations
Critical Perspectives on Voice, Image and Identity
Edited by Christine Daymon and Kristin Demetrious

Pathways to Public Relations
Histories of Practice and Profession
Edited by Burton Saint John III, Margot Opdycke Lamme and Jacquie L'Etang

Public Relations and Participatory Culture

Fandom, social media and community engagement

Edited by

Amber L. Hutchins and Natalie T. J. Tindall

LONDON AND NEW YORK

First published 2016
by Routledge

2 Park Square, Milton Park, Abingdon, Oxfordshire OX14 4RN
52 Vanderbilt Avenue, New York, NY 10017

Routledge is an imprint of the Taylor & Francis Group, an informa business

First issued in paperback 2019

British Library Cataloguing in Publication Data
A catalogue record for this book is available from the British Library

Library of Congress Cataloging in Publication Data
Public relations and participatory culture : fandom, social media and
community engagement / edited by Natalie T.J. Tindall and
Amber Hutchins.
    pages cm. – (Routledge new directions in public relations and
communication research)
    Includes bibliographical references and index.
    1. Public relations. 2. Participation. 3. Social media. 4. Political
participation. I. Tindall, Natalie T. J., 1978- editor. II. Hutchins, Amber,
editor.
    HD59.P7844 2016
    659.2–dc23
                    2015031292

ISBN: 978-1-138-78772-8 (hbk)
ISBN: 978-0-367-35901-0 (pbk)

Typeset in Bembo
by Taylor & Francis Books

Amber L. Hutchins: Dedicated to Justin, who is my sounding board and my comedic relief.

Natalie T. J. Tindall: This book is dedicated to my Words with Friends partner and listening post (my mother), my wartime consigliere (my father), and my James Bond and Trek-loving compatriot (my brother).

Contents

PART III
Brand perspectives: applying theories of public relations and fandom in corporate, government, and nonprofit spaces

List of illustrations

Figures

Tables

List of contributors

Melanie Bourdaa is associate professor at the University of Bordeaux in Communication and Information Sciences. She analyzes the new television environment and cultural convergence. She particularly studies American TV series, the phenomenon of fandom in the digital age, and production's strategies (i.e. Transmedia Storytelling). She also teaches courses on Audience and Programming, Television and Cultures, and Transmedia Storytelling.

Laura F. Bright (Ph.D., University of Texas at Austin) is an assistant professor in the School of Strategic Communication at TCU and co-directs TCU's Certified Public Communicator Program. Her research interests include media personalization, big data, and social media, all examined through the lens of advertising. Laura teaches channel planning, research, and new media.

Kelli S. Burns (Ph.D., University of Florida) is an associate professor in the School of Mass Communications at the University of South Florida. Burns received a master's degree in mass communication from Middle Tennessee State University and a bachelor's degree from Vanderbilt University.

Meta G. Carstarphen, Ph.D., APR, is a Professor at the University of Oklahoma in the Gaylord College of Journalism and Communication. Her research interests include rhetoric and writing, historiography, race/gender/class diversity, and tourism media and diversity. She teaches classes in race/gender/class and the media, public relations, and graduate rhetoric.

Bertha Chin's (Ph.D., Cardiff University) thesis explored community boundaries and construction of fan celebrities in cult television fandom. She has published extensively in internationally peer-reviewed journals and recently co-edited a special issue journal and book on crowdfunding. She is board member of the Fan Studies Network.

Patricia A. Curtin, Ph.D., is professor and Endowed Chair in Public Relations at the University of Oregon. Her research interests include critical/postmodern approaches to public relations theory, particularly as applied to marginalized publics and activism. She teaches courses in theory, methods, and globalization, and strategic communication issues.

Heidi Hatfield Edwards, Ph.D. is an associate professor, communication program chair, and associate head of the School of Arts and Communication at Florida Institute of Technology. Prior to joining Florida Tech, Edwards taught public relations at Pennsylvania State University. She has nine years professional experience in media, public relations, and marketing.

Sam Ford is Vice President of Innovation & Engagement at the digital and TV network Fusion. Previous to that, from 2008 to 2015, he worked for strategic communications and marketing firm Peppercomm, serving most recently as Director of Audience Engagement. He is also an affiliate of MIT's Program in Comparative Media Studies/Writing and teaches on Western Kentucky University's Popular Culture Studies Program. He co-authored the 2013 book *Spreadable Media*, from NYU Press, co-edited the 2011 book *The Survival of Soap Opera* from the University Press of Mississippi, and has written for *Fast Company*, *Harvard Business Review*, *The Boston Globe*, *Wall Street Journal*, and a range of other publications.

Karen Freberg (Ph.D., University of Tennessee) is an assistant professor in Strategic Communications at the University of Louisville. Freberg's research in crisis and social media has been published in several book chapters and in academic journals such as *Public Relations Review*, *Media Psychology Review*, *Journal of Contingencies and Crisis Management*, and *Health Communication*.

Romy Fröhlich is Full Professor of Communication Science and Media Research at Ludwig-Maximilians-University Munich, Germany. In research and teaching she specialized in PR & Organizational Communication, quant./qual. media content analysis & framing, gender studies). She was Visiting Scholar at Ohio State University (USA), the University of Newcastle (AU) and the University of Melbourne (AU). Currently, she is coordinator of an international cooperative EU FP7 research project on the role of media and strategic communication in violent conflicts (INFOCORE). She is member of the (Associate/Advisory/Review) Editorial Boards of *Communication, Culture & Critique, Journalism & Mass Communication Editor, Studies in Communication Sciences*, and co-edited *Women Journalists in the Western World* (Hampton).

Amber L. Hutchins (Ph.D., University of Utah) is the Robert D. Fowler Chair in Communication and the Assistant Director of Digital and New Technologies in the School of Communication and Media at Kennesaw State University. She earned a master's degree in mass communication and a bachelor's degree in journalism at The Walter Cronkite School of Journalism and Mass Communication Arizona State University. Her research interests include social media for strategic communication, fandom, and the intersection of journalism and PR ethics. She has also worked as a PR consultant.

Michelle Katchuck (M.A., M.B.A., University of Regina) is a communications and public relations practitioner whose experience spans corporate, public, and nonprofit organizations. She received her Bachelor of Arts in English and Political Science and master's degrees in English and Business Administration (MBA). Michelle teaches Public Relations and Communication at the University of Regina, Canada, and researches the use of gamification in PR and behavior change.

Amanda K. Kehrberg is a doctoral student in the Gaylord College of Journalism and Mass Communication at the University of Oklahoma. Her research focuses on technology, diversity, and public relations. She teaches classes for the University of Oklahoma and Arizona State University on new media, film, writing, and diversity in media.

Soojin Kim (Ph.D., Purdue University) is interested in the strategic management of public relations and public relations strategies. Specifically, her work so far has examined how organizations' behaviors or decisions along with other antecedents affect key publics' behaviors, and the impact of such behaviors on organizations' effectiveness. Her research interests also include how the theory and practice of PR conceptualize public relations strategy, and how the implementation of PR strategy influences organizational effectiveness. She is currently an assistant professor at Lee Kong Chian School of Business, Singapore Management University.

Arunima Krishna is a doctoral candidate at the Brian Lamb School of Communication at Purdue University. She received her M.A. degree in Public Relations from Purdue in 2013. Her areas of research include public behavior and strategic management of public relations, especially the impact that publics' communicative actions have on the development of social issues and problems. Her professional experience in marketing informs her research and drives her interest in bridging theory and practice of public relations.

Jacqueline Lambiase, Ph.D., is director of the School of Strategic Communication at TCU. She is co-director with Dr. Laura Bright of TCU's Certified Public Communicator Program. She teaches courses in writing, diversity, and communication planning, as well as conducting research on crisis communication, social media, and gendered media images.

Nicolle Lamerichs holds a Ph.D. in media studies at Maastricht University. Her doctoral thesis Productive Fandom (2014) explores intermediality and reception in fan cultures. She currently works at International Communication and Media at HU University of Applied Sciences, Utrecht. Her research focuses on participatory culture and new media, specifically the nexus between popular culture, storytelling, and play.

Cong Li (Ph.D., University of North Carolina at Chapel Hill) is an associate professor in the School of Communication at the University of Miami. He received his Ph.D. in mass communication from the University of North

Carolina at Chapel Hill. His primary research interests are centered around computer-mediated communication. He has published in a number of scholarly journals inside and outside the communication discipline.

Jiangmeng Liu is a doctoral student from the School of Communication at the University of Miami. Her research interests include corporate social media use for advertising and public relations purposes and word-of-mouth on social media. She is also interested in social media effects in terms of civic engagement, acculturation process, and psychological well-being.

Linjuan Rita Men, Ph.D., APR, is an assistant professor of public relations at the University of Florida. Her research interests include corporate communication, social media engagement, leadership communication, public relations evaluation and measurement, and organizational internal communication. She earned her Ph.D. in Communication from the University of Miami in 2012.

Michael North is a doctoral student studying communication at the University of Miami. His academic interests include advertising, journalism, and public relations along with social media, specifically Twitter. Currently, Michael is studying the practical application of social media for Fortune 500 companies from a strategic communication perspective.

Jimmy Sanderson (Ph.D, Arizona State University) is an assistant professor in the Department of Communication Studies at Clemson University where he directs the Sports Communication B.A. program. His research interests center on the intersection of social media and sport, as well as health and safety issues.

Clarissa Schöller is a Ph.D. student at the Department of Communication Studies and Media Research at Ludwig-Maximilians-University Munich, Germany. Her Ph.D. project is about Public Relation Consulting. Further research interests are organizational communication, Social Media, brand communication, and strategic communication.

Natalie T. J. Tindall (Ph.D., University of Maryland) is an associate professor in the Department of Communication at Georgia State University. Her research focuses on diversity in organizations, specifically the public relations function, and the situational theory of publics and intersectionality.

Wan-Hsiu Sunny Tsai is an associate professor in the School of Communication at the University of Miami. Her research areas include minority representations in advertising, multicultural and international advertising, and social media trends. She has investigated topics such as gay consumers' political consumption, and the global social networking phenomenon.

Justin A. Walden (Ph.D., Pennsylvania State University) is an assistant professor of public relations/organizational communication at North Dakota State University. He primarily researches employee communication, brand management, and media use routines. He wrote this book chapter as a member of the communication faculty at the College at Brockport, SUNY.

Jamie Ward (Ph.D., Bowling Green State University) is an assistant professor at Eastern Michigan University, with a specialization in public relations and storytelling for advocacy and engagement. She explores ideologies, frames, and stereotypes within popular culture in order to bring marginalized perspectives and experiences into dialogues with dominant narratives. Her work has been published in several academic journals. In addition to her work in academia, Jamie has worked over a decade in the communications field with nonprofit/advocacy-based organizations.

Richard D. Waters (Ph.D., University of Florida, 2007) is an associate professor in the School of Management at the University of San Francisco where he teaches strategic communication courses in the graduate programs in business, nonprofit, and public administration. His research interests focus on public relations theory and the use of new media in nonprofit organizations' communication efforts.

Brandi Watkins (Ph.D., University of Alabama) is an assistant professor at Virginia Tech. Her research interests include studying the use and influence of social media on relationship building efforts between an organization and its publics, in the context of sports. She teaches classes in public relations and social media.

Fan Yang is a doctoral student from the School of Communication at the University of Miami. Her research interests include corporate social media use and social media effects on individuals' psychological well-being. She is also interested in health interventions via social media.

Acknowledgement

The authors would like to thank the Routledge staff, especially the series editors, Kevin Moloney and Jacqueline Curthoys, for the opportunity to deliver this volume to a wider audience. Thank you to Sinead Walton for being eternally gracious and patient with us during the process. Our sincere appreciation goes to those who submitted proposals and to those who submitted the selected chapters. We were not sure if there was interest in this idea, and you demonstrated that many people have cogitated and researched in this area. Thank you for allowing us to see your work and for helping push this vision of participatory culture and fan studies into the public relations discipline. Without your insights and research, we would not have this book.

Part I

Foundations

1 Introduction

Amber L. Hutchins and Natalie T. J. Tindall

New media, especially social media, has changed the practice of public relations and challenged scholars to reconsider or reconceptualize what we consider "traditional" models and practices of PR. Experts believe that these changes will fundamentally redefine the purpose and practice of public relations, and that the future of public relations will become nothing like its past. The practice and scholarly study of public relations has evolved – and will continue to evolve – alongside technological advances, new techniques and communication channels, and new theoretical models of communication and persuasion.

As this new era of public relations – a *revolution*, as some are calling it – continues to take shape, scholars aim to reflect, understand, define, criticize, and ultimately enhance the practice of PR while also creating an intellectually rigorous area of academic study. We strive to create a balance between the two worlds. The most used definitions of public relations include the phrase "mutually-beneficial" and as PR scholars, many who have also served as practitioners, we aim for research and inquiry that is beneficial to both the professional and scholarly realms of PR. The most robust and useful research in this area creates a bridge between the scholarly and practical worlds of public relations.

The work included in this book provides closer examination of areas that are emerging as a result of participatory culture online, including fandom, social media, and community engagement.

Rethinking traditional models of publics

First, we must rethink current public relations models of *publics*. With the increasing importance of high-engagement publics in public relations efforts, practitioners are experiencing significant changes in their responsibilities and organizational roles, and the conception of the public in previous "traditional" models of PR are no longer valid across all campaigns. Traditional public relations models of publics, especially Grunig's Situational Theory of Publics (1984), define, categorize, and analyze the motivations and behaviors of publics.

Application and extensions of the Situational Theory of Publics have expanded our understanding of publics, but the research in this area is often aimed at managing publics and predicting behavior. Excellent research in this area can yield extensive insights into reception, process and psychology of persuasive messages, but under the traditional model of "publics," organizations often ignore individuals and groups who fall outside of the traditionally defined categories of active and latent publics (who are given the full attention of practitioners and scholars).

A significant limitation in publics research is that many studies are either designed or perceived as a way to solve a problem, that is managing conflicts or crisis. The dynamic between an organization and its publics is more likely to be seen as adversarial, and the public relations practitioner's role is limited to defusing activists and agitators. This contributes to the persistent perception of public relations as reactive rather than proactive and primarily interested in "damage control."

New publics, new responsibilities

Unlike the pre-Internet public relations environment, publics now have seemingly unlimited opportunities to become engaged with organizations, content, and each other. As part of a new set of professional responsibilities that reflect the increasing emphasis of online communication, PR practitioners are charged with creating, cultivating, and managing online brand communities, as well as the more complex task of establishing and maintaining the relationships created by active, *engaged publics.*

Examining publics that are already active and engaged is a necessary step in the new public relations world of social media. The term *engaged publics* moves us a step closer, but many researchers and practitioners are still measuring engagement via hyperlink clicks or website hits, and defining results based on business objectives like ROI. A shift in focus is necessary, away from research that continues to present a limited view of online communication as comparable to multimedia or interactivity, toward more robust analysis and models of online behavior by an individual or community.

Building, maintaining, and enhancing two-way communication and relationships between organizations and publics has always been an important function of public relations, but the importance of *community management* has expanded on a global scale, as evidenced by the number of international practitioners and entrepreneurs who now list community management as a job title or specialization, and the popularity of the topic in trade publications and at professional conferences. Many who manage social media on behalf of a client or organization are de-facto online community managers who focus on building and maintaining the strength of ties between publics via social media efforts.

Public relations scholars and professional experts are only now beginning research in this area. Although there has been some work on offline community management (also known as brand communities), these studies are typically limited to marketing or cultural studies, and pre-date social media or the Internet itself. Studies of brand communities, like Belk and Tumbat's "Cult of

Macintosh" (2005), which explores the evangelical connection between brand and publics, have provided a rationale for an exploration of online community management. The recent success of the PR-driven "Fiskateers" online community has been covered extensively in trade media and professional PR blogs (Jones, 2014), indicating a significant interest in the development of research and best practices in this area.

Examining the importance of online communities in PR is a natural extension of existing research that focus on the value of community to PR. For example, Starck and Kruckeberg (2001) suggest that by adopting a model of communitarianism and taking a more active role in the community, practitioners can fully realize two-way communication efforts, while Culbertson and Chen (1996) advocate for the empowerment of all members of a community and interconnectedness. The study of individuals within these communities is usually intended to develop best practices for activating key influencers and brand advocates, who serve as opinion leaders and tastemakers.

Because of social media and the *participatory culture* of online communities, publics are taking a more active role in the production and co-creation of messages, communication, and meaning. They have significant power in the relationship dynamic between the message, the communicator, and the larger audience, yet these publics cannot be defined using current theory and discourse. As a whole, publics have more ownership on a global scale, without the limitations of physical proximity, yet our current conceptions of public do not delineate between active and super-active publics, let alone discuss engagement with information beyond processing and seeking it or dealing with publics virtually who are highly motivated to communicate with organizations and brands.

Fandom, brandfans, and transmedia

Many of the engaged publics and members of online communities that are the focus of new public relations responsibilities fit the definition of *fans*, although public relations, as a discipline, has yet to determine what that term means to our field. Although public relations sometimes supplements its theory base with insights from other disciplines like marketing or rhetoric, work that examines fan studies is largely excluded from our interdisciplinary efforts.

In leading public relations and strategic communication journals, research on fans is rare, and the attempt to connect fandom research to segmentation and other public relations theory is nonexistent. In part because of Facebook's usage of "fan," the term has increased in usage in professional and scholarly PR settings, but usually indicates membership, affinity, approval, or support for an organization. Research that explores fans and fandom on a deeper level is usually considered the domain of cultural critical media audience studies.

Fan studies scholar Mark Duffet defines a "fan" as "a self-identified enthusiast, devotee or follower of a particular media genre, text person or activity" (Duffet, 2013, p. 293). Most fan studies scholars are primarily interested in fans of media texts (entertainment), but their exploration of fannish behavior, including community building, content creation and production, and engagement in fan–producer relationships, can greatly benefit public relations' foray into participatory culture and interaction with *brandfans*, who exhibit the same devotion to brands and non-media/entertainment organizations like corporate, government, and healthcare. Fans of brands and organizations also construct identity, values, and beliefs around the products and services (the "text") they love. They experience an emotional connection to each other as well as the org/producer, and they expect authentic, human connection and feel a sense of ownership in the brand, organization, or product.

Fan studies, which often considers public relations activities as part and parcel of marketing, promotions, and advertising, can also benefit from PR theory, models, and research. As fan–producer interactions increase, and the line between producers and consumers (*prosumers*) continues to blur, public relations research can help explain organization-side strategies, ethical standards, and best practices. Scholars like Henry Jenkins, whose work highlights the two-way communication between fans and organizations (2006) that has been made infinitely more robust thanks to social media, have piqued the interest of a wide range of scholars. By positioning the study of fan practices and culture within a blended context of both industry/professional (PR, marketing, and media management studies) and critical media studies, public relations and fan studies both stand to gain valuable insights from each other's discipline.

Given the similarities in behavior and attributes of engaged publics, fans, and brandfans, it's not surprising to see more interest in entertainment strategies from public relations managers and experts. Steve Rubel, Edelman's Chief Content Strategist, advises practitioners to incorporate *transmedia* (Rubel, 2010) and *drillable media* (Aufferman, 2012) – two terms with foundations in media scholarship – into strategic public relations and corporate communication efforts. Elements of transmedia, including storytelling across platforms, gamification, immersive experiences, and collective intelligence and problem-solving, are becoming integrated with public relations and strategic communication campaigns for nonprofits and corporate clients.

Transmedia is one of a number of opportunities for public relations to provide leadership for organizational communication efforts. With the integration of entertainment, marketing, public relations, games, and advertising, there are new roles for professional communicators that require traditional public relations techniques. Social media management, content strategy, relationship and experiential marketing rely on relationship management and two-way communication. As the field that has the strongest roots in these important areas, public relations needs to be at the forefront of research, management, and new techniques across professional communication.

Forward into the future of public relations

We present this book as the beginning of a conversation between PR professionals and scholars, the purpose of which is to re-evaluate our discipline in the context of participatory culture; to reaffirm foundations, models, and theory that can continue to provide guidance for professional communicators, and to focus our attention on the concepts and challenges ahead. The purpose of this volume is to integrate stakeholder and publics theories with those of participatory cultures and media studies/fan perspectives; to add new, fresh insight into the public relations discipline's concept of publics and segmentation; and to advance the existing theoretical framework of PR.

The chapters selected for inclusion in this volume explore the challenges, opportunities, and the diversity of fan activity and relationships. The situations analyzed also reflect the diversity of communication situations that involve fan-publics, that is, not limited to entertainment products. Through close examination of ground-breaking cases like the ALS "Ice Bucket" social media fundraising campaign, The Baltimore Ravens and the Ray Rice controversy, and Battlestar Galactica's transmedia fan engagement strategies, this book adds new, fresh insight into the public relations discipline's concept of publics and explores challenges, opportunities, and the diversity of fan activity and relationships in an international and intercultural public relations context. These chapters aim to help answer the question: How, as practitioners, can we create meaningful, ethical, and mutually beneficial relationships between brands/organizations and fans?

References

Aufferman, K. (2012, April 5). Digital impact recap: Social media lessons from the press. Retrieved November 2, 2015, from: http://www.prsa.org/SearchResults/view/9707/1048/Digital_Impact_Recap_Social_media_lessons_from_the#.Vd3dSixVhHw

Belk, R. W., & Tumbat, G. (2005). The cult of Macintosh. *Consumption, Markets and Culture*, 8(3), 205–217.

Culbertson, H. M., & Chen, N. (1996). *International public relations: A comparative analysis*. Mahwah, NJ: Lawrence Erlbaum and Associates.

Duffet, M. (2013) *Understanding fandom*. New York: Bloomsbury.

Grunig, J. E. & Hunt, T. T. (1984). *Managing public relations*. New York: Wadsworth Inc Fulfillment.

Jenkins, H. (2006). *Convergence culture: Where old and new media collide*. New York: New York University Press.

Jones, S. (2014, January). Fiskateers update: You can't kill community. Retrieved November 2, 2015, from: http://askspike.com/2014/01/27/fiskateers-update-cant-kill-community/

Rubel, S. (2010, October 11). The rise of the corporate transmedia storyteller. Retrieved August 26, 2015, from: http://www.forbes.com/2010/10/11/google-eric-schmidt-bieber-facebook-social-networking-storytelling-steve-rubel-cmo-network.html

Starck, K., & Kruckeberg, D. (2001). Public relations and community: A reconstructed theory revisited. In R. L. Health and contributing editor G. Vasquez (Eds.), *Handbook of public relations* (pp. 51–59). Thousand Oaks, CA: Sage Publications.

2 Social media, promotional culture, and participatory fandom

Bertha Chin

In the last few years, fan and digital culture studies scholars have turned their attention to social media and the increasingly complicated relationship between media content creators and their fans (Marwick and boyd, 2010, 2011; Chin, 2013; Bennett and Chin, 2014). In *Convergence Culture*, Henry Jenkins talks of the collaboration that is taking place between the media industry and its audience, suggesting that "[convergence] ... is both a top-down corporate-driven process and a bottom-up consumer-driven process. Corporate convergence coexists with grassroots convergence. ... Sometimes, corporate and grassroots convergence reinforce each other, creating closer, more rewarding relations between media producers and consumers" (2006, p. 18).

The media industry is constantly looking for ways to keep fans engaged, ensuring and building loyalty to the brand. One of the ways in which it keeps the audience engaged is through the narrative strategy of "transmedia story-telling," where a story "unfolds across multiple media platforms, with each new text making a distinctive and valuable contribution to the whole" (Jenkins, 2006, pp. 95–96). The most loyal fans would move across different platforms such as digital games, comics, exclusive web content, and so forth to uncover layers of storyline related to the source text. This also includes collaborating with fans, as texts like *Teen Wolf* (2011–) and *Outlander* (2014–) have built spaces on their official websites to accommodate fans, even curating fan transformative works like fan art.[1]

There is a push and pull industrial reaction to this turn to increased fan participation, Jenkins (2006) notes, in which the media industry is constantly giving out mixed signals about how much fans should be co-opted into fan–producer collaborations. Scholars like Suzanne Scott (2008) and Matt Hills (2012) caution against being too celebratory of the media industry's turn towards collaborating with, and producing ancillary content for, niche audiences. Scott (2008) argues that ancillary content which offers back stories for secondary characters hinders fan creativity, while Hills proposes that, despite the seemingly open gesture of inviting fans into participation, the media industry is in fact "responding to, and anticipating, fan criticisms, as well as catering for specific fractions of fandom who might otherwise be at odds with the unfolding brand, and attempting to draw a line under fan resistance to diegetic and production changes" (2012, p. 410), a concept he calls "fanagement." Therefore, we can read the development of transmedia storytelling as a form of inviting audience participation, but it is also possible that media producers are using these strategies to circumvent fan criticism.

Furthermore, Hills also reminds us that elaborate transmedia storytelling is characteristic of major Hollywood productions, something that is not always possible for public service television such as the BBC in the UK, thus non-major Hollywood productions may be disadvantaged with creating ancillary content for fan consumption. This is also the case for independent productions dependent on fans' word-of-mouth and engagement to succeed. For many independent productions, fan engagement on social media remains a way in which content creators can create awareness about their work through directly interacting with fandom.

In 2014, I was asked to consult for a short film, *The Portal* (Jonathan Williams, 2014), at a time when the producers were applying for funding to adapt the short into a web series.[2] My expertise was sought because I am a fan studies scholar and have published widely on the subject. As a Social Media and Audience Engagement consultant, my role was to help the producers and director understand fandom and how to engage with fans, particularly since one of the show's actors – Tahmoh Penikett (*Battlestar Galactica, Dollhouse, Supernatural*) – has considerable cultural capital as a genre actor. The 2-minute trailer released on YouTube showcased Penikett's return to his science fiction roots, but gave an added comedic element rarely seen in his body of work, generating much talk amongst fans on social media. The science fiction and fantastic elements of the short inspired fan creativity, and the filmmakers began showcasing fan art on their official social media networks. They also released exclusive materials such as behind-the-scenes photos and gifsets, directly encouraging fans to use the materials for their artworks.

In return, Penikett's fans were instrumental in spreading the word about his new project on Twitter, Tumblr, and Facebook, leading the trailer to obtain over a million views on YouTube. Having earned a reputation for being extremely fan-friendly, the filmmakers continued to keep fans engaged with the story through the release of the short film online, as well as the filming of the web series, and culminating in a successful Kickstarter campaign[3] to raise funds for post-production work. As Williams, the director, wrote in an update after the end of the Kickstarter campaign:

> this has been a fan-driven project from Day 1 – and I really think of you guys as an extension of our crew. During this campaign I got to know some of you a lot better, and I hope you stick with us going forward. I hope to create many more opportunities to participate and engage with the cast and creators as Riftworld launches.
>
> (2015, n.p.)

For independent projects such as *The Portal / Riftworld Chronicles*, keeping an open channel of communication with fans worked in the producers' favor. Penikett's fans shared and donated to the crowdfunding campaign, and they created artworks that were inspired by the source text using images released by the filmmakers for fans' creative and transformative use.

Crowdfunding, in fact, has become an important source of funding for independent content creators or celebrities intending to develop projects that are outside traditional studio and network production contexts. Paul Booth (2015) draws attention to the importance of acknowledging temporality in digital fandom, especially in relation to a practice like crowdfunding. Using the concept of "spimatic fandom … [where the] production and reception [are integrated] as coexistent paradigms," Booth (2015, p. 150) argues that this enables us to further understand the complexity of the relationship between content creator and fan/funder. In other words, crowdfunding campaigns that "engage their fans in a more participatory manner – acknowledging previous fan work, noting the saliency of fan activities in the past, appealing to fan attention in the future" (Booth, 2015, p. 151) have a higher chance of success as the content creators engage with their fans through the entire process of creation to crowdfunding and beyond. Indeed, fans not only want to interact with content through transmedia storytelling, they also want to interact with content creators, particularly if they are expected to invest in the content creators' visions via crowdfunding. And certainly for independent projects that require fan support, remaining open and available to fans becomes even more imperative for success.

This turn to audience participation and interaction is not limited to studios and networks, however. Actors such as Orlando Jones (*Sleepy Hollow*, 2013–), Stephen Amell (*Arrow*, 2012–), and Felicia Day (*The Guild*, 2007–2013) have been successfully utilizing social media networks such as Twitter, Facebook, and Tumblr as platforms for communicating with their fans, mobilizing them into action for social and charitable causes such as F★ck Cancer, and engaging fans in conversation about media representations of gender and ethnicity, as well as controversies such as Gamergate. As Nick Muntean and Anne Helen Petersen (2009) note, "celebrity tweeting has been equated with the assertion of the authentic celebrity voice. … With so many mediated voices attempting to 'speak' the meaning of the star, the Twitter account emerges as the privileged channel to the star him/herself."

Much like the independent filmmaker intending to promote their work or launch a crowdfunding campaign, these actors are also bypassing traditional gatekeepers such as entertainment news media and PR firms to engage with fans directly. Hollywood has clearly noted the importance of an actor's social media presence; as industry and entertainment website, The Wrap, recently noted, "a sizeable social media following" (Hod, 2015) could further help an actor land an acting job, in a sense guaranteeing that their projects will receive the attention of fans. Ms. In the Biz, a Hollywood industry website catering specifically to women in entertainment, similarly featured a guide (Bobiwash,

2015) for the website's users on how to tweet or maintain a positive social media presence, especially when one is working on an independent project and one's fans could help raise awareness of it.

Looking forward, it is important to note that narrative strategies such as transmedia storytelling and celebrities utilizing social media networks to directly engage with their fans is becoming increasingly common. While these attempts at engagement are often met with encouragement from fans, they do not prevent controversies from occurring, even with media-savvy actors like Orlando Jones. The perception of always being available to fans could lead to potentially tense exchanges when actors do not respond to a fan's request immediately, or if the request, such as for a follow or to respond to a personal query, violates the unspoken line between actors/producers and celebrities.[4]

Matt Hills highlights a further concern, arguing that Jenkins's convergence culture presents a homogenous assumption about media industries without taking into account transnational and/or transcultural industry practices, and this assumption of homogeneity also extends to fandom. Citing Nick Couldry, Hills reminds us "it can be helpful to consider convergence 'cultures' in the plural" (2012, p. 413), especially considering that independent productions featuring actors or producers with different social and cultural capital would need different strategies for engaging with their fans.[5] Similarly, some actors and producers would be more comfortable engaging with fans than others, thus able to maneuver around the oft-complicated interactions with different fan factions on different social media networks.

Hills's warning serves as a reminder for all scholars interested in the intersection of public relations and fan studies; that these are interesting times to be observing fan–celebrity/producer interactions on social media, where both parties are essentially sharing a symbolic space, to different purposes and with different skillsets. However, it is also important to remember that fandom is not homogenous, that industrial practices have different cultural norms across different transnational borders, and that rather than merely celebrating these developments – for they are interesting developments – we should also take heed of what and how these heightened interactions change and influence fan interactions with actors and producers, as well as how social media networks are used in these contexts.

Notes

1 See, for example, The Collective (www.collective.mtv.com/teenwolf/art/) and the Outlander Community (www.starz.com/outlandercommunity/home.html), which invites fans to sign up and share their fan art.
2 The web series was renamed *Riftworld Chronicles*.
3 The Kickstarter also remains very interactive, as the filmmakers continue to take suggestions from fans, adding perks, raffles, challenging fans to gifsets competitions, and getting producers involved in these challenges as well.
4 In fandom, the most common faux pas is usually when actors/producers are pushed to acknowledge fan fiction, either by fans themselves or by those around the actors/producers.

5 Consider, for instance, *Riftworld Chronicles*'s Kickstarter campaign, whereby pledges trickled in steadily but slowly. It wasn't until the final moments of the campaign that funding reached its goal, achieving CAD $61,518 of the $55,000 aimed for. On the other hand, two actors of Joss Whedon's cult favourite *Firefly* (Nathan Fillion and Alan Tudyk), launched a crowdfunding campaign for a web series, *Con Man*, on March 10, and within 3 days, achieved 360% of their US$425,000 funding goal.

References

Bennett, L. (2014). Fan/celebrity interactions and social media: Connectivity and engagement in Lady Gaga fandom. In L. Duits, K. Zwaan, & S. Reijnders (Eds.), *The Ashgate Research Companion to Fan Cultures* (pp. 109–120). Rotterdam: Ashgate.

Bennett, L., & Chin, B. (2014). Exploring fandom, social media and froducer/Fan interactions: An interview with *Sleepy Hollow*'s Orlando Jones. *Transformative Works and Cultures*, 17. Retrieved November 2, 2015, from: http://dx.doi.org/10.3983/twc.2014.0601.

Bobiwash, J. (2015, March 10). Just another hashtag … or how to tweet better. Retrieved March 10, 2015, from: http://msinthebiz.com/2015/03/10/just-another-hashtagor-how-to-tweet-better/.

Booth, P. (2015). Crowdfunding: A Spimatic application of digital fandom. *New Media & Society*, 17(2), 149–166.

Chin, B. (2013). The fan-media producer collaboration: How fan relationships are managed in a post-series X-Files fandom. *Journal of Science Fiction Film and Television*, 6 (1), 87–99.

Hills, M. (2012). Torchwood's trans-transmedia: Media tie-ins and brand "fanagement." *Participations: Journal of Audience & Reception Studies*, 9(2), 409–428.

Hod, I. (2015, March 10). How Hollywood actors' Twitter followings have become as important as talent. Retrieved March 10, 2015, from: http://www.thewrap.com/how-hollywood-actors-twitter-followings-have-become-as-important-as-talent/.

Jenkins, H. (2006). *Convergence culture: Where old and new media collide*. New York: New York University Press.

Marwick, A. E., & boyd, danah (2010). I tweet honestly, I tweet passionately: Twitter users, context collapse, and the imagined audience. *New Media & Society*, 13(1), 114–133.

Marwick, A. E., & boyd, danah (2011). To see and be seen: Celebrity practice on Twitter. *Convergence: The International Journal of Research into New Media Technologies*, 17(2), 139–158.

Muntean, N., & Petersen, A. H. (2009). Celebrity Twitter: Strategies of intrusion and disclosure in the age of technoculture. *M/C Journal*, 12(5). Retrieved November 2, 2015, from: http://journal.media-culture.org.au/index.php/mcjournal/article/view Article/194.

Scott, S. (2008). Authorised resistance: Is fan production frakked? In T. Potter & C. W. Marshall (Eds.), *Cylons in America: Critical studies in Battlestar Galactica* (pp. 210–223). New York: Continuum.

Williams, J. (2015, March 10). Letter from the writer/director – Riftworld Chronicles by First Love Films. Retrieved March 10, 2015, from: https://www.kickstarter.com/projects/1208035306/riftworld-chronicles/posts/1161086?ref=backer_project_update.

3 Public relations and the attempt to avoid truly relating to our publics

Sam Ford

In the past few decades, new means of communication have arisen which enable companies to more directly tell their stories, show their expertise and passion, listen to those they seek to reach, and engage in two-way communication.[1]

However, public relations – and adjacent marketing disciplines – have too often held to the corporate logics of the broadcast world.

Underpinning this persistence of outdated approaches, and the desire to preserve the logics that formerly governed public relations, is an inclination to view people as "audiences," a group who primarily exists in response to the company's messages. As Henry Jenkins, Joshua Green, and I (2013) argue in the book *Spreadable Media*, viewing these people as audiences drastically differs from understanding them as "publics," socially connected individuals whose existence doesn't revolve around your brand. Publics' interests may occasionally align with a company or perhaps come into direct conflict with it. But – even more often – publics will operate by very different motivations than the capitalistic logic that drives the company's raison d'être.

I joined the public relations world as an academic researcher. After almost eight years in the PR world, it's been my observation that public relations as a discipline has spent the majority of its history doing all it can to avoid truly relating to its publics.

In the broadcast era, we could argue we had little opportunity to really engage relevant publics, since one-to-many communication was the primary mode and much of the PR discipline's work depended on traditional media companies. Brands weren't publishers themselves. Instead, marketers/corporate communicators went to those who owned the printing presses or had the broadcast licenses, either in hopes they'd include the brand in the stories they told or else let the brand buy some space to hawk products and services between those stories.

As I entered PR in 2007/2008, the discipline was navigating new terrain. These were the early days of social network sites. It was the rise of the blogosphere, the moment in which microblogging became possible, and the period in which self-distributing multimedia content became feasible. (Some) companies were realizing that bringing their brochureware and marketing-speak online might not be the most useful way to engage those people they sought to reach. And everyone was trying to figure out how to navigate in a world where imagined audiences became real ... and talked back.

The PR profession still hasn't figured it all out. As we've tried to hang onto the logics of the broadcast world from whence this discipline was birthed, we have tried to measure success in today's era by means of "stickiness," getting people to experience our messages in ways we control and that gives us the most data to report back to the C-Suite. We have embraced the idea of "Big Data," and – with it – the desire to even further imagine those publics as analytics and statistics rather than as people. We have developed campaigns which seek to "go viral," positioning those publics as vehicles for the pandemic we want to infect them with and treating them as carriers for our messages rather than as interconnected human beings with agency and their own motivations. We have worked feverishly to identify and quantify "influencers" that we pretend the rest of the audience will follow blindly. And we have often defined those publics we seek as "brand communities" we imagine to be built around our companies/clients.

One of the potential antidotes to this harmful way of thinking comes through what the world of PR can learn from more than two decades of research in the burgeoning academic "discipline" of fan studies – which puts its primary focus not on what storytellers get their fans to do but rather what networks of fans do with and around media texts.

My journey into public relations

I came to the world of PR intentionally seeking to intervene in the ways companies imagine their audiences. I was trained in MIT's Program in Comparative Media Studies, with its focus on "applied humanities." There, in addition to studying how publics were finding new ways to engage actively with one another and with media producers/texts, we aimed to bring our research into conversation with industry practice. As a student, I helped launch the Convergence Culture Consortium – a project partnering with media companies, brands, and agencies to consider how the media landscape was changing and how companies should shift their logics accordingly. After graduating, I stayed on at MIT – teaching and helping manage the Consortium's research initiatives.

Meanwhile, PR and marketing firm Peppercomm reached out to me to do some consulting with them while in my position at MIT. They were in the midst of grappling with how to best serve clients when the communication environment was changing around them. The agency realized that, to fully make sense of this new terrain, they might not find all the answers within the PR world. And I realized that working with them – and their clients – might provide the means to make a more impactful intervention into changing the ways in which particular companies or the PR world approach those publics they seek to reach.

Peppercomm didn't quite know what they were looking for when they entered into conversation with a fan studies researcher who examines and writes about participatory culture. And I didn't know quite what I was looking for, either, talking with an agency. But we carved out a position that has allowed me, over the course of seven years, to divide my time into three roughly equal parts.

Studying participatory culture – and applying it to public relations

In my seven years working full-time at Peppercomm, I have engaged in a range of academic projects studying participatory culture – for example, from understanding the struggles of the U.S. soap opera to adapt to a digital age (i.e. Ford, De Kosnik, & Harrington, 2011) to exploring the complex ways pro wrestling fans engage with and around the narrative of the entertainment property (i.e. Ford, 2016b). I've examined how the concept of "ownership" is negotiated between the organizations who create stories and those fans who make those stories relevant through the ways they engage with them and make them their own (Ford, 2015). I've written about the future of "fan studies" as a discipline and what our approaches into understanding participatory culture might have to teach those who study communication outside of media fandom (Ford, 2014a). And, coming out of my work at MIT, I contributed to a six-year research initiative looking at what happens when the process of circulating media texts increasingly becomes a role for "the audience," which culminated in the aforementioned book, *Spreadable Media* (Jenkins, Ford, & Green, 2013). That time spent continuing to think about issues outside the PR world has, I hope, helped bring new ways of thinking to my role at Peppercomm.

Throughout my time in PR, I've also participated in the wider dialogue about the future of public relations: with trade organizations like the Word of Mouth Marketing Association and the Council of Public Relations Firms; via initiatives like a cross-agency statement on ethical engagement practices with Wikipedia I helped put together in 2014; and through speaking and writing, not only with PR industry events and trade publications but in the larger "business world" as well.

Much of my work has centered on issues of ethics in the public relations space – a particular challenge in an industry where space and time to talk about shifts in our logics is quite limited (Ford, 2016a). My focus has been to advocate for companies to become more human in their approach and to embrace the logics of a participatory culture.

I have also sought to contribute to Peppercomm's evolution over that time by trying to focus more heavily on representing the interests of those publics our clients seek to reach instead of solely representing our clients and by applying that way of thinking to the counsel I have given clients. When I first met the organization, Peppercomm was a traditional PR firm trying to figure out what's next. Today, the agency has that roadmap. The organizational tag-line is "Listen. Engage. Repeat." And, as the agency describes in its "Approach" on the Peppercomm website:

With our work, Peppercomm serves two constituents: the companies we partner with and the communities they want to reach. We listen to our client's audiences, and we look at the company from their eyes. From this perspective, we then help our clients better align their messages to serve their audiences. Our goal is to provide our clients with the strategies they need and audiences with engaging content they find so useful they will want to spread.

Peppercomm's co-founder, Steve Cody, has taken it a step further, writing in 2014 that:

> [A]fter 18 years of trying, we've figured out exactly WHY we come to work each day, what our specific purpose in the communications universe is AND how we can best serve our clients and their target audiences. We advocate before we communicate. But, and this is a big but, we advocate not only for the client that pays our bills, but for each, and every, constituent audience they wish to reach as well.

One of the ways we have tried to operationalize that approach is in how we build processes of listening and empathy into our workflow at Peppercomm. (See more details on that approach in Ford, 2014b.) For instance, our "Audience Experience" offering is aimed at helping clients see their company and its communications from their audience's view rather than their own, taking the tenets of "design thinking" and applying it to how an organization approaches not just products and services but communication experiences as well.

These are not approaches Peppercomm has perfected. But we are now describing and thinking about our work using frameworks aimed at the future instead of clinging to the logics of the past. The PR industry must evolve its approach and operations to embrace a world where companies tell their stories directly and where communication practices around those stories are heavily participatory.

The way forward

My years in the world of public relations and marketing strategy don't provide a tale of unabashed success. I come from a humanities background traditionally averse to engaging in dialogue with corporate interests. This has led to no shortage of challenges in translating my academic work into the commercial logic governing our agency and its clients. In return, I've had much to learn to understand how marketing, public relations, and the broader corporate world operate. And I've encountered no shortage of roadblocks in how the logics of the public relations world continue to cling to the broadcast mentality.

But one thing is clear to me. The discipline of public relations has the potential to lead the corporate world forward into a more participatory culture.

That's only possible as long as we aren't limiting our understanding of the role of public relations to being a vendor rather than a partner, focusing our efforts on wordsmithing what the organization wants to tell the world and trying to persuade audiences to think the way the organization would like to them to think.

Instead, we must be counsel to corporate decision-makers: listeners more than orators; ombudsmen for what publics want and need from the company rather than agents for aligning publics with the corporate POV; and strategic advocates for how a company should change its logics to be true participants in today's communication reality rather than tacticians for executing campaigns.

But that will only happen if the industry today pushes itself toward new logics built for a participatory culture and demands the corporate world to expect something more from the public relations discipline. It will only happen if those who study and explore the nature of public relations broaden their definition of what PR is and should be. And it will only happen if we are challenging the PR professionals of tomorrow to guide the industry toward what it must become rather than what it has been.

The very existence of this collection gives me hope that it's possible for public relations to live up to its name. But there's much work to be done to make that happen.

Note

1 Sam wrote the initial draft of this essay while serving as Director of Audience Engagement for strategic communications and marketing firm Peppercomm. In August 2015, he joined digital and TV network Fusion as Vice President of Innovation and Engagement. Since this essay was written while Sam was working in the public relations space, we have left it in the current tense.

References

Cody, S. (2014). Advocate before you communicate. *RepMan*, 5 June. Retrieved November 2, 2015, from: http://www.repmanblog.com/repman/2014/06/advoca te-before-you-communicate.html.

Ford, S. (2014a). Fan studies: Grappling with an undisciplined discipline. *Journal of Fandom Studies* 2(1), pp. 53–71.

Ford, S. (2014b). Listening and empathizing: Advocating for new management logics in marketing and corporate communications. In Derek Kompare, Avi Santo, & Derek Johnson (Eds.), *Making Media Work: Cultures of management in the entertainment industries*. New York: New York University Press, pp. 275–294.

Ford, S. (2015). Social media ownership. In Peng Hwa Ang & Robin Mansell (Eds.), *International encyclopedia of digital communication & society, Vol. 1.* Chichester, UK: Wiley, pp. 1–10.

Ford, S. (2016a). Perfectly "compliant": The devaluation of ethics in corporate communications industry discourse. In Paul Booth & Amber Davisson (Eds.), *Controversies in Media Ethics*. London: Bloomsbury Press.

Ford, S. (2016b). I was stabbed 21 times by crazy fans: Pro wrestling and popular concerns with immersive story worlds. In P. Booth & L. Bennett (Eds.), *Representations of fandom in media and popular culture*. London: Bloomsbury Academic.

Ford, S., De Kosnik, A., & Harrington, C. L. (Eds.) (2011). *The survival of soap opera: Transformations for a new media era*. Jackson, MS: University Press of Mississippi.

Jenkins, H., Ford, S., & Green, J. (2013). *Spreadable media: Creating value and meaning in a networked culture*. New York: New York University Press.

Peppercomm (n.d.) Approach: Listen first. last & always. Retrieved November 2, 2015, from: http://www.peppercomm.com/about/approach.

Part II

Theoretical approaches to public relations, engagement, and fandom

4 Encouraging the rise of fan publics

Bridging strategy to understand fan publics' positive communicative actions

Arunima Krishna and Soojin Kim

The identification and engagement of supportive publics or fan publics to being a part of an organization's communication efforts and activities has very recently emerged as a key agenda among public relations scholars and practitioners. While discussions on fandom and fan activism can be found extensively in the social sciences (e.g., Lee, 2011; Parry, Jones & Wann, 2014; Millward & Poulton, 2014), public relations as a field is yet to address fans as a public of interest. A few efforts have been made to build the connections between relationship management research (e.g., Bruning, Dials, & Shirka, 2008), public relations, and fandom (e.g. L'Etang, 2006; Dimitrov, 2008), yet these efforts remain few and far between. This edited volume presents a positive step in rectifying this issue, recognizing what L'Etang pointed out:

> To date sports literature does not seem to appreciate that public relations defines and analyses key stakeholders and newly emergent publics and interest groups with a view to understanding not only their perceptions of, and relationships with, the organisations but also with each other.
>
> (2006, p. 245)

While L'Etang (2006) focused specifically on sports fans, the logic extends to other types of organizations and their publics too. In this chapter we attempt to understand fan publics related to universities, and present research on university–student relationships.

The advent of social media and digital media has allowed various publics to engage in word-of-mouth behaviors about organizations and brands that they have strong feelings for, and for public relations practitioners to monitor and attend to such behaviors (Krishna & Kim, 2015). Fan publics of an organization may actively engage in supportive behaviors for an organization including positive communicative behaviors. Given the nature of social and digital media, such messages have the potential to reach a large number of people in a short space of time, and therefore may have consequences on the decision or behaviors of the organization (Kim & Rhee, 2011; Bach & Kim, 2012) and vice versa (Grunig, Grunig, & Dozier, 2002).

The focus of this chapter is on individuals who have strong positive relationships with an organization, or fan publics. Specifically in this chapter we examine the university–student dynamic, investigating how a university may encourage the development of fan publics in its student body through its communicative actions. In a university setting, students who perceive a high quality university–student relationship should be considered fan publics who can positively support, and pose strategic opportunities for the university. Their positive word-of-mouth behaviors may influence prospective students, community residents, investors, media, and other important stakeholders of the university. In contrast, students could also be hostile publics who can pose a threat for the university by engaging in negative word-of-mouth behaviors about the university if they are not satisfied with the university and if they find its behaviors and decisions to be problematic.

Interestingly, few public relations scholars have addressed university–student relationships as being an important area of inquiry. Students are a key internal public for a university as they not only interact with it on a regular basis, their affiliation with the university has the potential to last a lifetime in the form of alumni giving (Hueston, 1992), and university identification (Mael & Ashforth, 1992). Yet few studies of public relations have examined current students as publics who display communicative behaviors and may engage in alumni giving in the future (Sung & Yang, 2009). In this study we focus on students who perceive high quality relationships with the university, fan publics, to understand the factors that contribute to their development as well as communicative outcomes enjoyed by universities due to fan publics.

We investigate the relationship between a university's public relations strategy and student publics' communicative actions about their university. We aim to (a) conceptualize fan publics as publics who have positive relationships with the organization; (b) propose the bridging strategy as a proactive public engagement strategy that promotes mutually beneficial relationships between the organization and publics which helps create fan publics; and (c) test relationships between the bridging strategy and its multiple outcomes. In testing those relationships we look at how an organization's public relations strategy influences the quality and type of organization–public relationships that create fan and hostile publics' communication behavior.

Literature review

Conceptualization of fan publics

People talk about organizations, products, and brands. Corporate communicators and marketers have begun to acknowledge the significant change in consumer empowerment (Kucuk, 2008; Shaw & Duff, 2002; Harrison, 2005) – which means that active consumers proactively seek to engage in and to influence products and services through their actions (Shaw, Newholm, &

Dickinson, 2006). With the power of social media and networks, consumers have the power to voice their opinions about an organization (Kucuk, 2008).

However, people show different levels of activeness in their communication behavior. Specifically, hardcore groups of people, or extreme publics, exhibit high levels of either supportive or hostile behavior about an organization, which may either be a strategic opportunity or threat to the organization. According to Lee et al. (2014), extreme publics are more likely to express their opinions about a problem or an issue than others, regardless of their minority position. Their findings indicate that hardcore groups of people freely engage in active communication behavior without fear of backlash from the mainstream and that there is a possibility of this group being the majority.

While it is important to focus on activeness levels in publics' communicative actions, of more interest to marketers and communicators is the valence and quality of those behaviors. Kim and Rhee's (2011) conceptualization of mega-phoning and its antecedents is of value here. In their study, Kim and Rhee found that employees who perceive high-quality organization–public relationships actively spread positive messages about their employers to external publics. A logical extension of their argument, then, may find validity in conceptualizing fan publics. Extending Kim and Rhee's (2011) discussion of megaphoning, in this study we seek to understand student fan publics as those who (a) perceive high organization–public relationships and (b) engage in positive commu-nicative behaviors about the university. Fan publics are conceptualized as pub-lics who evaluate their relationship with an organization positively and support the organization by engaging in positive word-of-mouth behavior.

Still lacking in current research is an understanding of the motivations behind these empowered publics' communication behaviors, and the factors that encourage or discourage these behaviors. Hostile and antagonist consumer behaviors and their impact on organizational performance have received scho-larly attention (e.g., Bach & Kim, 2012; Blodgett, Granbois, & Walters, 1993; Day & Landon, 1976; Richins, 1983; Singh, 1988, 1990a, 1990b). However, little research has attempted to explain the conditions under which the rise of such antagonistic publics may be preempted through organizational actions, and fan publics may be encouraged. A central question for public relations research, and the guiding question for this study, then, is *how an organization can create fan publics*. Every organization wants to increase positive reactions from target publics and to build a group of supportive fans, while decreasing hostile reac-tions from consumers and activist groups. In the next section we outline how public relations strategy may be used to answer this question.

Bridging strategy to create fan publics

In the previous section we discussed the creation of fan publics as being a central theme for public relations scholarship. In this section we explore one way in which organizations can encourage fan publics to emerge, that is, through their own behaviors and communication strategy.

The term public relations strategy is still an ambiguous one among scholars and practitioners alike (Steyn, 2007; Tibble, 1997). Extant literature on public relations strategy focuses on messaging strategy (e.g. Werder, 2006) and relationship cultivation strategy (e.g., Ki & Hon, 2008, 2009). The focus of both public engagement and relationship cultivation strategies remains to be on favorable, long-term relationships between the organization and publics. In fact, previous work on student loyalty to their universities revealed that students who evaluate their relationship with the university positively were more likely to stay at the university rather than drop out (Bruning & Ralston, 2001). Understanding which kinds of public relations strategies may help encourage positive university–student relationships then becomes an important context for study.

This study draws upon Kim's (2014, 2015) work on public relations strategy, specifically, on her adaptation of Grunig's (2009) paradigms of public relations, bridging, and buffering, as public relations strategies. Bridging refers to a public relations strategy by which an organization makes or revises its behaviours or policies to be compatible to the needs of its strategic publics and makes efforts to narrow gaps between the stances of the organization and its publics. Buffering is conceptualized as a public relations strategy by which an organization seeks to shape and control publics' perceptions of itself, without actually rectifying any problem-causing behaviors (Kim, 2014, 2015).

In this chapter, the bridging strategy is proposed as a public relations strategy that may help create fan publics, and the attendant supportive communication behavior towards the organization. An organization that employs the bridging strategy addresses and adjusts the differences in interests between publics and the organization and takes responsibility for its actions. In addition, bridging strategies include an organization's strategic communication of these proactive problem solving approaches. By doing and communicating its efforts to listen and reflect publics' voices into the decision making process, the organization is able to have favorable relational outcomes: it encourages the creation of fan publics who not only are committed to the relationship with the organization but also exhibit strong supportive behavior towards the organization.

Relational outcomes of bridging strategy: type and quality of organization–public relationship

Stoker and Tusinski (2006) say that the goal of communication should be to achieve authenticity. Shen and Kim (2012) applied the concept of authenticity on organizational behavior which has been used for leadership. Authenticity can be achieved by meeting multiple dimensions including truthfulness, transparency, and consistency. When an organization uses two-way symmetrical communication it is likely to be perceived as being authentic, which will promote a favorable organization–public relationship (Shen & Kim, 2012).

Since an essential element of the bridging strategy is the use of dialogue to bridge the gap between the management and publics, a logical extension of Shen and Kim's (2012) study would be that the use of a bridging strategy will be positively associated with perceived authenticity. An organization adopting a bridging strategy is likely to be consistent and transparent in its words and actions so that they will be perceived as genuine in the publics' eyes. As a result publics are likely to favorably evaluate their relationships with the organization and to engage in supportive behavior for the organization. Hence, the following hypotheses are posited:

H1:   Perceived use of bridging strategy is positively associated with perceived authenticity.

H2:   Perceived authenticity will be positively associated with quality of organization–public relationship.

H3:   Publics who perceive good quality relationship with the organization (fan publics) are likely to engage in positive word-of-mouth behavior about the organization.

H3–1: Publics who perceive poor quality relationship with the organization are likely to engage in negative word-of-mouth behavior about the organization.

The use of a bridging strategy and organization–public relationship should also be discussed in the context of type of relationship that publics have with the organization. Type of relationship will be one of outcomes from the adoption of the bridging strategy and affect publics' communication behavior. According to Hon and Grunig (1999), there are two types of relationships: communal and exchange relationships. In a communal relationship entities provide benefits for one another out of care for the other, while those in an exchange relationship do so out of expected reciprocity.

Waters (2008) found that repeated donors are more likely to perceive their relationship with the organization as a communal relationship while one-time donors are more likely to perceive theirs as an exchange relationship. To encourage supportive publics, or fan publics, like repeated donors, it is necessary for an organization to utilize a proper public relations strategy to engage those key publics. If an organization fails to communicate well with its key publics, students in this case who are likely to be future donors, it is likely to have exchange relationships with them and it will be difficult to have a high quality organization–public relationship with them. Hung-Baesecke and Chen (2013) suggest that the type of relationship affects the quality of the organization–public relationship and that a communal relationship contributes to relational trust while an exchange relationship does not contribute to enhancing a quality organization–public relationship.

Based on the above discussion, it would be reasonable to expect that those in exchange relationships with the organization will evaluate their relationships with the organization negatively, and engage in negative behaviors about it, as they believe that their relationships exist only when they are needed by the organization. In contrast, people in communal relationships with the organization will evaluate their relationship with the organization favorably and engage in positive behavior for the organization. Therefore, the type of organization–public relationship will be an immediate outcome of the perceived use of the bridging strategy, which will affect the quality of the organization–public relationship and communication behavior. Therefore the following hypotheses are posited:

H4: Perceived use of a bridging strategy is positively associated with a communal relationship.

H4–1: Perceived use of a bridging strategy is negatively associated with an exchange relationship

H4–2: Publics who evaluate their relationships with the organization as communal relationships are likely to evaluate their relationship with the organization positively.

H4–3: Publics who evaluate their relationships with the organization as exchange relationships are likely to evaluate their relationship with the organization negatively.

Method

Data collection

An online survey was conducted at a large Midwestern university (September–December 2013). The survey used Qualtrics software and participants were recruited through the university's research system in exchange for course credit. A total of 684 university students responded with 611 valid responses to 110 questions. Among the respondents, 256 students were male (41.9%) while 355 students were female (58.1%). A large majority of the students, 548 respondents (89.7%), were domestic students and 63 students (10.3%) were international students.

Measures

To measure perceptions of the use of a bridging strategy, Kim's (2014) scales were used (total 7 items) (Cronbach's alpha=.847). The OPRA scale as revised and updated by Shen and Kim (2012): trust (9 items), commitment (6 items), control mutuality (4 items), and satisfaction (4 items) was utilized to measure organization–public relationships. Cronbach's alpha values were respectively: trust=.853, control mutuality=.667, commitment=.624, and satisfaction=.918. Exchange and communal relationships were measured using Hon and Grung's (1999) items (4 items). Based on Kim and Rhee's (2011) work, 7 items for positive megaphoning and negative megaphoning behaviors respectively were adopted (Cronbach's alpha for positive megaphoning=.887; for negative megaphoning=.904). (Table 4.1).

Table 4.1. Reliability values

Variable name	Cronbach's alpha	Number of items
Authenticity	.853	4
Bridging	.847	7
Trust	.853	9
Satisfaction	.918	4
Control mutuality	.667	4
Commitment	.624	4
Communal relationship	.582	3
Exchange relationship	.775	4
Positive communicative behavior	.887	7
Negative communicative behavior	.904	7

Data analysis

To conduct a data analysis and test the complex relationships between multiple variables, SEM (Structural Equation Modeling) was used. SEM also allows researchers to correct for the distorting influences of measurement errors. In addition, it is a good method to measure mediating relationships. Maximum likelihood (ML) procedures were selected for data analysis with AMOS. These techniques allow researchers to have consistent parameter estimates even when assumptions of normality might be violated (Yuan & Bentler, 2007, p. 17). Missing data was treated using Expected Maximization (EM) imputation.

Results

Structural model analysis and hypothesis testing

To evaluate the structural equation model, the following model fit indices were used: CFII$\geq$.90 (moderate fit), CFII$\geq$.95 (good fit), .08$\leq$RMSEA$\leq$.10 (moderate fit), RMSEA$\leq$ .08 (good fit) (MacCallum et al., 1996), 0$\leq$SRMR$\leq$1.0 (moderate fit), SRMR$\leq$.08 (acceptable) (Hu & Bentler, 1999), and NFI$\geq$.90 (good fit) (McDonald & Ho, 2002). The proposed models were tested as initially specified and then modifications using error covariance were made. The first structural model to test dynamics between bridging strategy, the effect of communal relationship, organization–public relationship, and positive megaphoning behavior demonstrated a good data–model fit (CFI=.906 SRMR=.079 RMSEA=.058 Chi-square[df]=2160.835[708] p=.000) (Figure 4.1). The second structural model to test relationships between bridging strategy, authenticity, the effect of exchange relationship, organization–public relationship and negative megaphoning behavior yielded a good data–model fit (CFI=.919 SRMR=.078 RMSEA=.053 Chi-square[df]=2166.835[708] p=.000) (Figure 4.2).

The first hypothesis posited that when publics perceive an organization adopting high level of bridging strategy they will perceive the organization's behaviour as authentic. The standardized path coefficient was positive and significant (path=.710★★★ p<.001). Therefore **H1** was supported (Figure 4.1). Next, it was predicted that perceived authentic organizational behavior will mediate the relationships between bridging strategy and quality of organization–public relationship. The standardized path coefficient between perceived authentic organization behaviour and quality of organization–public relationship was positive and significant (path=.774★★★ p<.001), providing strong support for **H2** (Figure 4.1).

We then proposed that perceived quality of organization–public relationship will have a positive effect on positive megaphoning (**H3**) (Figure 4.1) and a negative effect on negative megaphoning (**H3–1**) (Figure 4.2). These hypotheses on publics' communication behaviors were also supported (H3: path=.737★★★ p<.001) (Figure 4.1) (H3–1: path=-.456★★★ p<.001) (Figure 4.2). In terms of the nature of the relationship, first we hypothesized that there will be a positive relationship between bridging strategy and communal relationships (**H4**) (Figure 4.1) and a negative relationship between bridging strategy and exchange relationship (**H4–1**) (Figure 4.2). Next, we predicted that when publics perceive their relationships with the organization as communal they are likely to evaluate their relationship with the organization positively (Figure 4.1) (**H4–2**), while those in an exchange relationship are likely to evaluate it negatively (**H4–3**; Figure 4.2). All hypotheses were also strongly supported (H4: path=.529★★★, H4–1: path=-.130★★ p<.01, H4–2: path=.204 p<.001, H4–3: path=.-.086★★ p<.01).

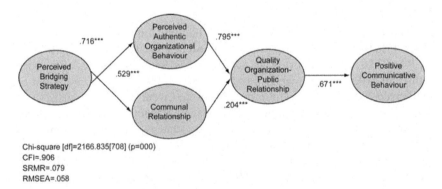

Chi-square [df]=2166.835[708] (p=000)
CFI=.906
SRMR=.079
RMSEA=.058

Figure 4.1 Model for associations between fan publics' positive communication behavior, and perceived use of bridging strategy, authenticity and relationship type and quality.

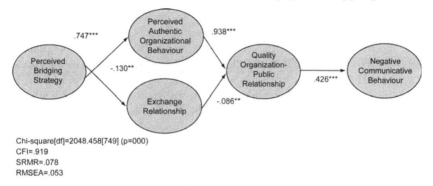

Chi-square[df]=2048.458[749] (p=000)
CFI=.919
SRMR=.078
RMSEA=.053

Figure 4.2 Model for associations between fan publics' negative communication behavior, and perceived use of bridging strategy, authenticity and relationship type and quality.

Discussion

In this study we sought to understand how organizations can use public relations strategies to promote the rise of fan publics. By specifically looking at university–student relationships in this regard, we sought to propose a new conceptualization for fan publics, as those who perceive high quality organization–public relationships and engage in positive communication behaviors about the organization. Our findings show that by adopting a bridging strategy, that is, a public relations strategy where the organization attempts to integrate the publics' perspectives and needs in its decision making and functioning, organizations can encourage their publics to engage in supportive behaviors, thereby creating fan publics.

The results of this research have several important implications for the theory and practice of public relations. First, this study represents one of the few scholarly efforts to understand university–student public relationships from the perspective of public relations. As Bruning and Ralston (2001) pointed out, public relations should attempt to understand students' intentions and behaviors towards their universities. Accordingly, the results of this study help bring university–student relationships into conversation with public relations theory, and propose a theory of students' relationships and communicative behaviors.

Second, this study furthers how public relations scholarship understands fan publics. By proposing a new conceptualization of fan publics as supportive publics who perceive high quality relationships and engage in positive communicative behaviors about the organization, this study helps situate the idea of fandom within public relations literature. For years public relations scholars have advocated that cultivation of strong positive organization–public relationships help increase publics' loyalty towards the organization (Bruning & Ralston, 2001). This study extends scholars' thought from just loyalty to fandom, explicating the behavioural outcomes that emerge from fan publics' loyalty.

Third, the results of this study further the arguments for universities to have dedicated public relations activities and for them to adopt theoretical principles for more effective functioning. That public relations has been relegated to primarily managing reputation rather than cultivating relationships, has been established in public relations scholarship (Bruning & Ralston, 2001). The results of this study offer evidence-based arguments for universities to employ public relations strategies to encourage and cultivate positive university–student relationships, and promote the emergence of fan publics among their student body. These fan publics, then, may help promote the university to external publics by engaging in positive communication behaviors about it, as was seen in this study.

Finally, the results of this study will also help practitioners understand fan publics better, and provide mechanisms for them through which they may encourage the rise of fan publics. As seen in this study, adoption of the bridging strategy is an effective tool to cultivate and encourage the emergence of fan publics, and discourage hostility from non-fan publics.

However, there are a few limitations associated with this study. Since it was conducted in a university setting the results from this study may not be generalizable to other industries or types of organizations. We also acknowledge that the bridging strategy is not a one-cure-fits-all for all public relations problems. It is important to note, however, that the bridging strategy does not discount the importance of strategic messaging. The main assertion of the bridging strategy is simply that strategic messaging can be most effective when backed by organizational behavior.

References

Bach, S. B., & Kim, S. (2012). Online consumer complaint behaviors: The dynamics of service failures, consumers' word of mouth, and organization–consumer relationships. *International Journal of Strategic Communication*, 6(1), 59–76.

Blodgett, J. G., Granbois, D. H., & Walters, R. G. (1993). The effects of perceived justice on complainants' negative word-of-mouth behavior and repatronage intentions. *Journal of Retailing*, 69(4), 399–428.

Bruning, S. D., Dials, M., & Shirka, A. (2008). Using dialogue to build organization–public relationships, engage publics, and positively affect organizational outcomes. *Public Relations Review*, 34(1), 25–31.

Bruning, S. D., & Ralston, M. (2001). Using a relational approach to retaining students and building mutually beneficial student university relationships. *Southern Journal of Communication*, 66(4), 337–345.

Day, R. L., & Landon, E. L., Jr. (1976). Collecting comprehensive consumer complaining data by survey research. In B. B. Anderson (Ed.), *Advances in consumer research, 3* (pp. 263–268). Ann Arbor, MI: Association for Consumer Research.

Dimitrov, R. (2008). Gender violence, fan activism and public relations in sport: The case of "Footy Fans Against Sexual Assault". *Public Relations Review*, 34(2), 90–98.

Grunig, J. E. (2009). Paradigms of global public relations in an age of digitalization. *Prism*, 6(2). Retrieved November 2, 2015, from: http://www.prismjournal.org/filea dmin/Praxis/Files/globalPR/GRUNIG.pdf.

Grunig, L. A., Grunig, J. E., & Dozier, D. M. (2002). Excellence in public relations and communication management: A review of the theory and results. In *Excellent public relations and effective organization: A study of communication management in three countries* (pp. 1–30). Mahwah, NJ: Lawrence Erlbaum.

Harrison, R. (2005). Pressure groups, campaigns and consumers. In R. Harrison, T. Newholm, & D. Shaw (Eds.), *The ethical consumer* (pp. 55–67). London: Sage.

Hon, L. C., & Grunig, J. E. (1999). Guidelines for measuring relationships in public relations. Paper for the Commission on Public Relations Measurement and Evaluation. Institute for Public Relations Research, Gainesville, FL.

Hu, L. T., & Bentler, P. M. (1999). Cutoff criteria for fit indexes in covariance structure analysis: Conventional criteria versus new alternatives. *Structural Equation Modeling: A Multidisciplinary Journal*, 6(1), 1–55.

Hueston, F. R. (1992). Predicting alumni giving: A donor analysis test. *Fund Raising Management*, 23(5), 19–22.

Hung-Baesecke, C. J. F., & Chen, Y. R. R. (2013). The effects of organization–public relationship types and quality on crisis attributes. In K. Sriramesh, A. Zerfass, & J.-N. Kim (Eds.) *Public relations and communication management: Current trends and emerging topics* (pp. 225–243). New York: Routledge.

Ki, E., & Hon, L.C. (2008). A measure of relationship cultivation strategies. *Journal of Public Relations Research*, 21(1), 1–24.

Ki, E.-J., & Hon, L. (2009). Causal linkages between relationship cultivation strategies and relationship quality outcomes. *Journal of Public Relations Research*, 3(4), 242–263.

Kim, J. N., & Rhee, Y. (2011). Strategic thinking about employee communication behavior (ECB) in public relations: Testing the models of megaphoning and scouting effects in Korea. *Journal of Public Relations Research*, 23(3), 243–268.

Kim, S. (2014). *Understanding two paradigms of public relations strategies: Buffering and bridging.* Unpublished doctoral dissertation. Purdue University, West Lafayette.

Kim, S. (2015). Bridge or buffer: Two ideas of effective corporate governance and public engagement. *Journal of Public Affairs.* DOI:10.1002/pa.1555.

Krishna, A. & Kim, S. (2015). Confessions of an angry employee. *Public Relations Review* 41(3), 401–410.

Kucuk, S. U. (2008). Consumer exit, voice, and "power" on the Internet. *Journal of Research for Consumers*, 15, 1–13.

Lee, H. K. (2011). Participatory media fandom: A case study of anime fansubbing. *Media, Culture & Society*, 33(8), 1131–1147.

Lee, H., Oshita, T., Oh, H. J., & Hove, T. (2014). When do people speak out? Integrating the spiral of silence and the situational theory of problem solving. *Journal of Public Relations Research*, 26(3), 185–199.

L'Etang, J. (2006). Public relations and sport in promotional culture. *Public Relations Review*, 32(4), 386–394.

MacCallum, R. C., Browne, M. W., & Sugawara, H. M. (1996). Power analysis and determination of sample size for covariance structure modeling. *Psychological Methods*, 1(2), 130–149.

Mael, F., & Ashforth, B. E. (1992). Alumni and their alma mater: A partial test of the reformulated model of organizational identification. *Journal of organizational Behavior*, 13(2), 103–123.

McDonald, R. P., & Ho, M-H. R. (2002). Principles and practice in reporting structural equation analyses. *Psychological Methods*, 7, 64–82.

Millward, P., & Poulton, G. (2014). Football fandom, mobilization and Herbert Blumer: A social movement analysis of FC United of Manchester. *Sociology of Sport Journal*, 31(1), 1–22.

Mintzberg, H. (1987). The strategy concept I: Five Ps for strategy. *California Management Review*, 30(1), 11–24.

Parry, K. D., Jones, I., & Wann, D. L. (2014). An examination of sport fandom in the United Kingdom: A comparative analysis of fan behaviors, socialization processes, and team identification. *Journal of Sport Behavior*, 37(3), 251–267.

Richins, M. L. (1983). Negative word-of-mouth by dissatisfied consumers: A pilot study. *Journal of Marketing*, 47(1), 68–78.

Shaw, D., & Duff, R. (2002). Ethics and social responsibility in fashion and clothing choice. Paper presented at the European Marketing Academy Conference, Portugal.

Shaw, D., Newholm, T., & Dickinson, R. (2006). Consumption as voting: An exploration of consumer empowerment. *European Journal of Marketing*, 40(9/10), 1049–1067.

Shen, H., & Kim, J.-N. (2012). The authentic enterprise: Another buzz word, or a true driver of quality relationships? *Journal of Public Relations Research*, 24, 371–389.

Shen, H., & Kim, J.-N. (2013). Linking ethics congruence, communication strategies, and relationship building. *Public Relations Journal*, 6(3), 1–35.

Singh, J. (1988). Consumer complaint intentions and behavior: Definitional and taxonomical issues. *Journal of Marketing*, 52, 93–107.

Singh, J. (1990a). Voice, exit, and negative word-of-mouth behaviors: An investigation across three service categories. *Journal of the Academy of Marketing Science*, 18(1), 1–15.

Singh, J. (1990b). A typology of consumer dissatisfaction response styles. *Journal of Retailing*, 66(1), 57–99.

Steyn, B. (2007). Contribution of public relations to organizational strategy formulation. In E. L. Toth (Ed.), *The future of excellence in public relations and communication management: Challenges for the next generation* (pp. 137–172). London: Routledge.

Stoker, K. L., & Tusinski, K. (2006). Reconsidering public relations' infatuation with dialogue: Why engagement and reconciliation can be more ethical than symmetry and reciprocity. *Journal of Mass Media Ethics*, 21(2–3), 156–176.

Sung, M., & Yang, S. U. (2009). Student–university relationships and reputation: A study of the links between key factors fostering students' supportive behavioral intentions towards their university. *Higher Education*, 57(6), 787–811.

Tibble, S. (1997). Developing communication strategy. *Journal of Communication Management*, 1(4), 356–361.

Tomlinson, M., Buttle, F., & Moores, B. (1995). The fan as customer: Customer service in sports marketing. *Journal of Hospitality & Leisure Marketing*, 3(1), 19–36.

Waters, R. D. (2008). Applying relationship management theory to the fundraising process for individual donors. *Journal of Communication Management*, 12(1), 73–87.

Werder, K. P. (2006). Responding to activism: An experimental analysis of public relations strategy influence on attributes of publics. *Journal of Public Relations Research*, 18(4), 335–356.

Yuan, K.-H., & Bentler, P. M. (2007). Robust procedures in structural equation modeling. In S.-Y. Lee (Ed.). *Handbook of latent variable and related models* (pp. 367–397). Amsterdam: Elsevier.

5 Extending the conversation

Audience reactions to dialogic activity on Twitter

Brandi Watkins

Since the emergence of the website as a tool for public relations, scholars have studied various online platforms to determine their usefulness for increasing engagement with the public (Waters & Williams, 2011). To date, much of this research has focused on the use of social media to build relationships with publics. A defining work in this area is the dialogic principles proposed by Kent and Taylor (1998), which provide strategies for engaging the public in dialogue in an online environment – a key first step to relationship building. Of all the social media platforms available, the one that has been consistently lauded for its relationship building potential is the microblogging site Twitter (Waters & Williams, 2011). Scholars have applied these principles to research in contemporary social media platforms including websites, blogs, and Facebook, with largely the same result – the dialogic capabilities of social media are underutilized. Collectively, these results indicate a need for research that goes beyond examining the activity of the organization but to continue through the communication process in order to better understand the audience perspective of this activity.

Through built-in and motivated fan bases, sports teams are able to encourage interaction and engagement with fans on social media (Wallace, Wilson, & Miloch, 2011). Social media use is prevalent in the sports setting and has provided fans with increased accessibility to sports teams and athletes (Gantz & Lewis, 2014). The high levels of involvement exhibited by sports fans is a relevant aspect of participatory culture that can provide insights into how social media is used to promote dialogue and facilitate relationship building between an organization and its publics.

This chapter explores the audience perspective of dialogic activity on social media as a way to extend the dialogue, specifically how sports fans react to the activity of professional athletes on Twitter. The role of dialogue and the importance of online relationship building are discussed, followed by an in-depth review of the current research on dialogue, social media, and public relations. Results of a survey of sports fans are presented along with implications for research on dialogue and sports.

Literature review

Online relationship building and the role of dialogue

Building relationships with publics is a key function of public relations (Bruning, Dials, & Shirka, 2008). Recently, social media has opened the door to new strategies and tactics for those working in the industry. Through the two-way communicative capabilities of the Internet, public relations practitioners can enhance their communication strategies with key publics (Kelleher, 2009). Smith (2010) describes social media sites as places for "interactivity and information exchange where issues are debated and defined" (p. 330). Many social media platforms offer specialized features and functions that allow organizations to personalize interactions with publics as well as maintain two-way conversations.

Two-way conversation is essential for relationship building efforts. Kent and Taylor (1998) explain, "for a dialogic relationship to exist, parties must view communicating as the goal of a relationship" (p. 324). Bruning et al. (2008) add "dialogue helps an organization manage the organization–public relationship by providing publics with the opportunity to ask questions, express viewpoints, and better understand organizational processes" (p. 241). However, in order for any form of dialogue to be effective, there must be a buy-in on the part of the organization (Kent & Taylor, 2002). The organization itself must demonstrate a commitment to dialogue and engagement on social media by providing opportunities to the public to be involved.

It is not enough for an organization to merely have an account on social media or use that account to disseminate mostly one-way messages. A dialogic orientation, or an engaging and interactive approach to social media, can help an organization with its relationship-building efforts (Bruning et al., 2008). Saffer, Sommerfeldt, and Taylor (2013) found support for the influence of interactivity on organization–public relationships. In their study, they found that the higher the level of interaction on Twitter, the higher the respondents perceived the quality of the organization–public relationship. The researchers go on to suggest that organizations should fully participate in the communication process instead of just acting as a sender of one-way messages. Similarly, a study by Bruning et al. (2008) found relationship attitude and dialogue to have a positive influence on evaluations of an organization.

In addition to being an effective strategy for relationship building, dialogue is also viewed as an ethical form of communication between the organization and public (McAllister-Spooner & Kent, 2009). Through dialogue, organizations are better able to maintain communication that is more transparent and develop relationships that are more open (McAllister-Spooner & Kent, 2009). Similarly, Kent and Taylor (2002) suggested five tenets of dialogue: (1) mutuality, or the idea that organizations and publics are linked together; (2) propinquity, if the public is willing to voice their opinion then the organization should listen; (3) empathy, a spirit of trust should exist between both parties; (4) risk, or the acceptance that some control is lost in the communication exchange; and (5) commitment, where both parties are committed to the relationship.

Dialogic principles

The principles include: (1) the dialogic loop, (2) usefulness of information, (3) generation of return visits, (4) intuitiveness/ease of interface, and (5) the rule of conversation of visitors. The dialogic loop principle states the website should contain a mechanism that allows the public to pose questions directly to the organization and the organization is able to provide a response.

Usefulness of information indicates that information provided by the organization on the website should meet the public's needs. Information must provide some sort of value for the public. Generation of return visits asserts the organization should develop a website with features and content that encourage the public to visit the site multiple times; in other words, the website should be updated regularly with information the audience will find valuable and worth the repeat visit. Related specifically to studies of websites, the intuitiveness or ease of interface principle suggests websites should be easy to navigate and information relevant to the public should be readily available. And finally, the rule of conservation of visitors states the organization should keep the public engaged in their online spaces, not their competitors. Visitors to the website should be able to easily find their way back to the page.

Applying dialogic principles in research

Earlier studies of dialogic capabilities on the Internet began with studies of organization websites. Results of research from Taylor and Kent (2004), Gordon and Berhow (2009) and Igenhoff and Koelling (2009) all found that the dialogic capabilities of websites were not fully realized. Park and Reber (2008) found that dialogic activity on websites could promote control mutuality, trust, satisfaction, openness, and intimacy. Seltzer and Mitrook (2007) asserted that blogs were actually more effective than websites at promoting dialogic principles.

Bortree and Seltzer (2009) studied the dialogic strategies of environmental advocacy groups on Facebook. They found that among the groups in their study, most of these organizations were not engaging their publics in dialogue using Facebook. Waters, Burnett, Lamm, and Lucas (2009) found that non-profit organizations were not using all of the Facebook applications available to them. However, Waters, Canfield, Foster, and Hardy (2011) found that university health centers with a large following on Facebook were more likely to employ dialogic principles on their page. Sweetser and Lariscy's (2008) study of Facebook comments during midterm elections found that people who wrote on a candidate's wall considered themselves to be "friendly" with the candidate, even though they rarely responded.

According to Waters and Williams (2011), information sharing is the primary focus of social media use among public relations practitioners, particularly on Twitter. In an analysis of the use of Twitter among 73 nonprofit organizations, Lovejoy, Waters, and Saxton (2012) found that the organizations are using the site to primarily distribute one-way messages to audiences rather than involving stakeholders. In their study, only about 20 percent of tweets were coded as conversations. Similarly, Linvill, McGee, and Hicks (2012) found that colleges and universities use Twitter primarily as an outlet for disseminating messages.

Other researchers have taken to studying the use of dialogic principles and structural features of Twitter. Rybalko and Seltzer (2010) found that among Fortune 500 companies, organizations with a dialogic orientation were more likely to employ the conservation of visitors principle. In a study of the Twitter activity of professional athletes, Watkins and Lewis (2014) found the dialogic capabilities of Twitter is underutilized, but the use of certain structural features of Twitter (i.e., hashtags and multimedia) do allow for some interaction with fans. McAllister-Spooner and Kent (2009) evaluated the relationship between dialogue and relationship building and found that useful information and the dialogic loop are significant predictors of responsiveness to organizational communication efforts.

These research findings support Levenshus (2010) who asserted that public relations practitioners were not fully utilizing the capabilities of social media and the Internet for relationship building, but practitioners did believe that these platforms were beneficial for meeting communication objectives. However, some have argued that the reason for the lack of dialogue evident in organizations' social media could be attributed to a lack of understanding of how organizations are defining dialogue and interaction as part of their social media strategy (Himelboim, Golan, Moon, & Suto, 2014). One area related to dialogue and social media that has not received as much attention in the research is the expectations of the public when it comes to interacting with organizations. This chapter focuses on an important area of participatory culture – the interactions between sports fans and athletes.

Sports fandom and engagement

Sports fans represent a highly engaged aspect of participatory culture that frequently use social media platforms to connect with their favorite teams, athletes, and other fans (Pegoraro, 2010; Browning & Sanderson, 2012). Throughout history, sports have played an important role in bringing people together. As early as the 1800s, the sport of baseball was credited with helping the nation come back together after the Civil War (Pedersen, Miloch, & Laucella, 2007). Today, the Internet is continuing this tradition by bringing together sports fans despite their geographic boundaries. Gantz and Lewis (2014) explains: "fans spend more time following sports than they did before and now follow sports using multiple platforms simultaneously" (p. 19).

Sports go beyond the on-field competition to become part of a person's identity (Fisher & Wakefield, 1998). Social identification theory has been used to explain the connection that sports fans have with their favorite team or athlete. Social identification is the knowledge that a person is a member of a social group and the emotional significance they place on membership with that group (Tajfel, 1982). The emotional connection a person has with the sports team or favorite athlete is what separates sports fans from casual spectators (Boyle & Magnusson, 2007). Because being a sports fan is so intertwined with a person's identity, the sports fan looks for ways to publicly express their fandom (Gantz & Lewis, 2014). Social media provides such an outlet for this outward expression of fandom and for connecting with other members of the group.

Now more than ever, sports fans have numerous resources for publicly expressing their fandom including social networks, mobile apps, and message boards. The interactive features of social media allow sports fans to not only consume sports-related content, but they can contribute their own content (Gantz & Lewis, 2014). Gantz and Lewis (2014) refer to this as extending their fanship networks. Technology allows fans to follow along with games when they are not able to watch, interact with other fans, participate in fantasy sports leagues, and comment on relevant sports stories.

As previously discussed, creating opportunities for dialogue with key publics is an important component of relationship building, but as much of the research has shown, direct two-way dialogue between an organization and the public on social media is lacking in practice. One area that is less discussed in the research is the perception of this activity on the part of the audience. The next logical question in this line of research should be what does the audience expect from the activity of organizations (or in this case athletes) they follow on social media? To extend the conversation, so to speak, and examine the audience perspective of dialogic activity on social media, the following research questions are proposed:

RQ1:   What factors motivate sports fans to engage with professional athletes on Twitter?
RQ2:   How do sports fans interact with professional athletes on Twitter?
RQ3:   How do sports fans feel about the use of dialogue on Twitter?
RQ3a: How does the use of the dialogic principles on Twitter influence social media outcomes?

Methodology

To address the research questions posed in this study, sports fans using Twitter to follow professional athletes were surveyed to determine their perception of the Twitter activity of professional athletes.

Measures and scale reliability

Engagement. Scales for determining respondents' engagement with athletes was developed from research by Kang (2014). The original 13-item public engagement scale included measures for affective commitment, affectivity, and empowerment. To fit the needs of the current study, the scale was modified to an 8-item scale measuring affective commitment and affectivity using a 5-point Likert scale. Empowerment was not applicable to this study and was left out of the survey. Cronbach's alpha for the engagement scale was .93.

Social Media Activity. Social media activity was measured by (1) consuming Twitter content from professional athletes, (2) contributing content for professional athletes on Twitter, and (3) motivations for interacting with athletes on Twitter with scales developed based on previous research by Men and Tsai (2013) and Muntinga, Moorman, and Smit (2011). Consuming Twitter content included asking respondents how often they read tweets from professional athletes on Twitter or consumed multimedia content (i.e., watching videos or looking at pictures posted by the athletes). Contributing content included questions related to how often respondents would respond to, or answer tweets posed by professional athletes and how often they would retweet messages from or tweet messages to professional athletes. Motivations for following professional athletes on Twitter included entertainment, social interaction, personal identity, information seeking, and reward. All items were measured using a 5-point Likert scale and were found to be reliable consuming social media content ($\alpha = .94$), contributing content ($\alpha = .87$), and motivations for following athletes on social media ($\alpha = .84$).

Dialogic Principles. To determine the audiences' attitude towards dialogic activity on social media, survey scales were developed based on coding categories from previous research of dialogic principles on social media (Watkins & Lewis, 2014). Usefulness of information was measured by asking respondents whether or not they liked it when an athlete tweeted about upcoming games, events they were attending, information about their team or sport, and practices. Conservation of visitors was measured by asking about activity on Twitter including clicking on links to external websites and using the athletes' other social media platforms. To determine attitudes related to the use of the generation of return visits principle, respondents were asked how they felt about an athlete sharing pictures, videos, or web links on social media and the frequency that they check the athletes' account. Finally the use of the dialogic loop principle asked respondents to what extent they feel like professional athletes want to interact on Twitter and their expectations that athletes will respond to them. All scales were found to have acceptable reliability: usefulness of information ($\alpha = .94$), conservation of visitors ($\alpha = .73$), generation of return visits ($\alpha = .90$), dialogic loop ($\alpha = .83$).

Analysis

Data was analyzed using SPSS 22.0. Means and standard deviations for all variables and specific survey questions are reported. A Pearson's correlation was used to determine existing relationships between the variables.

Results

Sample responses and descriptive data

College students were recruited to participate in this survey. A total of 193 surveys were completed. The average age of the respondents was 19 (SD = 1.235) with 42% males (n = 81) and 53% female (n = 111). The majority of respondents were white/Caucasian (n = 149, 77.2%) followed by Asian, (n = 23, 12.2%), Hispanic (n = 8, 4.1%), African American (n = 7, 3.6%), and 2.6% preferred not to answer (n = 5). Eighty-two percent of respondents indicated they were sports fans (n = 158). Of those 71% indicated they were football fans (n = 137), basketball fans (n = 100, 51.8%), and baseball (n = 62, 32.1%). Less than 20 percent of the sample indicated they were fans of hockey (n = 34), soccer (n = 32), tennis (n = 31), swimming (n = 27), and golf (n = 21).

Engagement

RQ1 investigated factors that lead to engagement with professional athletes on Twitter. Overall, the engagement scale had a mean of 2.61 (SD = .904). An examination of the individual items revealed that respondents were more likely to follow an athlete on Twitter because they were interested in the athletes' life (M = 3.33, SD = 1.151) and were generally attentive to what athletes had to say on Twitter (M = 2.95, SD = 1.183). Respondents did not indicate that they felt like they were part of the athletes' inner circle by following them on Twitter (M = 1.96, SD = .986).

Social media activity

RQ2 examined the social media activity of sports fans on Twitter. Overall, motivations for consuming social media content had the highest mean score of these three variables (M = 2.78, SD = .842) and most respondents followed athletes on Twitter for the entertainment value (M = 3.56, SD = 1.044) and to get information (M = 3.26, SD = 1.194). Second, respondents tended to show more of a propensity to consume Twitter content from athletes (M = 2.77, SD = 1.12) rather than contribute content (M = 1.66, SD = .744). For consuming Twitter content, respondents indicated that they looked at pictures from athletes (M = 3.02, SD = 1.252) and read their tweets (M = 2.91, SD = 1.204) more than other activities. As far as contributing content to Twitter, respondents indicated they were more likely to retweet a tweet from an athlete

(M = 2.49, SD = 1.299). The lowest scores were for answering questions from athletes (M = 1.31, SD = .718), asking athletes questions (M = 1.32, SD = .693), and tweeting to athletes (M = 1.42, SD = .839). Interestingly, in content analyses of dialogue on Twitter, these activities are generally coded as the dialogic loop principle.

Dialogic principles

RQ3 investigated the attitude of sports fans towards use of the dialogic principles. Respondents in the study were more interested in tweets that were considered useful (M = 3.55, SD = .947) followed by the generation of return visits (M = 3.08, SD = .972), conservation of visitors (M = 2.74, SD = .934), and dialogic loop (M = 2.09, SD = .834). These findings are similar to a content analysis of dialogic activity by professional athletes on Twitter (see Watkins & Lewis, 2014). Generation of return visits and usefulness of information were used the most among athletes in the sample. Survey results indicated that respondents tend to view these activities favorably.

A Pearson's correlation was run to determine if there was a relationship between the dialogic principles and the social media outcomes (RQ3a). Each variable was significantly and positively correlated with the dialogic principles. In other words, the more these principles were used on Twitter, then the more likely people would engage in the online activities under investigation.

The generation of return visits principle had the highest correlations with the social media outcomes: motivation (r (191) = .758, p < .001); consume (r (191) = .752, p < .001); engage (r (191) = .706, p < .001); and contribute (r (191) = .502, p < .001). The conservation of visitors principle correlated higher with consuming Twitter content (r (191) = .727, p < .001); motivation (r (191) = .674, p < .001); engagement (r (191) = .632, p < .001); and contributing content (r (191) = .611, p < .001). Usefulness of information was correlated with motivation (r (191) = .687, p < .001), consume (r (191) = .657, p < .001), and engagement (r (191) = .687, p < .001). Finally, the dialogic loop principle yielded the lowest correlations with social media outcomes: engagement (r (191) = .585, p < .001); motivation (r (191) = .492, p < .001); contribute (r (191) = .389, p < .001); and consume (r (191) = .175, p < .05).

Discussion

Dialogue is a complex and complicated concept (Kent & Taylor, 2002) and in order for it to be used as a public relations tactic, there must be buy-in from the organization. The organization must be willing to devote the time and resources to managing this endeavor. Recent research has revealed that organizations from various sectors are buying in to social media as a tool for communicating with key publics, but most of the research in this area revealed that most of these messages utilize one-way communication more frequently. The goal of this chapter was to examine the other side of this perspective, to look at how users respond to activity on Twitter and how that influences their social media activity.

Among the social media activities under investigation, motivation and consuming content had the highest mean scores. This finding indicates that from a participatory perspective the respondents in the sample were motivated to follow athletes for entertainment and information purposes and were more likely to consume content rather than contribute content or engage with the athlete. In order for a conversation to take place, there must be two willing participants. In this case, at least, direct interaction with athletes was not a priority on Twitter.

Related to the dialogic principles, respondents tended to look more favorably on the usefulness of information principle and generation of return visits. Employing each of these principles relies heavily on one-way communication (i.e., producing tweets with relevant information and creating content that keeps users coming back to the Twitter feed). The dialogic loop scored the lowest among respondents. This could be a result of audiences being conditioned to receiving one-way messages from organizations, or in this case from professional athletes.

The results of the correlation analysis revealed positive, significant correlations among all of the variables in the study, which indicates employing these principles on Twitter could lead to increased levels of engagement, consuming, contributing, and motivations to follow an organization on Twitter. As much of the literature has heralded the use of two-way communication, these results indicate some level of support for using all of the principles, including the ones that rely more on one-way communication tactics. Theunissen, Norbani, and Noordin (2012) argue that dialogue has not been clearly defined in the literature and has "been uncritically equated to two-way symmetrical communication" (p. 5). Put another way dialogue and two-way symmetrical communication are not the same and much of the current research on dialogue and social media defines dialogue in this way. These results show that other types of activity besides what has traditionally been conceptualized as dialogue can result in a positive influence on attitudes toward social media activity.

In participatory culture, such as sports, there must be a willingness from both the organization and the fan to engage in activity whether in real life or online. Waters and Williams (2011) concluded:

> there are times in organized communication campaigns when one-way messages are preferred and more helpful than taking a symmetrical approach; there are others when conversations and negotiation will yield the most gain for an organization. It is up to the public relations practitioners representing the organization to decide which model, or models, will produce the desired results for the organization.
>
> (pp. 359–360)

Dialogue and social media is an important aspect of public relations research and has implications for different aspects of participatory culture, especially sports. Dialogue has been noted as a key component of relationship building and study of its use should be continued. These findings suggest that other principles outside of direct, two-way communication can also engage audiences and perhaps enhance relationships. Continued research focused on how the audience interacts with content produced by the organization is necessary.

References

Bortree, D. S., & Seltzer, T. (2009). Dialogic strategies and outcomes: An analysis of environmental advocacy groups' Facebook profiles. *Public Relations Review*, 35, 317–319. doi: 10.1016/j.pubrev.2009.05.002.

Boyle, B. A., & Magnusson, P. (2007). Social identity and brand equity formation: A comparative study of collegiate sports fans. *Journal of Sport Management*, 21, 497–520.

Browning, B. & Sanderson, J. (2012). The positives and negatives of Twitter: Exploring how student-athletes use Twitter and respond to critical tweets. *International Journal of Sport Communication*, 5, 503–521.

Bruning, S. D., Dials, M., & Shirka, A. (2008). Using dialogue to build organization–public relationships, engage publics, and positively affect organizational outcomes. *Public Relations Review*, 34, 25–31.

Fisher, R. J., & Wakefield, K. (1998). Factors leading to group identification: A field study of winners and losers. *Psychology & Marketing*, 15(1), 23–40.

Gantz, W., & Lewis, N. (2014). Fanship differences between traditional and newer media. In Andrew C. Billings and Marie Hardin (Eds.), *Routledge handbook of sport and new media*. New York: Routledge.

Gordon, J., & Berhow, S. (2009). University websites and dialogic features for building relationships with potential students. *Public Relations Review*, 35, 150–152. doi: 10.1016/j.pubrev.2008.11.003.

Himelboim, I., Golan, G. J., Moon, B. B., & Suto, R. J. (2014). A social networks approach to public relations on Twitter. *Public Relations Review*, 26, 13–22. doi: 10.1080/1062726X.2014.908724.

Igenhoff, D., & Koelling, A. M. (2009). The potential of websites as a relationship building tool for charitable fundraising NPOS. *Public Relations Review*, 25, 66–73.

Kang, M. (2014). Understanding public engagement: Conceptualizing and measuring its influence on supportive behavioral intentions. *Journal of Public Relations Research*, 26 (5), 399–416. doi: 10.1080/1062726X.2014.956107.

Kelleher, T. (2009). Conversational voice, communicated commitment, and public relations outcomes in interactive online communication. *Journal of Communication*, 59, 172–188. doi: 10.111/j.1460–2466.2008.01410.x.

Kent, M. L., & Taylor, M. (1998). Building dialogic relationships through the world wide web. *Public Relations Review*, 24(3), 321–334.

Kent, M. L., & Taylor, M. (2002). Toward a dialogic theory of public relations. *Public Relations Review*, 28, 21–37.

Levenshus, A. (2010). Online relationship management in a presidential campaign: A case study of the Obama campaign's management of its internet-integrated grassroots effort. *Journal of Public Relations Research*, 22(3), 313–335. doi: 10.1080/10627261003614419.

Linvill, D. L., McGee, S. E., & Hicks, L. K. (2012). Colleges' and universities' use of Twitter: A content analysis. *Public Relations Review*, 38, 636–638. doi: http://dx.doi.org/10.1016/j.pubrev.2012.05.010.

Lovejoy, K., Waters, R., & Saxton, G. D. (2012). Engaging stakeholders through Twitter: How nonprofit organizations are getting more out of 140 characters or less. *Public Relations Review*, 38(2), 313–318.

McAllister-Spooner, S. M., & Kent, M. L. (2009). Dialogic public relations and resource dependency: New Jersey community colleges as models of web site effectiveness. *Atlantic Journal of Communication*, 17, 220–239, doi: 10.1080.15456870903210113.

Men, L. R., & Tsai, W. S. (2013). Beyond liking or following: Understanding public engagement on social networking sites in China. *Public Relations Review*, 39, 13–22. doi: 10.1016/j.pubrev.2012.09.013.

Muntinga, D. G., Moorman, M., & Smit, E. G. (2011). Introducing COBRAs Exploring motivations for brand-related social media use. *International Journal of Advertising*, 30(1), 13–46.

Park, H., & Reber, B. H. (2008). Relationship building and the use of web sites: How Fortune 500 corporations use their web sites to build relationships. *Public Relations Review*, 34, 409–411. doi: 10.1016/j.pubrev.2008.06.006.

Pedersen, P. M., Miloch, K. S., & Laucella, P. C. (2007). *Strategic Sport Communication*. Champaign, IL: Human Kinetics.

Pegoraro, A. (2010). Look who's talking. Athletes on Twitter: A case study. *International Journal of Sport Communication*, 3, 501–514.

Rybalko, S. & Seltzer, T. (2010). Dialogic communication in 140 characters or less: How Fortune 500 companies engage stakeholders using Twitter. *Public Relations Review*, 36, 336–341. doi: 10.1016/j.pubrev.2010.08.004.

Saffer, A. J., Sommerfeldt, E. J., & Taylor, M. (2013). The effects of organizational Twitter activity on organization–public relations. *Public Relations Review*, 39, 213–215. doi: 10.1016/jpubrev.2013.02.005.

Seltzer, T., & Mitrook, M. A. (2007). The dialogic potential of weblogs in relationship building. *Public Relations Review*, 33, 227–229.

Smith, B. G. (2010). Socially distributing public relations: Twitter, Haiti, and inter-activity in social media. *Public Relations Review*, 26, 329–335. doi: 10.1016/j.pubrev/2010.08.005.

Sweetser, K. D., & Lariscy, R. W. (2008). Candidates make good friends: An analysis of candidates' uses of Facebook. *International Journal of Strategic Communication*, 2(3), 175–198. doi: 10.1080/15531180802178687.

Tajfel, H. (1982). Social psychology of intergroup relations. *Annual Review of Psychology*, 33, 1–39. doi: 10.1146/annurev.ps.33.020182.000245.

Taylor, M., & Kent, M. L. (2004). Congressional web sites and their potential for public dialogue. *Atlantic Journal of Communication*, 12(2), 59–76.

Theunissen, P., Norbani, W., & Noordin, W. (2012). Revisiting the concept "dialogue" in public relations. *Public Relations Review*, 28, 5–13. doi: 10.1016/j.pubrev.2011.09.006.

Wallace, L., Wilson, J., & Miloch, K. (2011). Sporting Facebook: A content analysis of NCAA organizational sport pages and Big 12 conference athletic department pages. *International Journal of Sport Communication*, 4, 422–444.

Waters, R. D., Burnett, E., Lamm, A., & Lucas, J. (2009). Engaging stakeholders through social networking: How nonprofit organizations are using Facebook. *Public Relations Review*, 35, 102–106.

Waters, R. D., Canfield, R. R., Foster, J. M., & Hardy, E. E. (2011). Applying the dialogic theory to social networking sites: Examining how university health centers convey health messages on Facebook. *Journal of Social Marketing*, 1(3), 211–227. doi: 10.1108/204267611111170713.

Waters, R. D., & Williams, J. M. (2011). Squawking, tweeting, cooing, and hooting: Analyzing the communication patterns of government agencies on Twitter. *Journal of Public Affairs*, 11(4), 353–363. doi: 10.1002/pa.385.

Watkins, B., & Lewis, R. (2014). Initiating dialogue on social media: An investigation of athletes' use of dialogic principles and structural features of Twitter. *Public Relations Review*, 40, 853–855. doi: 10.1016/jpubrev.2014.08.001.

6 Gamification in PR

Michelle Katchuck

Offering a balance between theory and practice, this chapter examines how games and gamification are becoming widely used public relations strategies that have gone beyond simple entertainment. These games do more than just inform or instruct. Gamified activities and campaigns now motivate and impact behavior in areas from health (Göbel, Hardy, Wendel, Mehm, & Steinmetz, 2010; Wong et al., 2007), to acculturation (Kayali, 2011), to sustainability (Zografakis, Menegaki, & Tsagarakis, 2008). This chapter provides an overview of relevant and related communication theories that are put into practice through gamification, with concrete examples used in public relations today.

"Gamification" refers to the use of game mechanics or techniques, such as rules, competition, challenges, and so on within communication environments that are not in and of themselves games. For example, this could include motivating users to perform some sort of action like purchasing something, or increasing brand awareness and loyalty. According to Sebastian Deterding, founder and organizer of the Gamification Research Network, "Gamification is an informal umbrella term for the use of video game elements in non-gaming systems to improve user experience (UX) and user engagement" (Deterding, Khaled, Nacke, & Dixon, 2011, p. 1). Gamification is defined by Bunchball (2010) – a gamification application developer – as: integrating game dynamics into your site, service, community, content, or campaign, in order to drive participation (p. 2).

Gamification: what it is, what it is not

At their core, games are about engagement, they are a chance to engage our brains playing solo, they are a chance to engage with family or friends (Game night, anyone?), and they are a chance to engage with people we haven't even met yet as is the case with social gaming. What better way to persuade than by engaging audiences and consumers with a fun experience that taps into their emotions and desires – their own motivations – not just to directly change their behavior or purchase intent, but to endear them to your message or brand?

Engaging people creates fans, and fans are more valuable than a catchy tag line that makes people take one action, one time. Fans will not only change their behavior or meet your call to action, but will become advocates, engaging their friends and networks, instagramming photos and retweeting messages that they identify with and believe in.

The motivation for fandom is largely thought to boil down to a sense of belonging and identity, but the reasons for fan devotion can be extremely wide-ranging. The number of brands and ideological messages that we as individuals can be fans of at one time is large and diverse, so the ways we demonstrate that devotion may be as wide-ranging – from small actions like "liking" something on Facebook to larger actions like organizing a city-wide initiative in support of a cause. What is similar is the fact that we have attached an emotion to the message that we perceive to be encompassed in, or represented by, the brand or action or cause.

Public Relations practitioners have discovered that gamification can be a powerful, effective way to tap into this engagement, particularly in communications campaigns that target behavior change. Many researchers (Cheng, 2003; Davis, 2009; Fogg, 1998, 1999, 2002; King & Tester, 1999) believe that the information communication technology (ICT) itself can be persuasive, much like an extension of Marshall McLuhan's famous dictum, "the medium is the message."

Gamification techniques were pioneered by video games, especially multi-player video games with systems of points, leaderboards, achievements, and interaction between players. Such gaming was made possible by connecting computers together, first on LANS, then via the Internet, engaging players in a unified and unifying, real-time activity. Drawing on this foundation, gamification as a Public Relations technique has blossomed, facilitated by the Internet as a communication channel in what is called computer mediated communication (CMC).

And while games themselves have a history predating the written word, CMC has changed gaming. "Just as the printing press and the cinema have promoted and enabled new kinds of storytelling, computers work as enablers of games, letting us play old games in new ways and allowing for new kinds of games that would not have been possible before computers" (Juul, 2005, p. 6). Gamification holds the potential to motivate audiences in ways that were not possible with traditional mass media communications. Game mechanics or techniques that are often used in these gamification environments are:

- Immediate feedback, and feedback loops
- Points – these are represented by levels, badges, achievements, loyalty points, leaderboards
- Onboarding – helping new users understand the gaming aspects of the environment (how to win the game), tutorial, or practice
- Intrinsic/extrinsic rewards – endogenous/exogenous cost vs. reward
- Missions/quests/journeys

- Solo/multiplayer
- Synchronous/asynchronous
- Authentic identity or anonymous identity
- Collaboration – cooperating with others
- Virtual currency – virtual goods or items that can be accumulated and exchanged for either virtual or real-world goods
- Gratification
- Social capital/social influence/reputation
- Measurement

Gamification experiences may begin online, but need not end there. Successful gamification can result in real life actions taken by players, either directly tied to the game or indirectly, as a result of shifts in attitudes that can be spurred by the game experience. Thus gamification can not only build a fan community, but also address real-world problems by making real-world actions more fun. For example, in a gamification project that I helped to develop, players were rewarded with points online for taking real-world actions that decreased their environmental impact by doing things like taking public transportation or car-pooling.

It is helpful here to note what gamification is not, as there are related communications strategies and online experiences that look similar. One type of game that is often confused with gamification is the field of serious games, which are often immersive game-like simulations designed to teach or enforce real actions. Notable serious game designer Jane McGonigal in her book, *Reality is Broken* (2011), makes a call to action for games to address real-world problem-solving. For example instead of playing SimCity, people could play something like her game, World Without Oil, where they address the problem of living in peak oil real-world simulations. McGonigal's game *SuperBetter*, in contrast, is more typical of what we mean by gamification as players choose a personal health goal and get points for doing things to help achieve it. For example, a player can choose an exercise challenge and earn points by going for a walk around the block.

Gamification does not mean social games, although social engagement is often an important feature of gamification. Social games, as a category, are games like those from Zynga or other Facebook-like network games and smartphone game apps, in which people are most often playing with a profile that is closely tied to their real-world identity, such as Facebook profiles. However, while marketers and advertisers use these types of games as advertising vehicles, these are not considered gamification as they are purely entertainment, with no larger goal of imparting new knowledge, or changing attitudes or behaviors in the real world. A simplified delineation of these different game environments is that serious games focus on the world, social games focus on the game, while gamification focuses on the player, and for PR practitioners, this means your audience.

The game begins: communication theories behind gamification, why it's fun and why it works

While gamification may be new, the fact that communications can have an effect on individual behavior has been studied for decades, beginning with the research of the Chicago School of theorists (Harold Lasswell, Paul Lazarsfeld, Kurt Lewin, and Carl Hovland). These communication theories now inform the use of gamification in communication. If communication, at its heart, is the use and interpretation of words and symbols, then "gamifying" communication seems intuitive. Wittgenstein, in *Philosophical Investigations* (Wittgenstein and Anscombe, 2001), considers the use of language itself game-like, in its use of rules, like those of a game, which are neither true, nor false, neither fact, nor fiction, but simply used to facilitate the purposes of communication.

Gamification can influence communication – and behavior – by using game elements, or game mechanics, (e.g. rules, rewards, levels, challenges, etc.) to produce new knowledge, which in turn can influence participants. According to Singhal and Dearing (2006), this influence can happen in two ways: "First, it can influence audience individuals' awareness, attitudes, and behavior towards a socially desirable end. … Second, it can influence the audience's external environment to help create the necessary conditions for social change at the system level" (p. 202). The argument is not necessarily that games or gamification can impact behavior directly, but rather that they may have an impact on various motivators such as social norms or perceived control of actions. It may be possible to impact factors in the environment of an audience, which will in turn lead to behavioral change.

Another mechanism by which gamification can influence participants is described by theories concerning narrative persuasion (Green & Brock, 2000; Hinyard & Kreuter, 2007; Kreuter et al., 2007), which posits that narratives and storytelling techniques can encourage audiences to relate to the information in a more personalized way by empathizing with characters or events in a narrative. Successful gamification that enlists players as actors within a story can thus make an emotional appeal.

Research in the effects of mass communication led to conceptualizing theories of Uses and Gratification as a factor in how communication affects audiences.

> Uses and Gratifications is a psychological communication perspective that examines how individuals use mass media. An audience based theoretical framework, it is grounded on the assumption that individuals select media content to fulfill needs and wants … individuals use media and experience gratifications.
>
> (Papacharissi, 2008, p. 137)

This framework applies to gamification because the Internet and mobile technology can impart a range of gratifying experiences for individual users through communication messages that appeal to their own distinct motivations.

The use of gamification as a communication strategy allows a high degree of audience involvement in this way. In fact, early research in Uses and Gratification examined why people listen to radio quiz shows, highlighting various intrinsic motivations, such as audience members learning something about themselves, or feeling good about knowing the answers (Herzog, 1942; Lazarsfeld and Stanton, 1941, 1979). Papacharissi (2008) notes that, "despite the diversity of contexts and interests, [Uses and Gratification] studies tend to share a common frame of analysis that focuses on motives, social and psychological antecedents, and cognitive, attitudinal, or behavioural outcomes" (p. 139).

The concept of motivation is essential to the theoretical underpinning of gamification – and it is a concept that has evolved greatly over decades and engendered much debate among communication and psychology theorists. A century ago, Freud (1914) discussed human drives, or instincts, that motivate behavior, asserting that the main human drives are sex and aggression. Such theories have been expanded by others (e.g., Hull, 1942), and most notably in Maslow's well-known hierarchy of needs, which is based on motivations towards behaviors that satisfy human needs from basic (food, shelter, security), to emotional and intellectual needs.

These early theories emphasized extrinsic motivations as drivers of human behavior – that is, positive rewards outside of a person, which they earn from repeating certain behaviors. Later studies turned to the idea of intrinsic motivation, which is thought of as doing an action for its own sake, but is also used to refer to a motivation that is considered to be internal, such as a satisfying feeling on the part of the person performing the behavior. Consider recycling: some do it out of a personal conviction (intrinsic motivation) that recycling is a moral, ethical act, regardless of personal gain, while others do it to cash in the 5- or 10-cent deposit per container – an amount that is essentially a bounty put on recyclable material by governments to create an extrinsic, monetary reward for recycling.

One common criticism of gamification is that it focuses mainly on extrinsic rewards, such as the points and badges typically associated with games. This stems from longstanding research questioning the value of extrinsic rewards as a motivator for behavioral change (e.g., Skinner, 1953), as well as the use of extrinsic rewards as a strategy to impact intrinsic motivation (e.g., Deci, 1971). In gamification terms, an intrinsic reward may be the desire for self expression, while an extrinsic reward might be winning enough points to be seen at the top of a leaderboard. Kohn (1999) posits that behavior cannot be changed by rewards alone. His theory that behaviourism – the attempt to change behaviors by conditioning, such as offering positive rewards for the desired actions – actually undermines real, sustainable behavioral change. This theory, known as overjustification effect, has been widely debated both positively and negatively (Cameron, Banko, & Pierce, 2001).

However, the theoretical battle between intrinsic and extrinsic motivation might best be described as "game over." A more contemporary view of motivation, for example, Brophy (2010, p. xi), posits that, "theorizing about motivation has evolved, culminating [currently] in notions of intrinsic motivation or flow as an ideal state."

Go with the flow

Motivation research – and gamification/game design in general – is particularly interested in the idea of "flow," a concept from the field of positive psychology put forth by Mihályi Csíkszentmihályi (1990, 1991), who proposes flow as a way to understand "experiences during which individuals are fully involved in the present moment ... [a] phenomenon of intrinsically motivated, or autotelic, activity" (1990, p. 89). What Csíkszentmihályi and others (Bernhaupt, 2010; Chen, 2007; Deterding, 2011; Kim, 1998; McGonigal, 2011; Nakamura & Csíkszentmihályi, 2002; Pink, 2005; Reeves & Read, 2009; Von Ahn & Dabbish, 2008; Zichermann & Cunningham, 2011) posit is that understanding flow can lead to a better understanding of individuals' intrinsic motivations for behavior. In game terms, if you've ever fired up your Xbox One or dropped into a game of Farmville "just for minute" and suddenly found that hours have flown by, you've experienced "flow."

From this perspective, gamification makes use of extrinsic motivators to obtain engagement by offering prizes, and once players are motivated to participate, this can lead to intrinsic motivation – such as the positive experience of flow – and thus to positive changes in attitudes toward the issue or brand. However, even flow can't explain all the motivations that compel people to participate in gamified experiences, and all the avenues by which a gamified campaign can change people's behavior outside the game. Reiss (2012) identified several universal reinforcements that motivate people, claiming that:

> Human motives are just too diverse to fall into just two categories. ... Moreover, extrinsic motivation (a means to an end) arises from the pursuit of the intrinsically valued goal it produces; thus, it is not a separate and distinct category of motivation.
>
> (p. 3)

Among the motivations or reinforcements that Reiss (2005, 2012) identified as motivations for attitude and behavior are: collecting, sharing, altruism, and competing.

Also of interest to the design of gamified campaigns is a proposition put forth by Self-Perception Theory (Bem & McConnell, 1970; Bem, 1973; Laird, 2007), which holds that attitudes may follow behavior. This theory is often used in public relations, marketing, and communication campaigns as a process for attitude change. Self-perception theory holds that there is a possibility for these campaigns to cause participants to analyze their attitudes regarding these behaviors and see them more positively. What does all this look like in the real world? One player in a recent research project/gamified campaign was an interesting example of tension between forms of motivation. The campaign encouraged students to adopt sustainable behaviors, such as conserving energy or using less water. This particular player had a high number of points and was one of the most engaged players. During the post-campaign interviews I learned that his primary motivation for playing was competition – he simply wanted to beat his friends. He had no particular interest in the pro-environmental messages delivered through the campaign. However, at the same time, he reported learning a great deal about sustainability and was considering changing his college major to something related to sustainability. Clearly, the gamified communications campaign tapped into an intrinsic motivation of which this student was not even consciously aware.

Putting gamification into practice

Public Relations practitioners should keep in mind that, in terms of gamification, player engagement is more likely to be achieved, and to be longer lasting, when intrinsic motivation is higher than extrinsic. This type of motivation is best suited to the social aspects of gamified experiences, such as activities that encourage sociality, social capital, achievement or status, and immersion and engagement. When well orchestrated, these experiences create a condition in which an audience is fully engaged in consuming the information, or performing gamified tasks – in other words, flow. Further conditions that also foster flow include clear goals throughout the game, immediate feedback and reward for actions, balance between challenge and skills, and intrinsic motivations. Another perspective is that, "arousal, pleasure, and individualism act as particularly potent drivers of higher-order needs in virtual world channels" (Deci & Ryan, 1985, p. 7).

Gamification is used to drive sales, build fan communities, spread awareness, inspire action, educate, and influence. An example of early attempts to use gamification factors to an advantage are loyalty rewards cards or points from credit card companies, air miles points, or Nike+, which first used RFID and web technologies to track and provide feedback to engage runners, and now the Nike+ Fuel band, which can track a range of activities and use this feedback for gamified motivation and engagement.

What makes fans engage beyond the game to build a relationship with a brand or complete a real-world action? Unlike the loyalty programs that simply and directly rewarded repeat customers, the goals for gamification in Public Relations often are social or personal rather than direct engagement with a brand, product, or service, such as sharing the game with friends, or supporting a cause. Perhaps the best way to understand how gamification is used for Public Relations and communications campaigns is to look at a few cases using gamification. The following examples highlight a variety of gamification tactics and strategies being used by organizations and companies in all sectors: corporate, nonprofit, government, and education.

Uses and cases: building and engaging a fan community

As part of its campaign for environmentally friendly cars, car maker Volkswagen ran a public relations contest it called The Fun Theory, asking people to submit ideas for making it more fun to change behavior for the better. While contests alone are not considered a gamification technique, some of the contestants naturally turned to gamification elements to "make things more fun." The first winner in 2010 devised a Speed Camera Lottery – where speeders are fined, while drivers obeying the speed limit were entered into a lottery to win cash collected from the fines. Volkswagen and The Swedish National Society for Road Safety actually tried it out and found that the potential to win a reward for obeying the speed limit was compelling; the result was a 22% reduction in speeding.

Step2, maker of childrens' toys and products, has gamified its web program called Customer Buzz (www.step2.com/loyalty), which uses points, leaderboards, and badges to reward users for reviewing products on the Step2.com website. Reviewers also earn points and badges when their reviews are rated. The gamification system relies on a desire for social capital as players are rewarded with points, not monetary credits or discounts. High-level players are designated as influencers. Brand and segment influencers are a very valuable audience that gamification makes easier to identify. Step2 may target influencers with product or other communications, knowing that this highly engaged and motivated audience will essentially become their marketing partners, helping to spread the word about Step2's brand.

The use of gamification as a PR engagement strategy extends not just to commercial brands, but to scientific research or social good. Fold.It is a web-based gamified science project (http://fold.it/portal/) that allows users to play puzzle games in pursuit of creating protein bundles for the purposes of protein structure prediction that can be used in real scientific and medical research. Puzzle solutions are scored and the website uses leaderboards and challenges. Players can create their own challenges and form groups to solve puzzles collaboratively. This particular type of gamification system is often called Citizen Science, where research or tasks for science projects are essentially crowd-sourced; however, it is important to note that not all citizen science projects are games or use gamification.

Recyclebank (www.recyclebank.com) is an organization that wants everyone to take care of the environment by adopting better eco-behaviors. To engage its audience in learning more about how their actions impact the environment the Recyclebank website awards users with points for completing activities ranging from educating themselves about an issue, completing quizzes, or making a change in personal habits. Points can be redeemed via partner organizations and retailers for discounts and items.

Pop band Coldplay gamified the album release for its 2013 album *Ghost Stories*. The band organized a global scavenger hunt for handwritten lyrics to the album's songs. Clues were posted on Twitter and one of the hidden lyrics contained a Golden Ticket that would award the finder tickets and a trip to see the band live in concert. This game not only engaged current fans of the band, but also gained new fans who became interested via the scavenger hunt. This seems an especially effective use of gamification for Public Relations in an industry that is shifting dramatically, calling for new ways to engage music fans.

Gamification is used not just to engage current fans, but also collaboratively by brands to find new fans. Fashion clothing and accessories brands have signed up to be a part of the fashion gamification app Covet Fashion (www.covetfashion.com). Players use virtual currency to purchase virtual replicas of brands' shoes, accessories, and clothing. Covet Fashion then challenges users to dress and style an avatar for various situations or events that are set up as the game challenges. Everyone is a winner at Covet Fashion – people earn more in-game currency by voting on these user-created looks and the players whose looks get the most votes earn prizes. The app is really designed to gamify, and make fun, discovering new brands and products for each new fashion season. Players who like their own or another player's looks can discover and purchase the real thing.

Using gamification to make fans out of employees

Gamification is also used for Internal Communications and Employee Engagement. Pep Boys, an aftermarket automotive company, used gamification to engage employees in learning workplace safety and product loss information through quizzes, rewards, and real-time feedback used to individualize gameplay. The gamification developer, Axonify, and Pep Boys stated that by using this gamified system, the company saw a 45% reduction in workplace safety incidents, and a 55% reduction in inventory shrink (Axonify, 2014).

Achievers.com (www.achievers.com/platform) uses badges/rewards, challenges/quests, leaderboards, near real-time feedback, and social recognition to engage employees in a variety of engagement activities including health and wellness challenges and brand product knowledge. Achievers uses public recognition as a motivator and social engagement strategy that will ultimately drive sales and encourage employees to better engage with customers.

Enterprise gamification developer Badgeville has one of the largest gamification software applications that businesses can purchase to motivate and engage employees. Badgeville's gamification system uses badges, challenges, levels, leaderboards, quizzes, and rewards to increase participation in customer facing engagement by employees – turning employees into brand fans and champions.

The primary driver for such employee gamification apps is engagement. Companies want their employees to be fans of the organization, to enjoy working there, and to be engaged; because engaged people do better work and foster a better corporate culture.

Keep your eye on the prize

Gamification is still relatively new, and research on its uses and effects is ongoing. Communication campaigns in general, however, have long been studied for their potential effects on attitude and behavior change (see: Ajzen and Fishbein, 2005; Cacioppo, Petty, Kao, & Rodriguez 1986; Cappella, Fishbein, Hornik, Ahern, and Sayeed, 2001). Atkin and Salmon define a communication campaign as having four essential elements (2010, p. 420):

1   A campaign intends to generate specific outcomes or effects.
2   Audience is a relatively large number of individuals.
3   Has a specified time frame.
4   Has an organized set of communication activities.

These foundational elements are essential if gamification is to achieve its goal as a PR or communication strategy. Just adding a leaderboard to a campaign is not likely to be effective at engaging a brand's audience or fans. Gamification is a tactic, not a goal unto itself, to be implemented when Public Relations professionals conclude that it can be an effective means of engaging an audience and eliciting a desired effect from that audience as part of a larger communications strategy. Before undertaking a gamified communications campaign, designers must be able to answer: Why are we using this tactic? What do we want people to learn and/or do in the real world as a result of participating? Why is gamification the best method for achieving that outcome?

There is a wide variety of avenues for gamification – serious games, persuasive games, entertainment, learning or education games. Game elements from each of these may be useful to an organization but require a very different method of implementation, from small gamification tactics (e.g. leaderboards, reward points, etc.) to full game platform or app development. As these case studies demonstrate, gamification is an effective new way to reach audiences, build brand loyalty, and change behavior. The modern Public Relations professional would do well to master the techniques of gamification and understand the communication theories that inform their effective use.

References

Achievers. (2015). http://www.achievers.com/.

Ajzen, I., & Fishbein, M. (2005). The influence of attitudes on behavior. In D. Albarracín, B. T. Johnson, & Zanna (Eds.), *The handbook of attitudes* (pp. 173–221). Mahwah, NJ: Lawrence Erlbaum.

Atkin, C., & Salmon, C. T. (2010). Communication campaigns. In C. R. Berger, M. E. Roloff, & D. R. Roskos-Ewoldsen (Eds.), *Handbook of communication science* (2nd ed., pp. 419–435). Los Angeles, CA: Sage.

Axonify. (2014). Axonify case study pep boys. Brochure, n.p.

Bem, D. J. (1973). Self-perception theory. In L. Berkowitz (Ed.), *Advances in experimental social psychology* (Vol. 6, pp. 1–62). New York: Academic Press.

Bem, D. J., & McConnell, H. K. (1970). Testing the self-perception explanation of dissonance phenomena: On the salience of premanipulation attitudes. *Journal of Personality and Social Psychology*, 14(1), 23–31.

Bernhaupt, R. (2010). *Evaluating user experience in games: Concepts and methods.* London: Springer Publishing Company, Incorporated.

Brophy, J. E. (2010). *Motivating students to learn* (3rd ed.). New York: Routledge.

Bunchball. (2010). Gamification 101: An introduction to the use of game dynamics to influence behavior. Brochure, n.p.

Cameron, J., Banko, K. M., & Pierce, W. D. (2001). Pervasive negative effects of rewards on intrinsic motivation: The myth continues. *The Behavior Analyst*, 24(1), 1–44.

Cacioppo, J. T., Petty, R. E., Kao, C. F., & Rodriguez, R.. (1986). Central and peripheral routes to persuasion: An individual difference perspective. *Journal of Personality and Social Psychology*, 51(5), 1032–1043.

Cappella, J. N., Fishbein, M., Hornik, R., Ahern, R. K., & Sayeed, S.. (2001). Using theory to select messages in antidrug media campaigns. *Public communication campaigns*, 214–230.

Chen, J. (2007). Flow in games (and everything else). *Communications of the ACM*, 50(4), 31–34.

Cheng, R. (2003). Persuasion strategies for computers as persuasive technologies. Department of Computer Science, University of Saskatchewan.

Covet Fashion. (2015). http://www.covetfashion.com.

Csíkszentmihályi, M. (1990). *Flow: The psychology of optimal experience.* New York: Harper and Row.

Csíkszentmihályi, M. (1997). Flow and education. *NAMTA Journal*, 22(2), 2–35.

Csíkszentmihályi, M. & Csíkszentmihályi, M. (1991). *Flow: The psychology of optimal experience.* (Vol. 41). New York: Harper and Row.

Davis, J. (2009). Design methods for ethical persuasive computing. In Proceedings of the 4th International Conference on Persuasive Technology (p. 6). ACM. PERSUASIVE '09, April 26–29, Claremont, California, USA. ISBN 978-1-60558-376-1/09/04.

Deci, E. L. (1971). Effects of externally mediated rewards on intrinsic motivation. *Journal of Personality and Social Psychology*, 18(1), 105–115.

Deci, E. L., Koestner, R., & Ryan, R. M. (1999). The undermining effect is a reality after all – extrinsic rewards, task interest, and self-determination: Reply to Eisenberger, Pierce, and Cameron (1999) and Lepper, Henderlong, and Gingras (1999). *Psychological Bulletin*, 125(6), 692–700.

Deci, E. L., & Ryan, R. M. (1985*). Intrinsic motivation and self-determination in human behavior.* New York: Plenum Press.

Deterding, S., Sicart, M., Nacke, L., O'Hara, K. & Dixon, D. (2011). Gamification: Using game design elements in non-gaming contexts. In *CHI 2011 Extended Abstracts on Human Factors in Computing Systems*, 2425–2428.

Fogg, B. J. (1998). Persuasive computers: Perspectives and research directions. In Proceedings of the SIGCHI conference on Human factors in computing systems. April 18–23, 1998, Los Angeles, CA (pp. 225–232).

Fogg, B. J. (1999). Persuasive technologies. *Communications of the ACM*, 42(5), 27–29.

Fogg, B. J. (2002). *Persuasive technology: Using computers to change what we think and do.* Burlington, MA: Morgan Kaufmann.

Fold.It. (2015). http://fold.it/portal/.

Freud, S. (1914). *Psychopathology of everyday life* (Trans. A. A. Brill). New York: The Macmillan Company.

Göbel, S., Hardy, S., Wendel, V., Mehm, F., & Steinmetz, R. (2010). Serious games for health: personalized exergames. In 18th International Conference on Multimedia 2010. Italy: ACM Press.

Green, M. C., & Brock, T. C. (2002) The role of transportation in the persuasiveness of public narratives. *Journal of Personality and Social Psychology*, 79(5), 701.

Herzog, H. (1942). What do we really know about daytime serial listeners. *Radio Research*, 1943, 3–33.

Hinyard, L. J., & Kreuter, M. W. (2007). Using narrative communication as a tool for health behavior change: A conceptual, theoretical, and empirical overview. *Health Education & Behavior*, 34(5), 777–792.

Hull, C. L. (1942). Conditioning: Outline of a systematic theory of learning. In N. B. Henry (Ed.), *The forty-first yearbook of the National Society for the Study of Education: Part II, the psychology of learning* (pp. 61–95). Chicago, IL: University of Chicago Press.

Jull, J. (2005). *Half-real: Video games between real rules and fictional worlds*. Cambridge, MA: MIT Press.

Kayali, F. (2011). Serious beats: Transdisciplinary research methodologies for designing and evaluating a socially integrative serious music-based online game. Proceedings of the 2011 DiGRA International Conference, 'Think, Design, Play'. Utrecht School of the Arts, Netherlands.

Kim, A. J. (1998). Killers have more fun. *Wired News*, May.

King, P., & Tester, J. (1999). The landscape of persuasive technologies. *Communications of the ACM*, 42(5), 31–38.

Kohn, A. (1999). *Punished by rewards: The trouble with gold stars, incentive plans, A's, praise, and other bribes*. New York: Mariner Books.

Kreuter, M. W., Green, M. C., Cappella, J. N., Slater, M. D., Wise, M. E., Storey, D., et al. (2007). Narrative communication in cancer prevention and control: a framework to guide research and application. *Annals of Behavioral Medicine*, 33(3), 221–235.

Laird, J. D. (2007). *Feelings: The perception of self* (1st ed.). New York: Oxford University Press.

Lazarsfeld, P. F., & Stanton, F. (1941). *Radio research, 1941*. New York: Duell, Sloan and Pearce.

Lazarsfeld, P. F., & Stanton, F. (1979). *Radio research, 1942–1943*. Manchester, NH: Ayer Co Publishing.

Lewin, K. (1938). Will and needs. In W. D. Ellis (Ed.), *A source book of Gestalt psychology* (pp. 283–299). London: Kegan Paul, Trench, Trubner & Company.

McGonigal, J. (2011). *Reality is broken: Why games make us better and how they can change the world*. New York: Penguin.

Nakamura, J. & Csíkszentmihályi, M. (2002). The concept of flow. In S. Lopez & C. R. Snyder (eds), *Handbook of positive psychology* (pp. 89–105) New York: Oxford University Press.

Papacharissi, Z. (2008). Uses and gratifications. In D. W. Stacks & M. B. Salwen (Eds.), *An integrated approach to communication theory and research* (pp. 137–152). New York: Taylor & Francis.

Pink, D. H. (2005). *A whole new mind: Moving from the information age to the conceptual age*. New York: Riverhead Books.

Recylebank. (2015). https://www.recyclebank.com.

Reeves, B., & Read, J. L. (2009). *Total engagement: Using games and virtual worlds to change the way people work and businesses compete*. Boston: Harvard Business School Press.

Reiss, S. (2005). Extrinsic and intrinsic motivation at 30: Unresolved scientific issues. *The Behavior Analyst*, 28(1), 1–14.

Reiss, S. (2012). Intrinsic and extrinsic motivation. *Teaching of Psychology*, 39(2), 152–156. doi: 10.1177/0098628312437704.

Singhal, A. & Dearing, J. W. (2006). *Communication of innovations: A journey with Ev Rogers*. Thousand Oaks, CA: Sage Publications Pvt. Ltd.

Skinner, B. F. (1953). *Science and human behavior*. New York: Free Press.

SuperBetter. *SuperBetter*. http://superbetter.com/.

Von Ahn, L., & Dabbish, L. (2008). Designing games with a purpose. *Communications of the ACM*, 51, 58–67. doi: http://doi.acm.org.eres.library.manoa.hawaii.edu/10.1145/1378704.1378719.

Volkswagen. (2011). *The fun theory*. http://www.thefuntheory.com.

Wittgenstein, L., & Anscombe, G. E. (2001). *Philosophical investigations: The German text, with a revised English translation*. London: Wiley-Blackwell.

Wong, W. L., Shen, C., Nocera, L., Carriazo, E., Tang, F., Bugga, S., & Ritterfeld, U. (2007). Serious video game effectiveness. In ACE'07, June 13–15, Salzburg, Austria.

Zichermann, G., & Cunningham, C. (2011). *Gamification by design: Implementing game mechanics in web and mobile apps*. Sebastopol, CA: O'Reilly Media.

Zografakis, Nikolaos, Menegaki, Angeliki N., & Tsagarakis, Konstantinos P. (2008). Effective education for energy efficiency. *Energy Policy*, 36(8), 3226–3232.

7 How the top social media brands use influencer and brand advocacy campaigns to engage fans

Kelli S. Burns

In a consumer culture, consumers often express their self-identity through their brand selections. The reputation of brands is established through marketing and public relations, and consumers may make certain brand choices to communicate an actual or idealized version of themselves to others. The importance of brands in the lives of consumers combined with easy access to social media tools that can be used to share brand love has contributed to much online chatter about brands.

Approximately 500 billion word-of-mouth impressions about brands occur on the social web each year in the United States (Zuberance, 2011). The sheer volume of brand mentions on the Internet suggests that companies are initiating some of this discussion and that consumers are interested in sharing brand experiences, talking about brand selections, and soliciting brand feedback through their networks. This chapter explores how the organizations behind popular brands are increasing their share of voice in social media, the social media sites used, and how they are being transparent about their involvement in directing brand conversation.

Two popular public relations campaign tactics that take advantage of the power of word of mouth include influencer outreach and brand advocacy programs. Although both predate social media and the Internet, today's online, networked environment makes these strategies both more effective and efficient. Social media provide a powerful mechanism to quickly distribute positive messages generated by passionate brand advocates or influencers to a wide and established network of connections. Both strategies are based on the concept of electronic word of mouth (eWOM), which research has deemed effective because of its immediacy, credibility, accessibility, and wide reach (Hennig-Thurau, Gwinner, Walsh, & Gremle, 2004). A McKinsey study found consumer-to-consumer word-of-mouth methods to be more effective than traditional advertising in driving sales (Bughin, Doogan, & Jørgen Vetvik, 2010).

In an example of influencer outreach, the women's fashion brand DKNY invited 30 influential fashion bloggers to their New York City and London stores to participate in the brand's Easter Twitter Scavenger Hunt. As "DKNY PR Girl" tweeted tips to the candy-filled Easter eggs, bloggers tweeted photos of the found eggs and their respective articles of clothing. In contrast, Chili's Grill & Bar energized its customers (aka Advocates) through a brand advocacy program to spread positive word-of-mouth messages. When users signed up to receive emails from Chili's, they were able to share a free queso offer with their online connections.

The concept of brand advocates differs from influencers in that online influencers tend to be bloggers, celebrities, or pundits with large followings while brand advocates are generally regular people who not only use and love a brand, but also have a desire to share their experiences with others. Ehrlich (2013) differentiated the two types by classifying brand advocates as being "high trust" and influencers as being "high reach."

Nielsen's 2013 Global Trust in Advertising and Brand Messages study provides a context for understanding how brand advocacy programs can succeed. The research showed that 84% of online users from the 58 countries surveyed said they consider a recommendation to be trustworthy when it comes from a friend or family member. Advertising on branded websites was trusted by 69% of respondents followed closely by consumer opinions posted online, trusted by 68% of respondents. Randall Beard, global head of Advertiser Solutions at Nielsen, had this to say about the results:

> While TV remains the front-running format for the delivery of marketing messages based on ad spend, consumers globally are also looking to online media to get information about brands. On the flipside, earned advertising channels have empowered consumers to advocate for their favorite brands, something that shouldn't go unnoticed by brand advertisers.

In contrast to advocacy programs, influencer campaigns may have fundamental problems in their ability to gain the trust of consumers. A study by Forrester found that only 18% of those surveyed trusted influencers defined as bloggers, pundits, and celebrities (Newman, 2014).

Literature review

Influence theory suggests that a small percentage of users can be effective at persuading others (Rogers, 1962) and that these influencers can inspire word-of-mouth discussion (Katz & Lazarsfeld, 1955). Katz and Lazarsfeld (1955) theorized that opinion leaders serve to mediate the flow of communication from the mass media to the public. In the decades since, the findings of Katz and Lazarsfeld, often called the two-step flow theory, have become the "dominant paradigm" of media studies (Gitlin, 1978). Rogers (1962) noted the role of innovators as influencers in the diffusion of innovations, and similarly, Gladwell (2002) explored the influence of hubs, connectors, and mavens.

More recent research has generated skepticism about influence theory, suggesting that the virality of a message or innovation depends on relationships among regular people and whether society is ready to embrace the message or innovation (Watts & Dodds, 2007). Watts and Dodds (2007) questioned whether recognition of influencers in an environment enhanced the importance of the role those influencers would play in forming public opinion. They found that, under certain conditions, influencers are significantly more responsible than average people at "triggering large-scale 'cascades' of influence," but that these conditions are the exception rather than the rule (Watts & Dodds, 2007, p. 442). Under most conditions, influencers are only slightly more effective than regular people. Their research findings even suggested that most change occurs because of "easily influenced individuals influencing other easily influenced individuals" (Watts & Dodds, 2007, p. 442).

A study by Bakshy, Hofman, Mason, and Watts (2011) found support for the two-step flow theory, but suggested that following this approach might lead to less effective results. After examining 1.6 million Twitter users and their 74 million tweets, Bakshy et al. (2011) concluded that those users with the largest number of followers and those that were most likely to be retweeted were the most influential. At the same time, they suggested that focusing a campaign on those influencers might result in incorrect targeting and reduced effectiveness and encouraged including a larger group of less influential users for enhanced effectiveness.

Several studies have sought to categorize consumers on the basis of their ability to be brand advocates. A Wildfire by Google study of 10,000 Facebook campaigns identified social media participants as falling into one of three categories: joiners, sharers, and advocates. Joiners, who comprise about 83% of total participants in the 10,000 campaign sample, participate in the social media sites of a brand but do not spread the word outside of their individual interactions. The remaining 17% include sharers and advocates who comprise approximately 15.4% of participants and just 1.5% of participants respectively. Sharers are participants who will share information about a brand within their network, while advocates "participate with a branded campaign, share about it, and have enough clout within their network to influence friends to convert into participants as well" (p. 3). Both sharers and advocates generate earned media, but the earned media created by advocates is considered more valuable. When the top-performing 10% of campaigns were examined, the study found those brands had a much higher percentage of sharers and advocates among their fans and also acquired 264% more earned media impressions than the average campaign.

Clancy and Paquette (2012) defined brand advocates as "consumers who not only use a brand, but also love it and want to help others get to know it." They classified approximately 5–10% of customers as brand advocates with loyalists representing about 15–20% of customers. They further estimated that Facebook fans are 1.5–2.5 times more likely to be brand advocates than non-Facebook fans. The researchers proposed that marketers determine the specific measures of passion that are most predictive of advocacy behaviors and then use these measures to identify advocates.

Sedereviciute and Valentini (2011) prioritized publics according to the two dimensions of connectivity (i.e., suggesting their influence over others) and content sharing. Unconcerned lurkers are low on both dimensions, unconcerned influencers are high in connectivity and low in content sharing, and concerned lurkers are low in connectivity and high in content sharing. The category most relevant to this study is that of concerned influencers, who are high in both connectivity and content sharing.

Despite the evidence that brand advocates can be particularly effective for marketers, research has generated some considerations for their use. For example, a study by Anghelcev (2015) has implications for advocacy programs that use incentives such as coupons, rewards, or discounts as the motivation to purchase or recommend a brand. This experimental study found that subjects who received a small monetary reward for a product recommendation were less intrinsically motivated to write the recommendation than those who did not receive a reward. In addition, the subjects who received the reward also wrote shorter recommendations than the other group. Applying motivation crowding theory to this study, Anghelcev argued that the extrinsic monetary reward crowded out intrinsic motivations, creating a situation where the subjects were less willing to engage in the behavior. The implications are that advocacy programs can backfire, making followers less likely to trust advocate recommendations (Anghelcev, 2015).

Other studies have compared the effectiveness of brand advocates to celebrity influencers. A Zuberance study from January 2012 found the primary reasons people recommend products are their positive experiences with the products and that they want to help others. Brand advocates elicit higher levels of trust than influencers and tend to create longer-lasting effects among followers (Baer, n.d.). Advocates may be more effective than influencers because they often have a more personal relationship with their online connections.

A study by EngagedSciences of 400 brands found that only 4.7% of fans contributed to all social referrals (Heath, 2014). The report suggests that too many marketers are trying to use celebrity influencers in their campaigns while overlooking this potentially valuable group of brand advocates who can offer much more reach than the typical engaged fan.

The power of brand advocates and influencers comes from source credibility, a widely researched variable in the study of the effectiveness of communication. After Hovland and Weiss first introduced this concept in 1951 with the dimensions of trustworthiness and expertise, subsequent studies have examined other dimensions, such as the impact of attractiveness on credibility (Ohanian, 1991). Goldsmith, Lafferty, and Newell (2000) later examined the relationship between corporate credibility and consumer reactions to brands. More recently, Eagar (2009) studied brand hero credibility and the impact on a brand community of this brand hero who is connected to both the brand and the community.

Another related concept is that of word-of-mouth communication. An early study of word of mouth was conducted by Dichter (1966), who first analyzed motivations to engage in this kind of conversation. More recently, Wallace, Bull, and de Chernatony (2012) found that consumers will offer positive word of mouth through social networks about self-expressive brands that reflect the consumer's inner or social self.

Although popular public relations strategies, influencer and advocacy programs have received little attention in the public relations literature and may even be limited to a 2011 study by Freberg, Graham, McGaughey, and Freberg that measured audience perceptions of social media influencers. Their study demonstrated that the California Q-sort could be applied to evaluate the quality and relevance of four social media influencers and also compare social media influencers to one another. The attributes that best described the influencers were verbal, smart, ambitious, productive, and poised. When compared to a previous study about CEOs (Freberg et al., 2010), the influencers were more likely to be viewed as giving advice or being turned to for advice than CEOs.

The present study intends to expand knowledge of brand advocacy and influencer programs that can be applied to their future implementation. The following research questions will be addressed based on campaigns by the top 50 social media brands from a two-year time period:

1   What type of campaign – brand advocacy or influencer – is more common?
2   What is the range of content generated by each type of campaign?
3   How are brands transparent about their sponsorship of these campaigns and the content they generate?

Methodology

The sample of brands for this study was drawn from the SocialBakers list of the Top 50 Facebook brands from January 2014 (see Table 7.1). Online searches were conducted to locate information on brand advocacy and influencer campaigns for each of these brands for a slightly more than two-year period starting in January 2012 and ending in February 2014. Keywords included "influencer campaign" and "brand advocacy campaign" along with the brand name.

For the purposes of this study, brand advocacy campaigns were defined as those that provided a means for the advocates to both engage with the brand and then attempt to engage their followers with the brand through voting or other similar methods. Simple campaigns where advocates tweet using a hashtag or share photos on Instagram were not included. Influencer campaigns were limited to those that used a celebrity, popular blogger, or other influencer to engage with the brand and then generate branded content. Celebrity endorsement campaigns were not included. A total of 31 influencer and brand advocacy campaigns were located, representing 25 different brands (indicated in bold in the table).

Campaigns were coded as either brand advocacy or influencer campaigns. Finally, the range of content created as a result of these campaigns and methods for increasing transparency were noted.

Results

Campaign type

After analyzing the 31 campaigns, it was determined that they fall into four classifications instead of two: 1) influencer campaigns, 2) brand advocacy campaigns, 3) campaigns that activate both influencers and brand advocates, and 4) campaigns that target influencers who are known or likely brand advocates. Approximately the same number of campaigns used influencer (n=11) and brand advocacy strategies (n=10) while fewer campaigns activated both influencers and advocates (n=3) and targeted influencers who are known or likely advocates (n=7). The following discussion provides multiple examples of each type of campaign.

Table 7.1 SocialBakers Top 50 Facebook brands (January 2014)

Ranking	Brand	Ranking	Brand
1	**Coca-Cola**	26	Kit Kat
2	Red Bull	27	**Levi's**
3	**Converse**	28	**Dove**
4	**PlayStation**	29	**ZARA**
5	**Starbucks**	30	**Ferrero Rocher**
6	Oreo	31	Mozilla Firefox
7	**Walmart**	32	Nutella
8	**Samsung Mobile**	33	**H&M**
9	**Pepsi**	34	Guarana Antarctica
10	iTunes	35	**Burberry**
11	**McDonald's**	36	Adidas Football
12	**BlackBerry**	37	Google Chrome
13	Skype	38	Heineken
14	Subway	39	Nike
15	**Pringles**	40	Louis Vuitton
16	Samsung Mobile USA	41	**Sprite**
17	**Skittles**	42	**Dr Pepper**
18	Victoria's Secret	43	Windows
19	Monster Energy	44	**BMW**
20	Intel	45	**Adidas**
21	**Xbox**	46	NESCAFE
22	Amazon.com	47	Macy's
23	**Target**	48	**Victoria's Secret Pink**
24	Adidas Originals	49	Tata Docomo
25	**Nike Football**	50	Fanta

Source: http://www.socialbakers.com/all-social-media-stats/facebook/.

Converse's "My Canvas Journey" campaign is an example of an *influencer campaign*. The company provided 23 influential Instagram users, including photographers, stylists, and sound engineers, a Converse duffel bag and challenged them to photograph their customization of the bag and its journey over a four-week period. The influencers posted the photos to Converse's Instagram account and also shared them on their own blogs.

To promote its line of commuter clothing in 2013, Levi's also conducted an influencer campaign. The company worked with 20 photographers in targeted cycling cities throughout the United States to generate photo content for Instagram, Twitter, and Facebook. The company tracked engagement rate and total engagement with the content as well as audience growth and potential impressions.

Target worked with three of Pinterest's most "tastemaking" pinners in an influencer campaign. Joy Cho (Oh Joy!), Jan Halvarson (Popptalk), and Kate Arends (Wit & Delight) created lines for Target's party-planning collections and used social media platforms such as their blogs, Pinterest, and Instagram to promote the products. Target benefitted by showcasing products designed by influencers with a built-in audience who were likely to purchase these products.

A 2012 Skittles *brand advocacy campaign* from Canada motivated Skittles fans to share a video called "Get Skittles Rich." Participants earned one virtual Skittle for every view that resulted from a video share and posted standings on a leaderboard. The fan at the top of the leaderboard at the end of the contest was dubbed the Skittles Millionaire and received 1 million Skittles delivered to his home.

Another brand advocacy campaign is BMW's "Experience the Dynamic 1," which took place in India during 2013. In the first part of the campaign, 10 winners were provided an all-expenses-paid trip to Germany to have a guided tour of the BMW Museum in Munich. These brand advocates also had an opportunity to be among the first to drive the BMW Series 1 with Indian cricketer Sachin Tendulkar and race car driver Armaan Ebrahim. BMW also hosted a three-day event at various malls in India. Participants used an iPad to virtually drive the car on the racetrack. These advocates could virtually invite their friends to compete and win prizes.

To promote the BOOST Energy running shoes by Adidas in Italy, the company used a campaign that targeted *both influencers and brand advocates*. First, they created a Facebook app to provide advocates with a way to create a personalized online "energy" card, which they then shared on their own Facebook timelines. Participants also asked friends for their votes, and the top 10 entries received an exclusive invitation to the BOOST launch afterparty. Influencers were also invited to create an energy card and received a personalized outreach gift box that included a t-shirt with his or her Twitter handle on it, a USB stick with a personalized video, and an invitation to join the afterparty.

Another example of a campaign that activated both influencers and brand advocates was Nike's launch of the Hypervenom football (soccer) cleat in the UK. The "Deadly Art of Attack" campaign used a gladiator-style environment in an old chapel in London as the setting for the event. The guests toured the chapel to learn about the new product, customized their own Nike cleats, and met with Nike ambassadors and World Cup 2014 participants. The event attracted 250 attendees, and a special invitation was sent to 30 influential "Football Obsessed Teens." The event generated posts by the advocates and influencers on Twitter and Instagram that reached 650,000 people with the #hypervenom hashtag.

For the launch of its e-commerce site in the United States, H&M's 50 States of Fashion campaign from 2013 asked fans to upload photos to Instagram using the hashtag for their state. Participants then spread the word to their friends to garner votes for the chance to win a $1,000 shopping spree and a trip to New York City during Fashion Week. H&M also selected 50 style ambassadors (one from each state) who could help promote the contest on their blogs.

Pringles partnered with the Star Wars franchise for The Force for Fun campaign that invited fans to make a Star Wars-themed video on behalf of Pringles. Although the main strategy of the campaign was the fan videos, the campaign also activated 10 superfans, who were heavy social media users and influencers, to generate additional interest in the campaign. The superfans were provided with extra content, such as behind-the-scenes footage and interviews with Star Wars filmmakers, and also hosted contests with prizes provided by Star Wars and Pringles.

Although the clothing retailer Zara does not generally rely on public relations tactics, it used a campaign that *targeted influencers who were known and likely brand advocates* for its 2013 launch of Zara.com in Canada. The company identified 700 influencers, mostly highly social, fashion-aware, young professionals who were already Zara customers or strong prospective customers and sent each of them a $150 gift card, encouraging them to visit the site before it had officially launched. The campaign generated social media content, mostly on Twitter.

In 2012, McDonald's assembled a group of 400 bloggers in the UK who were already fans of the brand to teach them how to use social media to become advocates for the brand. In exchange for favorable blog posts, the bloggers received free gifts and all-expenses-paid trips.

Range of content

Influencer and advocacy campaigns are particularly valuable for generating content and widespread distribution of that content, and a review of the campaigns in this study revealed no noted differences between the types of campaigns in terms of the content or social media sites used. Some campaigns analyzed in this study focused on creating content for one social media site, such as YouTube videos or photos shared on Instagram, while others utilized a range of social media sites including Twitter, YouTube, Instagram, Pinterest, and Tumblr. Despite being the largest social network, Facebook was mentioned much less frequently than other platforms.

Transparency

The campaigns analyzed in this study exhibited a range of transparency, but most were designed to expose the relationship between the influencer/advocate and the brand. Although campaigns revealed their sponsors through the following four methods, complete transparency may still be a concern.

First, influencer-created content is often hosted on the social media sites of the sponsor and tagged with the campaign's hashtag. When viewers see this content, they should assume that its creation was motivated by a contractual arrangement with the brand. The more high-profile the influencer, the more likely consumers should be to make this assumption. Issues may arise, however, when influencers post content on their own social media sites and fail to be transparent about why they are plugging the brand within that space.

For example, Burberry, in a 2014 campaign for its women's fragrance Brit Rhythm, utilized global influencers to create content tagged with #THISIS-BRIT to build excitement for live musical performances in several cities. The content was then shared across Burberry's social media channels, including its Sound and Rhythm Tumblr page, as well as the social media sites of the influencers.

Second, influencers often create content as a result of an invitation to an exclusive event hosted by the sponsor. Within this context, consumers should assume that the event encouraged or required the influencer to create content. In some cases, influencers, especially non-celebrities, are not paid to participate but are happy to receive free entertainment, food, beverages, and swag. Although financial arrangements will often be necessary to work with certain celebrities, consumers may mistakenly believe that the celebrities attended for the purpose of enjoying the event.

In an example of this type of transparency, Converse opened a pop-up space in downtown San Francisco during the summer of 2013 for the purpose of promoting both the brand and the opening of a new store. The company targeted a network of local musicians, tastemakers, and influencers who would be able to promote the Converse brand, rewarding them with a pair of premium shoes.

Third, experienced bloggers are generally aware that they are required to disclose their relationships with sponsors and already have practices in place in order to do so (Burns, 2012). When companies target influencers and advocates with free products or gift cards, they need to reinforce the requirement that the consumers provide full disclosure when, for example, they post about an event where they received freebies or share what they purchased with their gift cards.

The Walmart Moms panel, a strategy the company has been using since 2008, includes nine moms, all influential bloggers. The mom bloggers are transparent in their blog posts that they are part of the panel and are being compensated. The Walmart Moms webpage is also explicit in saying that participation is voluntary and that disclosure of compensation is required.

Finally, advocate campaigns are often designed around garnering votes from friends or sending branded messages to friends so in this context, the sponsor is obvious. For example, in 2012, Ferrero, maker of Ferrero Rocher, launched the e-commerce site Ferrero China. To promote the site, visitors could personalize, share, and send a Christmas greeting when they purchased a box of chocolates. The message could also be shared on social media sites with a virtual gift. The participants who sent virtual gifts were then eligible to win a Ferrero Christmas box set delivered to their home by a Ferrero ambassador.

The campaigns located for this study generally did not employ any methods that intentionally lacked transparency. However, two campaigns will be highlighted here for problems with transparency and incentivizing positive reviews. Through a campaign conducted by video entertainment network Machinima, Microsoft offered videogamers an opportunity to earn financial rewards by posting videos featuring the Xbox One on YouTube. To be paid, users had to include at least 30 seconds of gameplay or footage in their video, mention the specific game being played, and tag the video with XB1M13. The agreement between Machinima and Microsoft stated that all feedback must be positive and the terms of agreement must remain confidential in order for participants to be paid at the rate of $3 per thousand views. In other words, the videogamers could not disclose the arrangement, which is a direct violation of FTC guidelines. When the invitation from Machinima to videogamers was exposed, the backlash from the community toward Microsoft was damaging (Gibbs, 2014). Similarly, McDonald's UK campaign with 400 bloggers provided financial incentives for those who wrote favorable blog posts (Tepper, 2012). Both of these campaigns attempt to influence advocates to provide positive reviews through compensation, which is considered to be an unethical practice.

Conclusion

Influencer and brand advocacy campaigns take advantage of the power of social media, allowing influencers and advocates to easily share content within their networks. This chapter explores the execution of these types of campaigns as well as the ethical issues surrounding transparency. The present study found a range of advocacy and influencer campaigns among 25 of the Top 50 Facebook brands with some of the brands using more than one of these campaigns during the two-year time period studied. The content generated for these campaigns was either intended for one particular social media site, such as YouTube or Instagram, or for a variety of social media sites. Interestingly, Facebook was mentioned less frequently than other social media platforms for sharing content created through these types of campaigns. Finally, the execution of most of these campaigns made transparency practically unavoidable, but still raised some questions and considerations.

The present study was limited in that it only reviewed published accounts of campaigns from the top Facebook brands. Behind many of these brands are global corporations that run many different campaigns throughout the world managed by many different agencies. It is likely that many brand advocacy and influencer campaigns were overlooked because there was simply no information about them available on the web or they could not be located using the selected keywords.

Future research should explore variables that increase the effectiveness of brand advocacy and influencer campaigns. Suggestions include the compatibility of the influencer/advocate and the product as well as the variables of reach and trust as they relate to the influencer or advocate. Additional variables to explore include commitment or emotional connection to the brand, the role of incentives, and the ability of the influencer or advocate to communicate. Agencies are also still learning how to best locate and activate advocates and influencers, and future research could add valuable understanding to this process. The success of influencer and advocacy campaigns are often guided by Key Performance Indicators, metrics that should be further explored. Common KPIs related to these types of campaigns include the number of brand advocates/influencers and brand advocacy scores, such as the Net Promoter Score (Gleanster, 2011). Social network analysis could also be particularly useful in understanding the dissemination of conversation that is triggered by influencers or brand advocates. In addition to focusing on the influencer or advocate, future research should also examine the effectiveness of this strategy on the consumers who are exposed to these messages.

References

Anghelcev, G. (2015). Unintended effects of incentivizing consumers to recommend a favorite brand. *Journal of Marketing Communications*, 21(3), 210–223.

Baer, J. (n.d.). Social media influencers vs. brand advocates infographic. Convince and Convert blog. Available: http://www.convinceandconvert.com/social-media-info graphics/social-media-influencers-versus-brand-advocates-infographic/.

Bakshy, E., Hofman, J., Mason, W., & Watts, D. (2011). Everyone's an influencer: Quantifying influences on Twitter. Proceedings of the fourth ACM international conference on Web search and data mining, 9–12 February, Hong Kong, China (pp. 65–74).

Bughin, J., Doogan, J., & Jørgen Vetvik, O. (2010, April). A new way to measure word-of-mouth marketing. *McKinsey Quarterly* Available: http://www. mckinsey.com/insights/marketing_sales/a_new_way_to_measure_word-of-mouth_m arketing.

Burns, K. S. (2012). Mommy bloggers speak out: Reactions to the FTC's guidelines concerning the use of endorsements and testimonials. *Journal of New Communications Research*, 126–145.

Clancy, K., & Paquette, E. (2012). Measuring and motivating brand advocates: The state of science. The Copernicus Marketing Genius Series. Available: http://www.cop ernicusmarketing.com/assets/196/brand_advocates_v1.12.pdf.

Dichter, E. (1966, November/December). How word-of-mouth advertising works. *Harvard Business Review*, 44(6), 147–161.

Eagar, T. (2009). Defining the brand hero: Explorations of the impact of brand hero credibility on a brand community. *Advances in Consumer Research – North American Conference Proceedings*, 36, 488–493.

Ehrlich, S. (2013). The age of influencers: How to engage influencers to amplify your PR program. *Bulldog Reporter*, December 30. Available: http://www.bulldogreporter. com/dailydog/article/thought-leaders/the-age-of-influencers-how-to-engage-influen cers-to-amplify-your-pr.

Freberg, K., Graham, K., McGaughey, K., & Freberg, L. A. (2011). Who are the social media influencers? A study of public perceptions of personality. *Public Relations Review*, 37, 90–92.

Freberg, K., Graham, K., McGaughey, K., Rust, M., Blume, M., Menon, A., et al. (2010). Leaders or snakes in suits: Perceptions of today's CEOs. Poster presented at the 22nd Association of Psychological Sciences Annual Convention, Washington, DC.

Gibbs, S.(2014). Microsoft Xbox One prompts outrage after YouTube stealth-marking stunt. The Guardian. Available at:: http://www.theguardian.com/technology/2014/ jan/21/microsoft-xbox-one-youtube-stealth-marketing-outrage.

Gitlin, T. (1978). Media sociology: The dominant paradigm. *Theory and Society*, 6, 205– 253.

Gladwell, M. (2002). *The tipping point: How little things can make a big difference*. New York: Back Bay Books.

Gleanster. (2011, August). Gleansight: Social intelligence. Available: http://www.glea nster.com/reports/reports/26#.UQnLE79EH09

Goldsmith, R. E., Lafferty, B. A., & Newell, S. J. (2000, Fall). The impact of corporate credibility and celebrity credibility on consumer reaction to advertisements and brands. *Journal of Advertising*, 29(3), 43–54.

Heath, F. (2014, January 18). Study: Only 4.7% of a brand's fan base generates 100% of its social referrals. *Technorati*. Available: http://technorati.com/social-media/article/ study-only-47-of-a-brands1/.

Hennig-Thurau, T., Gwinner, K. P., Walsh, G., & Gremle, D. D. (2004). Electronic word-of-mouth via consumer-opinion platforms: What motivates consumers to articulate themselves on the Internet? *Journal of Interactive Marketing*, 18(1), 38–52.

Hovland, C. I., & Weiss, W. (1951). The influence of source credibility on communication effectiveness. *Public Opinion Quarterly*, 15, 633–650.

Katz, E., & Lazarsfeld, P. (1955). *Personal influence: The part played by people in the flow of mass communications*. New York: The Free Press.

Newman, D. (2014, February 25). Influencers: Be cautious when choosing your brand associations. *Forbes*. Available: http://www.forbes.com/sites/onmarketing/2014/02/ 25/influencers-be-cautious-when-choosing-your-brand-associations/.

Nielsen (2013, September). Global trust in advertising and brand messages. Report. Available: http://www.nielsen.com/us/en/reports/2013/global-trust-in-advertising-a nd-brand-messages.html.

Ohanian, R. (1991). The impact of celebrity spokespersons' perceived image on consumers' intention to purchase. *Journal of Advertising Research*, 31(1), 46–54.

Rogers, E. M. (1962). *Diffusion of innovations*. New York: The Free Press.

Sedereviciute, K., & Valentini, C. (2011). Towards a more holistic stakeholder analysis approach: Mapping known and undiscovered stakeholders from social media. *International Journal of Strategic Communication*, 5(4), 221–239.

Tepper, R. (2012). McDonald's to shower bloggers with parties and gifts for positive posts. Huffington Post. Available at:: http://www.huffingtonpost.com/2012/05/07/mcdonalds-bloggers-campaign_n_1497417.html?ref=food.

Wallace, E., Bull, I., & de Chernatony, L. (2012). Facebook 'friendship' and brand advocacy. *Journal of Brand Management*, 20, 128–146.

Watts, D., & Dodds, P. (2007). Influentials, networks, and public opinion formation. *Journal of Consumer Research*, 34, 441–458.

Wildfire by Google (n.d.). How superbrands breed superfans: Six best practices for 10x greater fan growth. White Paper. Available: http://cequityknowledge.files.wordpress.com/2012/08/2_20919_how_superbrands_breed_superfans_6_best_practices_for_10x_greater_fan_growth_-_8_7_121.pdf.

Zuberance. (2011). Brand advocate data & insights. Report. Available: http://www.zuberance.com/downloads/brandAdvocateInsights.pdf.

Zuberance. (2012). Three surprising facts about brand advocates. Report. Available: http://www.zuberance.com/brandadvocateresearch/Three_Surprising_Facts_About_Brand_Advocates_Zuberance.pdf.

8 Brand communities in social media

Strategic approaches in corporate communication

Clarissa Schöller and Romy Fröhlich

Social media are forcing companies to develop new approaches to addressing their target groups online (Hennig-Thurau et al., 2010; Ashcroft & Hoey, 2001). As the communication environment changes, traditional distinctions between communication disciplines are challenged and the shift in communication hierarchy demands new strategies (Gurău, 2008). Marketing, public relations, and customer service divisions need to unite their competencies and create new instruments for strategic communication under a broader umbrella of "relationship-management." In this chapter, we introduce the idea of brand communities as a specific tool for strategic communication via social media. Fifteen years ago, brand communities were rather uncommon (offline) gatherings of fans that proactively supported a certain brand. In recent years the social web, which is represented "by a class of web sites and applications in which user participation is the primary driver of value" (Gruber, 2008, p. 4), has expanded perceptibly. The number of company-initiated brand communities that now use social media platforms has grown. In this chapter we first discuss the characteristics of brand communities in general, develop a new definition, and briefly describe protagonists and the specifics of the communication processes. Furthermore, we discuss specific challenges to understanding brand communities as a tool for, and an instrument of, *strategic* corporate communication, and outline the most obvious risks and prospects of online brand communities.

In the second part of this chapter we present empirical findings from an exploratory interview study, which focuses on the actual strategic use and handling of web-based brand communities by companies. Based on these findings, we differentiate four types of strategic attempts used with brand communities in social web environments and describe the most obvious (existing) obstacles still faced by corporate communication practitioners today in their attempts to introduce brand communities and to make use of them professionally.

Theoretical background

Definition

Although brand communities are increasingly present on the web, little research is available on this topic (see for example Andersen, 2005).[1] Muniz and O'Quinn (2001) were the first to take a closer scientific look at brand communities. In a highly explorative attempt, they identified three traditional markers of community within brand communities: (1) consciousness of kind,[2] (2) shared rituals and traditions, and (3) a sense of moral responsibility. These findings led the authors to the conclusion that brand communities are indeed *a modern form of community* and are therefore a suitable means of binding their members to the alliance. Muniz and O'Quinn described the relationship between customers and brand as a triad, in which the brand is connected with the customers while, at the same time, the customers are in contact with each other. This model resembles a network rather than the traditional, linear concept of asymmetrical (imbalanced) communication between a company and its target groups.

In 2002 McAlexander, Schouten, and Koenig contributed another important aspect to the concept of brand community. In their study they conducted an ethnographic analysis of a brand community (a community of Jeep owners) and then tested their key findings through quantitative methods. They found that brand community members can easily differentiate between marketer, product, and brand and therefore enhanced Muniz and O'Quinn's triad into a "customer-centric model of brand community" (McAlexander et al., 2002, p. 39): the focal customer interacts with the marketer, the product, and the brand plus various other customers. This indicates that a well-constructed brand alone is no longer enough. If brand community members are unhappy with the way the company behaves they will express their concerns and can cause negative communication that might lead to decreased brand loyalty amongst brand community members. McAlexander et al. agreed with Muniz and O'Quinn that brand communities are a special form of community and recommended that shared customer experience be facilitated to strengthen ties between brand community members.

Both studies acknowledged the possibility of brand communities being entirely Internet-based. Muniz and O'Quinn implicitly highlighted this possibility by including the concept of "local independence" in their definition of brand communities: "A brand community is a specialized, non-geographically bound community, based on a structured set of social relations among admirers of a brand" (Muniz & O'Quinn, 2001, p. 412).

Although this definition has been widely used in brand community literature, we believe that a revision of the definition is necessary, especially with respect to the authors' specific understanding of brand community members: Muniz and O'Quinn name them "admirers" of a brand. Given the fact that social media enables people all over the world to interact within brand communities, it is very likely that not only admirers, but also "normal" customers will take part in brand community communication.

The brand communities examined by Muniz and O'Quinn (2001) and McAlexander et al. (2002) were all initiated by consumers of the respective brands. Nevertheless, the idea of brand communities intentionally created by companies was always an option. Since Arora (2009) differentiates between "customer initiated and managed brand communities and company initiated and managed brand communities" (p. 13), we aimed to include a more detailed understanding of *initiators* of brand communities in our definition. Furthermore, our definition also aimed to implicate the possibility of the *strategic use* of brand communities as tools for corporate communication. In doing so, we again turn to Arora's (2009) work, which summarizes the various advantages of brand communities that make them most promising as a strategic tool:

- Brand communities are capable of developing brand loyalty[3] among the customers of a brand.
- Increased brand loyalty amongst customers enables companies to increase brand equity in the market place.
- Loyal customers can become advocates of the brand and initiate positive word of mouth.
- Brand communities can help companies to gain new customers without any additional costs of attraction (p. 15).

These aspects are all linked to monetary aspects of corporate management. Goh, Heng, & Lin (2013) were even able to show that engagement in a brand community leads to a significant increase in consumer purchases (p. 103). However, we would like to add three more points that are specifically linked to corporate communication, being aware that communication always acts in monetary interests:

- Brand communities allow companies to interact with various target groups *directly* and *symmetrically*.
- Brand communities create *positive* communication about the brand that can also be perceived by mass media.
- Information retrieved from brand communities (such as feedback on products) can be used for *quality management* and *innovation management* (see also Sawhney, Verona, & Prandelli, 2005; Schau, Muniz, & Arnould, 2009).

Against the theoretical background briefly delineated here, we developed a new definition of the term "brand community" which is based on a definition of von Loewenfeld (2006) and our own research:

A brand community is an interest based, non-geographically bound community which is focused on one specific brand. Brand communities exist in offline and/or online surroundings. By creating a surrounding characterized by high identification potential, it interactively unites adherents and admirers of the brand, customers with general interest in the brand and/or a company's stakeholders sharing a professional interest in the brand. Brand communities are initiated by users or companies and may be strategically used by companies as tools for corporate communication.

(Fröhlich & Schöller, 2012, p. 90)

Protagonists and communication processes

Previous researchers agreed on two groups of protagonists in brand communities: *customers* and *admirers* of the brand on the one hand, and the *marketer* (representing the product and brand in its action) on the other. We believe these considerations take a one-sided view of the aspect of brand community members. Why should only fans and customers be target groups for brand communities? In principle, all stakeholders[4] of a company represent potential target groups for brand communities. Journalists in particular are very likely to use a brand community as source of information, even if they do not participate actively in the community.

This idea of active or passive participation leads us to another challenge: How can we distinguish different kinds of members of a brand community? Theoretical considerations allow us to develop an idea of intra-community communication roles, which might help to understand the intra-community *dynamics* of a brand community. Thus, we suggest consulting classic models of communication flow and applying those models to communication with and within brand communities. Lazarsfeld, Berelson, and Gaudet's (1948) model of the two-step flow of communication argues that mass-media information is proceeded by *opinion leaders*, who are trusted by their fellow citizens. Most people have more trust in opinion leaders they know (more or less personally) than in mass media (messages).

The model has been enhanced to the multi-step flow of communication model (Eisenstein, 1994), which introduces the idea of *virtual* opinion leaders such as anchorwomen or hosts of TV or radio shows. Marketing professionals quickly adopted the promising idea of opinion leaders: if opinion leaders love a product, their friends, families, co-workers, neighbors, and so on are likely to do so as well. Simmons (2008, p. 304) calls opinion leaders within online environments "tribal trendsetters." Muniz and O'Quinn (2005) even view brand communities themselves as a specific kind of opinion leader. While this idea is alluring, we stop short of calling brand communities opinion leaders. Instead, we believe that as in any other form of community, brand communities, too, assemble different kinds of tribal trendsetters/opinion leaders.

Apart from opinion leaders, we differentiate further between two other member groups in brand communities. We call them (1) *prosumers* and (2) *information consumers*. Prosumers[5] actively take part in the community by both generating content (e.g. by discussing with co-members or uploading pictures) and consuming information. In contrast to prosumers, information consumers remain almost invisible as members. They consult the brand community to find information they are looking for and visit the brand community (discontinuously) only if needed. It is important to note that of course, communication within the brand community is open and all groups of community-members will talk to one another (Mangold & Faulds, 2009, p. 359).[6] Although our assumptions about these different groups of brand community members have not yet been verified through empirical research, our considerations lead us to construct possible communication processes in and around the brand community, as the following models show (Figure 8.1 & 8.2).

The defined components of the model are as follows:

- *Corporate communication measures*: Communication activities of the marketer address the brand community, individuals outside the respective brand community, and mass media.
- *Media coverage*: Content from mass media is received by the respective company, members of the brand community, and individuals outside the brand community.
- *Research*: Journalists use brand communities for research issues and investigation.
- *Feedback* (from brand community members): Reaches the marketer directly and unfiltered.
- *Exchange of information:* Between online and offline opinion leaders in and around a brand community.
- *Word of mouth*: From opinion leaders to prosumers and information consumers both inside and around a brand community.

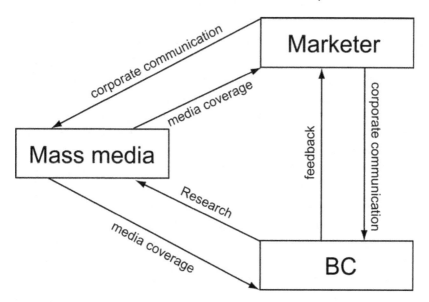

Figure 8.1 Communication processes in and out of brand communities

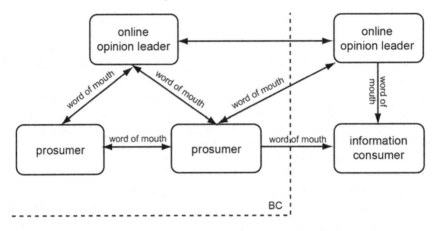

Figure 8.2 Communication processes in and out of brand communities.

This model of protagonists and communication processes in brand communities (see Figures 8.1 & 8.2) provides an idea of the range and the diverse
characters of all factors which could potentially interfere with companies'
(offline and online) communication strategies.

Brand communities as a tool for, and an instrument of, strategic corporate communication: specific challenges

As already mentioned brand communities can be initiated by customers and
fans of a brand or by the brand-owning company itself. In the following, we
take a closer look at *company*-initiated brand communities, and in doing so
concentrate on those that are consciously used as a tool for, and an instrument
of, corporate communication. Are they a public relations instrument, or a
means of marketing communication? According to Zerfaß (2015), who assigns
different objectives to marketing communication and public relations, marketing communication aims at selling and buying products, services, and resources,
while the aim of public relations is to legitimize and secure room for man-
oeuvre by cultivating social and political relationships (p. 80). He describes a
"traditional" way of regarding public relations and marketing communication:
marketing professionals sell the products, while public relations professionals
watch their back and take care of the company's image. Not all authors agree
on this segmentation. Concepts such as customer relationship marketing
(CRM) (Grönroos, 2004; Balmer & Greyser, 2006) try to incorporate relationship building into marketing. Sin, Tse, and Yim (2005) describe the tasks of
CRM as "attracting, maintaining, and enhancing customer relationships"
(p. 1265). Does this mean that marketing professionals build relationships with
customers and public relations practitioners with *stakeholders* and *journalists*?

With respect to online environments, long-effective classic distinctions are obviously losing their relevance, and with this the traditional hierarchy within corporate communications is experiencing a dramatic shift. In our view, corporate communication in and through social media (especially when using community surroundings) can no longer be divided into marketing communication and public relations, but instead demands convincing integrated approaches which also include *internal* corporate communication (see Huang, Baptista, & Galliers, 2013). Employees are stakeholders of a company as well (Donaldson & Preston 1995, p. 69; Cornelissen, 2004, p. 58) and are therefore not only potential, but also very important target groups for brand communities.

The concept of "integrated marketing communication" has suggested the integration of all forms of corporate communication. Kliatchko (2005) defines integrated marketing communication as "the concept and process of strategically managing audience-focused, channel-centred, and results-driven brand communication programmes over time" (p. 23). He suggests focusing on the objectives of communication measures rather than on the disciplinary background of the respective corporate unit that executes them. This might include units that are normally far away from corporate communication, such as product development or innovation or risk management. Brand communities seem to be the ideal tool for integrated marketing communication approaches, since different social software tools can be combined for different purposes to meet the different interests of relevant publics (Fröhlich & Schöller, 2012, p. 91).

In the social web, companies face fragmented publics which address the company with any issue related to its brand, its product and services, its philosophy and corporate culture, its environmental policy and so on. Communication professionals cannot possibly react to all of these inquiries. Therefore it is important to resort to valuable resources in the company: employees who have expertise in fields which are relevant for the brand community's target groups. Companies should systematically and strategically integrate employees into their concepts for online brand communities by, for example, giving them active roles in the respective communities.

Risks and prospects of online brand communities

A major issue in practitioners' discourse about social media is *control* and how to handle it. Prominent examples, such as customers' public irritation about a t-shirt of fashion label ZARA that resembled a WWII concentration camp prisoner's uniform in 2014, seem to prove how dangerous negative word-of-mouth communication in social web can be for companies. Arora (2009) even considers opponents' brand communities to be a threat as they might spread negative information about their "competitors" (p 15). Ewing, Wagstaff, and Powell (2013) found that brand community members use humor, epithets, and ridicule but also degenerative digital dialogue, malice, and insult to express their opinions about "rivalling" brands (p. 7).

Another risk may come out of the brand community itself: strong brand communities might not "allow" the company to improve or to change its brand due to the members' very high emotional attachment and involvement to the existing brand (Arora, 2009, p. 17). This happened to IKEA, when the company decided to end the much-loved EXPEDIT series in 2014. Research shows that companies need to "engage in engaging" (Brodie, Ilic, Juric, & Hollebeek, 2013, p. 112) consumers in brand communications in order to get accepted by the community. Advice on how to react to anger amongst brand community members exist, but are rarely followed by companies, according to Habibi, Laroche, and Richard (2014, p. 159). Strong communities are also known to become skeptical of new members (Muniz & O'Quinn, 2001, p. 419) and thus decelerate the brand community's growth.

These risks are countered by prospects that are the result of either the community specifics of a respective brand community or the fact that modern online brand communities are situated within a social media environment. Social software applications such as social network sites, weblogs, microblogs, and other dialog platforms enable companies to contact their target groups directly and symmetrically. Thus, brand communities in the social web provide the possibility of symmetrical corporate communication described by Grunig and Hunt (1984) as a model of "excellent public relations." However, real dialog can only be of use for companies if they are genuinely willing to interact at eye level and if they are well prepared to deal with this very demanding form of symmetrical communication.

Another advantage of online brand communities is the *directness* of communication already mentioned. Content can be delivered directly to the target groups without being filtered through mass media/journalists – a concept often referred to as "bypassing" (Cammaerts & Carpentier, 2009, p. 8). Nevertheless, companies should be aware that mass media (offline and online) still exist and that conflict issues leap into classic mass media (as happened in the aforementioned examples). Thus, journalists should not be excluded as potential participants in brand community communication.

The study

Focus and research interest

With respect to previous research, brand communities were mostly examined from their members' point of view (Brodie et al., 2013; Ewing et al., 2013; Goh et al., 2013; Habibi et al, 2014; Zaglia, 2013). However, few studies on brand communities in social media surroundings and out of the corporate perspective have been conducted to date; and if so, they discussed success strategies for company-initiated brand communities (Gensler et al., 2013; Huang et al., 2013). Thus, our research project aimed to gather information on the professional motives of companies in using brand communities as part of their corporate communication strategy. We were interested in how those companies actually handle brand communities, how they deal with dialog communication in brand communities, and what strategic approaches and concepts (if any) they actually use with brand communities. Another area of focus was intra-organizational aspects such as responsibilities and the use of resources through out the organization. Altogether, our goal was to gain insights into corporate communication techniques in the social web, concentrating on one (theoretically) particularly suitable tool: the brand community.

Methodology

Explorative methodology allows data from different interview partners to be compared on an individual basis. With the help of a theoretically based field manual, guided in-depth interviews were conducted with eleven representatives of different companies (including five international enterprises) who are in charge of company-initiated online brand communities. The field manual for the interviews consisted of 29 main questions and various sub-questions, for a more in-depth exploration.

Sample

We chose our interview partners by means of theoretical sampling: "Cases are selected because they are particularly suitable for illuminating and extending relationships and logic among constructs" (Eisenhardt & Graebner, 2007, p. 27). We interviewed corporate communication practitioners who were responsible for brand communities in their company (self-nomination). The brand community cases chosen can be differentiated from each other in three aspects: (1) the respective social media tools used with the brand community, (2) the size of the marketer (measured by the number of employees), and (3) the obvious target group of the brand community (B2B vs. B2C).

We defined the brand community as the decisive sampling unit. This means that in some cases we interviewed more than one responsible practitioner in one company. This was the case when a company either had more than one brand community or when a company named more than one professional as being responsible for its (single) brand community. The latter was naturally treated as a single case in terms of data analysis. Table 8.1 gives an overview of the interviewees, their companies, and brand communities. As all interviewees were guaranteed to remain anonymous, we refrain from naming the branches of trade to which the recruited enterprises belong.

Findings

Only four of the brand communities (C02, C03, C05, and C09) are situated on company-owned platforms. C05 is built around a weblog which is integrated into the corporate website. Some of the platforms are further linked to public social media tools. Eight out of nine brand communities use facebook.com, six

Table 8.1 Overview of interviewees, companies, and brand communities

Interviewee	Department of interviewee (official name)	Company	Number of employees	B2B	B2C	Brand community	Social Media tools used with brand community
B01	Corporate Human Resources	U01	405.000	x		C01	Facebook
B02	Marketing (Germany)	U02	96.200		x	C02	Facebook, YouTube, Twitter, company-owned platform
B03	CRM/Online Marketing	U03	14.000		x	C03	Company-owned platform, linked to Facebook
B04	Public Relations	U04	2.300		x	C04	Twitter, formspring.me
B05a	Marketing (Product management)	U05	800		x	C05	Company-owned platform, linked to other Social Media tools
B05b	Marketing (Product management)	U05	800		x	C05	Company-owned platform, linked to other Social Media tools
B06	Communication-Media - Licencing	U06	33	x		C06	Facebook, YouTube, Twitter, flickr, delicious
B07	Online Marketing	U07	16		x	C07	Twitter, Facebook
B08	BWS Segment Marketing	U08	5.300	x		C08	Twitter, Facebook, Google-Buzz, Xing
B09	Branding, Brand Strategy, Brand & Trade Communication	U08	5.300		x	C09	Numerous Social Media tools
B10	Corporate Communications/ External Communications	U08	5.300		x	C09	Numerous Social Media tools

out of nine are linked to or situated on (C04, C09) twitter.com – they are so-called "embedded communities" (Zaglia, 2013, p. 220).

Target groups

Social media is often said to be an environment in which very specific target groups can be addressed. However, three of our interviewed practitioners reacted by pondering when asked for the target groups of their brand communities. They explained that they are not trying to reach any specific well-defined target group, but are hoping that interested individuals will find their way to the brand community. Obviously, they see the brand community as an offer rather than an instrument aiming for its target with pinpoint accuracy. Nevertheless, after explaining their lack of a strategically defined concept for target groups they all named groups of people they are hoping to address through their brand community, such as customers, fans, or individuals with a general interest in the brand. Other interviewees, in contrast, have very clear ideas of their brand communities' target groups. *Customers* and *potential customers* are the number one target group. Another popular target group comprises *fans* of the brand and *people with a general interest* in the brand. During the interviews it became obvious that only two brand communities were actually not aimed towards customers: C01 and C06. The practitioners who "owned" these brand communities had good reasons for their direction: C01 was used as a human resources *recruiting instrument*, while C06 acted as a networking tool for *professionals* with a shared interest in the company's brand.

Journalists as potential target groups were explicitly named by two of the interviewees (C04 and C09) while four other practitioners stated that they are aware of the fact that journalists might use the brand community for research purposes. Both C04 and C09 (plus C07) are intended to attract *multipliers*. The two interviewees who named both journalists and multipliers as target groups worked in the public relations departments of their companies. The fact that none of the other interviewees involved mass media in their strategic thoughts could be interpreted as a sign of the professional blindness of some of the interviewees. Besides journalists and multipliers, no other stakeholder groups were mentioned as target groups.

Given the fact that most of the interviewees come from marketing backgrounds, customers and fans are the self-evident choices. This general orientation is reflected in the objectives to which the interviewees aspire with their brand communities.

Strategic objectives

Compared to the questions concerning target groups, the practitioners interviewed appeared to be much clearer and more decisive when talking about their *objectives*. Five of the brand communities had clearly defined main targets; all interviewees were able to name (commercial/economic or communication) targets they are trying to reach with their brand communities. Most of the objectives are of a communication-related nature: cultivation of the companies' image (11), customer retention (7), and information (5). The interviewees often named objectives linked to relationship building (9), but only one person actually used the term "relationship." Instead, the interviewees talked about "reaching the customer through bold and authentic communication" and, as a result, "creating a positive customer experience." The practitioners pointed out that although profit maximization was the single objective behind all corporate measures, it is only a subordinate strategic objective for the brand community.

"We're trying to really dialog with our customers, really get their feedback and of course, in the end we're always trying to sell something to them" (B08, f, 34, C08). B08 is one of three practitioners who work in B2B markets. All of these three interviewees were eager to actually dialog and build a trusted relationship with their target groups. This fits the picture: B2B marketers are used to communicating at eye level.

Beside the objectives described and the target groups to be found in the brand communities, the practitioners showed one other strong motive for getting into the social web: simply to be there. The fact that six of the brand communities were only set up because social media communication seems to be the current trend in corporate communication was not inevitably judged negatively by the interviewees. As B10 puts it:

> Social media is one part of the evolution of the Internet. [...] It is every company's duty not to miss trends like this, even if you don't know one hundred percent where this is going to take you and what the outcome will be. I don't think it's negative that some companies just say: Ok, there's an issue, we don't know it yet, but we need to stay tuned.
>
> (B10, m, 38, U08)

Five out of eleven interviewees also named personal enthusiasm as an important motive in starting the brand community. They spend a great deal of free time online and enjoy bringing social media into their working environment.

Dialogue

One of the most interesting topics examined in the interviews was the question of dialogue: Is there genuine dialogue in the brand communities? Do companies actually want it, and how do they handle it? All interviewees but one stated they wanted to dialog with their target groups in the brand community. Four of them (B05a, B06, B07, and B10) even explicitly consider dialog a strategic strength of their brand community. B05a and her colleague (B05b) are the interviewees who obviously have the clearest idea of social media communication. They were the only ones interviewed who had clearly dismissed the idea of coverage-driven marketing communication and were well on the way to a customer-centric, dialog-driven communication approach: their goal is not to reach as many potential consumers as possible, but to hold valuable conversations with a smaller number of customers and fans, encouraging and enabling follow-up communication about products and services.

In many of our cases dialog occurs as a company's reaction to negative feedback from brand community members. Four of the interviewees (B04, B07, B08, and B09) therefore use their brand community as an additional channel for customer service. While some of the practitioners commented on their experiences with negative feedback in a very frustrated way, they also experienced enthusiastic reactions of customers when problems were actually solved through the brand community:

> We have a Twitter tool only for customer service. If people talk negatively about [brand] on Twitter my colleague contacts them there: "Hey, what's going on, can I help you?" Like a direct feedback channel. It works fantastically. Because people are totally enthusiastic – "Hey, I got feedback on my criticism – that is sensational!" We help them – and that is really cool.
>
> (B07, m, 35, C07)

Typology of brand communities

On the basis of our interviews, we identified three dimensions which permit a typology of our sample brand communities to be developed: (1) the style of communication within a brand community, (2) the objectives of a brand community, and (3) the type of main target group(s) of a brand community. Our data showed significant variety in these three dimensions and thus allowed us to divide the communities examined into four types of brand communities: (1) fan communities, (2) service communities, (3) multipurpose communities, and (4) special interest communities (see also Fröhlich & Schöller, 2012). These four types represent the *strategic approaches* applied by companies selected.

(1) Fan communities

This type of brand community is very close to our general definition of brand community and the idea of brand communities held by early researchers. The main target groups of those communities are fans and customers of a brand. All fan communities in our sample are situated on company-owned social media platforms, a sign for the companies' high investment of resources. Lively communication among users is a characteristic of fan communities. Companies hold back and leave content control in the hands of the brand community members. Main objectives of fan communities are customer retention, innovation, and feedback.

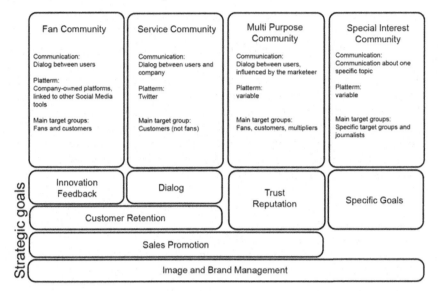

Figure 8.3 Typology of brand communities

(2) Service communities

The possibility to use the brand community for customer service purposes[7] was exploited by more than one of the communities examined, but only two brand communities focused solely on this strategic utilization. Communication inside service communities is very linear (between marketer and customer) and much less network-like than in fan communities. Most of the time, problems of customers with products and services of the brand are discussed and (ideally) solved. Accordingly, dialog and customer retention are the service communities' main objectives. Both brand communities in our sample which fit into the service community type consistently use Twitter as a platform, which allows for quick, precise, and direct dialog.

(3) Multipurpose communities

Multipurpose communities combine characteristics of service and fan communities. Typically, they use a multi-channel approach: one platform (e.g. Twitter) is used for customer service and another one for fans of the brand, while all applications are linked to each other. Communication styles vary depending on the single platform and its purpose. The main objectives of this type of brand community are trust and reputation. The latter includes the aim of picking up on new communication trends. Based on our data, we are unable to tell whether multipurpose communities really represent an original type of brand community or whether they are actually a hybrid of (1) and (2). Future (quantitative) research based on more cases should investigate this question.

(4) Special interest communities

Among all four types of brand communities, special interest communities are the furthest away from the original idea of brand communities, as the brand is not the members' most important object of identification. Instead, members share an interest in a certain topic. Communication in the brand community circles around these topics; the brand only provides the framework for the conversation. The technical platforms and the style of communication as well as the specific target groups vary. Both cases in our sample explicitly aim to attract journalists and emphasize specialized target groups. Special interest communities therefore represent a kind of borderline case which should be examined with more detail in further studies.

Whether our typology of brand communities is transferable to a broader sample cannot be answered here. In our data, the four types could be selectively distinguished from each other. Apart from testing more cases for their typology, it would be very interesting to take a closer look at dimensions such as type of dialog, characteristics of members, and nature of the social software used.

Intra-organizational mechanisms

Literature points towards an ongoing fusion of marketing and public relations measures in online corporate communications (Gurău, 2008). Nevertheless, most of our interviewees work in marketing, sometimes in specialized sub-departments such as online marketing. But do they revert to their companies' resources, for example by coordinating decisions with other (communication-) departments? The answer is: yes and no. Actually, *all* interviewees talk to other departments in their companies about the new phenomenon of "communication with and through the brand community." In some cases this coordination is even organized into formal processes, such as regular coordination meetings with the involved departments. The small companies in our sample (C06, C07) in particular use more informal methods for those coordination processes. Most of the practitioners coordinate with other *communication*-related departments in the company; four explicitly involve the customer service department in working with the brand community. Three practitioners (B04, B09, B10) involve other departments than marketing, customer service, and/or public relations. However, not all of the interviewees were supported by their management. In some cases we examined, only the personal motivation, interest, and enthusiasm of the person interviewed led to the brand community engagement of his/her company in the first place:

> Actually, there is no instruction from management. They are like: "Well – we need to do something there [in social web], somehow. But do it on top of your daily business." For a company like ours, which works a lot with communication – that's a bit difficult.
>
> (B09, m, 30, C09)

Five of the interviewees talk about resistance from other departments and even from colleagues of their own unit:

> In the beginning there was some resistance that lasted for quite some time. "Who is going to take care of the brand community every day? You need someone to monitor this constantly, not only every two or three days. You need resources."
>
> (B08, w, 34, C08)

The example illustrates the most dominant reasons for resistance: (1) fear of losing control and (2) concerns about the (enormous and additional) resources necessary for effective dialog. To overcome these concerns, clear decisions from top management are absolutely crucial.

Conclusion

From a theoretical point of view, brand communities seem to be the ideal cross-professional tool for corporate online communication in the social web. We see this assumption confirmed by our explorative study. However, some of the brand communities examined have not yet unfolded their full potential. This restriction has three reasons: First of all, management often hesitates to show genuine commitment to social web campaigns and initiatives. Second, and as a result of this, some companies do not provide enough resources for social media communication like brand communities. The third reason lies with the communication practitioners themselves: on the one hand, they have difficulties in abandoning established ways of working (for example, within the traditional communication hierarchies and borderlines between marketing and public relations) and, on the other hand, they have difficulties in truly engaging in social media communication with all its risks and prospects. The latter is naturally very hard to implement without full commitment and full back up throughout the top management, and all the more given that our interviewees are aware that using the social web is more than a momentary phase but a well-established part of many customers' communication behaviors.

Notes

1 Besides works on less specific and therefore more general "online" or "Internet" communities (for example Rothaermel & Sugiyama, 2001; Szmigin, Canning, & Reppel, 2005).
2 For more details about the understanding of *consciousness of kind* as innate collective feelings of similarity and belonging, see Giddings (1901).
3 Brodie, Ilic, Juric, & Hollebeek (2013) found that engaging consumers in brand community also enhances satisfaction, connection, emotional bonding, trust, and commitment (p. 112).
4 For the stakeholder concept see Donaldson & Preston (1995).
5 For the original sociological concept of the prosumer see Kotler (1986).

6 Gensler, Völckner, Liu-Thompkins, & Wiertz (2013) also discuss the possibility of networks between different brands (p. 251), which would allow further expansion of the model.

7 For more about the impact of new media explicitly on customer relationship, especially within the context of brand-building strategies, see for example Hennig-Thurau et al. (2010).

References

Andersen, P. H. (2005). Relationship marketing and brand involvement of professionals through web-enhanced brand communities: the case of Coloplast. *Industrial Marketing Management*, 34(1), 39–51.

Arora, H. (2009). A conceptual study of brand communities. *The Icfai University Journal of Brand Management*, 6(2), 7–21.

Ashcroft, L., & Hoey, C. (2001). PR, marketing and the internet: implications for information professionals. *Library Management*, 22(1), 68–74.

Balmer, J. M. T., & Greyser, S. A. (2006). Corporate marketing: Integrating corporate identity, corporate branding, corporate communications, corporate image and corporate reputation. *European Journal of Marketing*, 40(7/8), 730–741.

Brodie, R. J., Ilic, A., Juric, B., & Hollebeek, L. (2013). Consumer engagement in a virtual brand community: An exploratory analysis. *Journal of Business Research*, 66, 105–114.

Cammaerts, B., & Carpentier, N. (2009). Challenging the ideological model of war and mainstream journalism? *Observatorio (OBS*) Journal*, 9, 1–23.

Cornelissen, J. (2004). *Corporate communications. Theory and practice*. London: Sage Publications.

Donaldson, T., & Preston, L. E. (1995). The stakeholder theory of the corporation: Concepts, evidence, and implications. *The Academy of Management Review*, 20(1), 65–91.

Eisenhardt, K. M., & Graebner, M. E. (2007). Theory building from cases: Opportunities and challenges. *Academy of Management Journal*, 50(1), 25–32.

Eisenstein, C. (1994). *Meinungsbildung in der mediengesellschaft. Eine theoretische und empirische analyse zum multi-step flow of communication*. Opladen, Germany: Westdeutscher Verlag.

Ewing, M. T., Wagstaff, P. E., & Powell, I. H. (2013). Brand rivalry and community conflict. *Journal of Business Research*, 66, 4–12.

Fröhlich, R., & Schöller, C. (2012). Online brand communities: New public relations challenges through social media. In: S. Duhé (Ed.), *New media and public relations* (2nd ed.) (pp. 86–95). New York: Peter Lang.

Gensler, S., Völckner, F., Liu-Thompkins, Y., & Wiertz, C. (2013). Managing brands in the social media environment. *Journal of Interactive Marketing*, 27, 242–256.

Giddings, F. H. (1901). *Inductive sociology: A syllabus of methods, analyses and classifications, and previsionally formulated laws*. London: Macmillan.

Goh, K.-Y., Heng, C.-S., & Lin, Z. (2013). Social media brand community and consumer behavior: Quantifying the relative impact of user- and marketer-generated content. *Information Systems Research*, 24(1), 88–107.

Grönroos, C. (2004). The relationship marketing process: Communication, interaction, dialogue, value. *Journal of Business & Industrial Marketing*, 19(2), 99–113.

Gruber, T. (2008). Collective knowledge systems: Where the social web meets the semantic web. *Web Semantics: Science, Services and Agents on the World Wide Web*, 6(1), 4–13.

Grunig, J. E. & Hunt, T. T. (1984). *Managing public relations*. New York: Wadsworth Inc Fulfillment.

Gurău, C. (2008). Integrated online marketing communication: Implementation and management. *Journal of Communication Management*, 12(2), 169–184.

Habibi, M. R., Laroche, M., & Richard, M.-O. (2014). The roles of brand community and community engagement in building brand trust on social media. *Computers in Human Behavior*, 37, 152–161.

Hennig-Thurau, T., Malthouse, E. C., Friege, C., Gensler, S., Lobschat, L., Rangaswamy, A., & Skiera, B. (2010). The impact of new media on customer relationships. *Journal of Service Research*, 13(3), 311–330.

Huang, J., Baptista, J., & Galliers, R. D. (2013). Reconceptualizing rhetorical practices in organizations: The impact of social media on internal communications. *Information & Management*, 50, 112–124.

Kliatchko, J. (2005). Towards a new definition of integrated marketing communications (IMC). *International Journal of Advertising*, 24(1), 7–34.

Kotler, P. (1986). The prosumer movement: a new challenge for marketers. *Advances in Consumer Research*, 13, 510–513.

Lazarsfeld, P. F., Berelson, B. & Gaudet, H. (1948). *The people's choice. How the voter makes up his mind in a presidential campaign*. New York: Columbia University Press.

McAlexander, J. H., Schouten, J. W., & Koenig, H. F. (2002). Building brand community. *Journal of Marketing*, 66, 38–54.

Mangold, W. G., & Faulds, D. J. (2009). Social media: The new hybrid element of the promotion mix. *Business Horizons*, 52, 357–365.

Muniz, A. M., Jr., & O'Quinn, T. C. (2001). Brand community. *The Journal of Consumer Research*, 27(4), 412–432.

Muniz, A. M., Jr., & O'Quinn, T. C. (2005). Marketing communications in a world of consumption and brand communities. In A. Kimmel (Ed.), *Marketing communication. New approaches, technologies, and styles* (pp. 63–85). Oxford: Oxford University Press.

Rothaermel, F. T., & Sugiyama, S. (2001). Virtual internet communities and commercial success: Individual and community-level theory grounded in the atypical case of TimeZone.com. *Journal of Management*, 27, 297–312.

Sawhney, M., Verona, G., & Prandelli, E. (2005). Collaborating to create: The internet as a platform for customer engagement in product innovation. *Journal of Interactive Marketing*, 19(4), 4–17.

Schau, H. J., Muniz, A. M., & Arnould, E. J. (2009). How brand community practices create value. *Journal of Marketing*, 73, 30–51.

Simmons, G. (2008). Marketing to postmodern consumers: Introducing the internet chameleon. *European Journal of Marketing*, 42(3/4), 299–310.

Sin, L. Y.Tse, A. C. B., & Yim, F. H. K. (2005). CRM: conceptualization and scale development. *European Journal of Marketing*, 39(11/12), 1264–1290.

Szmigin, I., Canning, L., & Reppel, A. E. (2005). Online community: Enhancing the relationship marketing concept through customer bonding. *International Journal of Service Industry Management*, 16, 480–496.

von Loewenfeld, F. (2006). *Brand communities: Erfolgsfaktoren und ökonomische relevanz von markengemeinschaften*. Wiesbaden, Germany: Deutscher Universitäts-Verlag.

Zaglia, M. E. (2013). Brand communities embedded in social networks. *Journal of Business Research*, 66, 216–223.

Zerfaß, A. (2015). Corporate communication revisited: Integrating business strategy and strategic communication. In A. Zerfaß, B. van Ruler, & K. Sriramesh (Eds.), *Public relations research. European and international perspectives and innovations* (pp. 65–96). Wiesbaden, Germany: VS Verlag für Sozialwissenschaften.

9 Gearing toward excellence in corporate social media communications

Understanding the why and how of public engagement

Linjuan Rita Men and Wan-Hsiu Sunny Tsai

Given the ubiquity and dominance of social media, it is no longer an issue *whether* organizations should include social media in their communication channels, but *how* they can strategically use social media to engage digital-savvy stakeholders. Trade publications have reported that when publics search for information on a company, brand, or product, they now use social media more frequently than corporate websites (Dei Worldwide, 2008). In fact, many new businesses today rely solely on social media for their online presence (Goodfellow, 2014). Unlike the corporate "controlled" media, the open and crowdsourced social media enable individual users to serve as media gatekeepers and content-creators who collaboratively shape corporate image and reputation through "likes," "posts," and "shares" across online communities (Muntinga, Moorman, & Smith, 2011). For public relations, Web 2.0 technologies have triggered paradigm shifts in communication and relationship management, bringing unprecedented challenges and opportunities for organizations to engage publics in meaningful conversations and interactions.

Not surprisingly, social media and the related implications have received a tremendous amount of research attention. Early studies examined the common social communication strategies employed by organizations via content analyses (e.g., Men & Tsai, 2012) and interviews with public relations practitioners (e.g., Sweetser & Kelleher, 2011). Research has also examined publics' motivations of using social media in general (e.g., Phillips, 2008). Different social media stakeholders, including their salience and influence, are identified based on dimensions of connectivity and shared content (Sedereviciute & Valentini, 2011). Strategies for cultivating relationships via social media have also been explored (e.g., Levenshus, 2010).

As the use of social media in public relations becomes more sophisticated beyond the early function of information distribution, recent studies have adopted various theoretical frameworks to understand the mechanisms underlying publics' interactions with organizations on social media. For instance, Lee,

Kim, and Kim (2011) examined the roles of social identification and intrinsic motives of altruism in driving publics' involvement with user-initiated brand communities. Focusing on organization-public relationships (OPRs), Himelboim et al. (2014) identified different types of social mediators that connect organizations and their publics and their corresponding roles in mediating OPRs.

Additionally, within the constantly evolving and diversifying social media landscape, social networking sites (SNSs) (e.g., Facebook) are viewed as the dominant drivers of the media revolution (Vogt & Knapman, 2008). Recent media surveys report that Internet users spent the most time on SNSs (Fox, 2013). With the revolutionary advantages of a collaborative, communal, and democratizing communication process (Muntinga, et al., 2011), SNSs have fundamentally changed how organizations communicate and engage with stakeholders. Based on empirical findings of several studies, this chapter focuses on publics' engagement with organizations on corporate SNS pages to offer a normative model to address the following key questions concerning publics' social engagement: *What* is public-organization social media engagement? *Why* does social media engagement matter for organizations? *How* can companies effectively engage publics on social media?

Public engagement on social media

Recognizing that social media has sparked a revolution within the communication discipline, Edelman (2008) proposed a paradigm shift from public relations to public *engagement*. Bruce and Shelly (2010) defined stakeholder engagement as "the interaction between an organization and those individuals and groups that are impacted by, or influence, the organization" (p. 30). However, prior studies exploring stakeholder engagement on social media have predominantly focused on the strength of engagement and did not explore the nature and types of engagement behavior. Muntinga et al. (2011) theorized a typology on consumers' online brand-related activities that classifies not only engagement levels but also their associated activities. At the passive level, users' online engagement consists of *consuming* content on SNSs, such as viewing videos and pictures, reading product reviews, and downloading widgets. The moderate level of online activeness entails activities of *contributing* to SNS content by responding to organizations or fellow users, such as taking polls, engaging in wall post conversations, and commenting on the videos or pictures posted on corporate SNS pages. The ultimate level of activeness involves behaviors of *creating* user-generated content such as posting users' own product reviews and publishing and sharing videos and pictures on corporate SNS pages that others can consume and contribute to. Based on empirical data, we adopted the typology as a behavioral construct with hierarchical activity levels, and revised it into reactive message *consumption* and proactive *contributing* engagement activities (Men & Tsai, 2013) to examine the antecedents and consequences of public engagement on social media.

Why social media engagement matters

In contrast to the one-way communication model associated with traditional media, social media communication is not only interactive but also personal, and simultaneously communal, participatory, and collaborative, thus allowing organizations to engage publics in constant conversations, supportive behaviors, and meaningful relationships. Public engagement on social media thus contributes to important perceptual, relational, and behavioral outcomes.

Perceptual outcomes: corporate authenticity and transparency

In the midst of various communication trends driven by social media, corporate authenticity and transparency are two key perceptual factors that are directly influenced by publics' social engagement. Specifically, authenticity addresses an organization's central, enduring, and distinctive character perceived by stakeholders (Albert & Whetten, 1985). Being truthful to an organization itself and its publics is at the core of organizational authenticity (Shen & Kim, 2012). Further, an organization's conduct should be congruent with its values, mission, principles, and rhetoric (Molleda & Roberts, 2008). Thus, perception of corporate authenticity is an ongoing process by the publics to recognize and evaluate an organization's motives, policies, practices, and communications.

Corporate SNSs allow organizations to be embedded in publics' personal networks and to communicate in a personal, genuine, and friendly manner (Men & Tsai, 2013; Tsai & Men, 2013). Additionally, organizations can be imbued with a unique character and a genuine personality, be perceived as a relatable corporate person. Fans and followers can thereby experience para-social interactions and develop intimate interpersonal relationships with an organization's SNS representative, which further enhances public engagement (Men & Tsai, 2013; Tsai & Men, 2013). As a consequence, when publics are highly engaged with a company on the corporate SNS pages, they tend to perceive the organization as a personal friend and as an authentic corporate character (Men & Tsai, 2013; Tsai & Men, 2013).

The related construct of corporate transparency is an invaluable attribute of organizational reputation and character. In the Web 2.0 era, when any individual user can be a media gatekeeper and content-creator who actively monitors and publicizes corporate action, policy, and communication, there is unprecedented demand for corporate transparency (Molleda & Roberts, 2008). The open and user-empowered model of social media engagement has increased both users' expectations and organizations' opportunities to share information and knowledge, and in turn, reinforce organizational transparency.

Rawlins (2009) theorized that organizational transparency involves three aspects – substantial information, participation, and accountability. The informational aspect requires organizations to "make available publicly all legally releasable information – whether positive or negative in nature – in a manner which is accurate, timely, balanced, and unequivocal" (Heise, 1985, p. 209, cited in Rawlins, 2009). Cotterrell (2000) further argued that "Transparency as a process involves not just availability of information but active participation in acquiring, distributing and creating knowledge" (p. 419). Consequently, it is imperative to understand what publics need to know by involving stakeholder in identifying the information needed for decision-making. The third element of organizational transparency involves accountability – organizations being held accountable for their messages and actions, which are often readily seen and judged by the netizens of today. Specifically, corporate SNS pages provide companies an easily accessible tool to disseminate detailed and up-to-date information in a timely manner. The viral nature of social networking allows messages to rapidly reach a wider range of stakeholders. Most importantly, corporate SNS pages allow companies to listen closely to their fans and critics and incorporate their voice in deciding what information is needed by the publics. Disseminating detailed, complete, timely, and substantial information on a needed, collaborative basis contributes to greater organizational transparency. Therefore, the more the publics engage with social communications with an organization, the more they believe the organization as a transparent entity.

Relational outcome: organization–public relationships

Public relations contributes to organizational effectiveness by developing long-term quality relationships with various strategic publics (Grunig et al., 2002). Given the relationship-centric nature of social media, public engagement with the strategically managed corporate SNS pages naturally influence the quality of organization–public relationships. Specifically, SNS users who are more deeply engaged with corporate SNS pages tend to be more trusting of, more satisfied with, and more committed to the organization (Men & Tsai, 2013; Tsai & Men, 2013). In addition, when publics are actively engaged, they paid more attention and were more receptive to organizations' social messages. By participating in the conversations embedded in corporate SNS pages (e.g., responding to the organizations' posts, making suggestions and criticisms, sharing corporate messages with one's social connections), online stakeholders could directly engage the company and each other on a more personal level – a mechanism that gradually reinforces their relationships with the organizations. Further, through engagement with an organization's SNS pages, users become an integral part of the company's SNS community, fostering a sense of identification with the organization, which again contributes to the formation of lasting and committed relationships (Pronschinske, Groza, & Walker, 2012). As noted by Gummerus, Liljander, Weman and Pihlstrom (2012), even though users who participate in corporate SNS communities are believed to already have a baseline relationship with the organization, such a relationship can be strengthened via engagement with corporate SNS communities.

Behavioral outcome: public advocacy

Public engagement also exerts direct effects on the behavioral consequence of public advocacy – the voluntary promotion or defense of a company and its products, through such behaviors as positive word-of-mouth and defense against critics (Walz & Celuch, 2010). The more the publics are engaged with corporate SNS pages, the more likely they are to become advocates of a company to support, protect, and defend the organization, and to recommend it and its product or services within their personal networks (Men & Tsai, 2014).

Public advocacy has been recognized as one of the most important outcomes of public engagement, as it significantly extends the effectiveness and efficacy of the organization's communication efforts (Walz & Celuch, 2010). In particular, the communal and collaborative environment of social media readily contributes to publics' awareness that their advocacy or criticism can have a rapid and broad impact, and thereby increases the likelihood that they will engage in advocacy activities (Özdemir, 2012).

Motivations of public engagement

Knowledge of users' motivations for interacting with organizations on social media is a prerequisite for providing content that effectively engages users. The extensive literature on uses and gratification (UG) theory highlights the crucial role of motivation in dictating individual media choices and usage. Based on UG theory, research has explored motivations for using SNSs in general and reported that, although the key motivators for traditional media usage – entertainment, social integration, personal identity, and information – remain applicable to social media (Boyd, 2008), remuneration and empowerment emerge as original motivators distinct to publics' organization-related social media use (Muntinga, et al., 2011).

Specifically for publics' motivations of visiting, liking, and following an organization's corporate SNS pages, remuneration was found to be the primary reason that users often expect to gain certain economic incentives (e.g., discounts, free samples, and sweepstakes prizes) and even job-related benefits (e.g., information for job applications) (Tsai & Men, 2013). The second most common motivation is information-seeking, which is similarly based on utilitarian considerations of searching for product/brand/company-related information. SNS users also frequently visit corporate SNS pages for entertainment, indicating that publics appreciate the entertainment value of organization- or user-provided content on corporate SNS pages to relax, pass time, and experience aesthetic enjoyment (Tsai & Men, 2013). In sum, publics typically use a company's SNS page as a platform to search for discount or sales news, to exchange information with other members, and to have fun and seek leisure. Therefore, they are primarily driven by utilitarian reasons, rather than by motivations of gaining social support, managing social identities, or voicing their opinions and expectations. This indicates that the potential of social media to fulfill stakeholders' other identity-based, community-oriented, and empowerment needs is yet to be realized.

Antecedents of public engagement

Recognizing the significant influence of social media engagement, a growing number of studies have dedicated to identifying factors driving publics' social engagement with organizations. Overall, three categories of engagement antecedents have been theorized: individual, corporate communication, and relational factors.

Individual factors

Individual factors pertain to social media users' dispositional attributes and user habits, such as the user's *social media dependency* (Men & Tsai, 2013; Tsai & Men, 2013), *social media usage*, and *personality match* with a social media site (Pentina et al., 2014). While publics today are increasingly relying on social media as one of their primary information sources (Fuscaldo, 2011), there are variations among individual users regarding their level of dependency on social media and frequency of usage. Earlier research suggests that audience involvement with media influences their engagement with the messages conveyed by media personae or with other media users (Rubin & Step, 1997). Empirical evidence has also shown that media dependency influences various attitudinal and behavior outcomes such as trust (Georg & Jackob, 2010), involvement, and even purchasing behaviors (Enrique, Bias, & Tortes, 2006). Specific to the context of corporate SNSs, users who are more dependent on social media for information tend to exhibit a deeper social engagement with companies (Men & Tsai, 2013). Active social media users are more likely to consume messages and interact with companies on corporate social media pages.

Additionally, social identity theory suggests that similar attitudes, personality traits, background, and perceptions lead to people's categorization of social "in-groups." Therefore, for social media users, it is likely that they take perceived similarity into account when making decisions to trust, join, or continue using a social media site. For instance, Pentina, et al. (2014) study found that Twitter users who perceive their personalities matching with Twitter in aspects of extroversion, openness, and emotional stability tend to trust and engage more with the social media site. By the same token, social media users who perceive similar personality traits with a company's SNS page feel more identified with the online community and thus more engaged.

Corporate communication factors

Corporate communication factors address a company's characteristics such as *corporate character*, its social media *communication strategies* (i.e., being open, interactive, transparent, authentic, and responsive), and *messaging tactics* (i.e., conversational tone). Given that social media platforms are inherently inter-active, communal, and personal, they serve as an important social milieu that enables interpersonal communication with organizations (Men & Tsai, 2015). Notably, social media allow companies to exert a personal touch in their communications to build unique corporate character. Defined as "how a sta-keholder distinguishes an organization, expressed in terms of human character-istics" (Davies, Chun, Silva, & Roper, 2004, p. 127), corporate character significantly influences public engagement (Men & Tsai, 2015). In particular, among various corporate character traits identified in the literature (e.g., agreeableness, enterprise, competence, chic, and ruthlessness), agreeableness demonstrated strong positive effects on public engagement with companies on social media. When a company is perceived as friendly, pleasant, open, empa-thetic, and supportive, and acts like an honest, sincere, trustworthy, and responsible person (Davies, et al., 2004; Chun & Davis, 2006), publics are more likely to engage with the organization on its SNS pages. In other words, who the organization is, its inherent attributes, and how it is presented on social media is a crucial consideration for public engagement.

Another key factor is how the organization communicates and interacts with publics on its social platforms. Numerous studies have examined strategies companies use to build relationships with publics on social media. For instance, earlier studies (e.g., Kelleher & Miller, 2006; Sweetser & Metzgar, 2007) found that blog interactivity features and dialogical communication contributes to successful relationship cultivation. More recently, scholars have shown that disclosure, information dissemination, and interactivity and involvement are effective strategies to nurture quality relationships with publics on SNSs (Waters, Burnett, Lamm, & Lucas, 2009; Men & Tsai, 2012). Further, authentic communication involving sharing truthful and unbiased information in an open, transparent, timely manner is often appreciated by the publics (Men & Stacks, 2014). Thus, communicating in an authentic, genuine, personal, and consistent way works to foster public engagement and nurture relationships (Men & Tsai, 2014). Being responsive is another crucial factor for boosting public engagement. Being attentive and responsive to the publics' comments, inquiries, or even complaints indicate a company's commitment to its publics, showing openness in its communication and willingness to address the publics' needs and concerns. Such two-way communication facilitates dialogues, builds mutual understanding, and ultimately, quality relationships.

Regarding messaging tactics, research has shown that the use of a conversa-tional tone in corporate social media posting is more engaging than that of traditional formal messages (Sung & Kim, 2014). Kelleher (2009) reported that online users' perception of a "conversational human voice" of web content was positively correlated with relationship outcomes such as trust, satisfaction, commitment, and control mutuality. Sung and Kim (2014) found that com-panies which adopt a personalized approach in its social media communication and use a conversational tone in its messaging are rewarded with an enhanced perception of the organization's willingness to invest in relationship with the publics. Accordingly, a personal, conversational tone of messaging personifies the organization on social media and builds the corporate character, again contributing to public engagement.

Relational factors

Relational factors (e.g., *para-social interaction, community identification*) are additional categories of antecedents of public engagement. Specifically, para-social interaction (PSI) as theorized by media scholars in television studies, refers to the audience's illusion of having an intimate and personal relationship with media personalities, such as fictional TV characters and news hosts (Russell & Stern, 2006). Applied to SNS communications, we redefined PSI to address users' interpersonal involvement with a media personality (including companies' SNS representatives) through mediated communication (Tsai & Men, 2013). Companies' SNS representatives often act as "friends" and blend themselves in the followers' personal network. By engaging in a day-to-day interaction and conversation with the company's SNS representatives and observing how they interact with other fans or mind-alike others, publics gradually develop interpersonal relationships or even friendships with organizations' SNS representatives. Although the corporate SNS representative remains a mediated persona who represents a company and projects the intended corporate character, such pseudo-personal interactions and perceived intimate relationships effectively lead to greater public–organization engagement (Men & Tsai, 2013; Tsai & Men, 2013).

Another relational factor contributing to public engagement is publics' identification with the organization's SNS community. Corporate SNS pages are organic cyber communities where publics socialize not only with the corporate communicators but also with like-minded others who share similar interests in the organization. Users who "like" the same corporate SNS page also often "like" and comment on each other's posts. Such active group interactions and dynamics deepen a sense of belonging to the corporate SNS community. The communal atmosphere also encourages creating and sharing user-generated content, such as product reviews, photos, and videos shared by the community members, which enriches the attractiveness and informativeness of the corporate SNS community (Tsai & Men, 2013). For individual users, since those social activities (e.g., joining a fan page, commenting, etc.) are often visible to their online connections, publics could manage their social identities through their affiliations with and participation in the corporate SNS community. Such community identification stimulates group-oriented attitudes and behaviors (Zeng et al., 2009), as well as public engagement on corporate SNS pages (Men & Tsai, 2013).

Toward an integrated model of public–organization social media engagement

Based on the identified motivations, antecedents, and consequences of publics' social engagement with companies, an integrated organization–public engagement model can be conceptualized (see Figure 9.1). Public engagement with companies on social media involves activities of passive message consumption on the company's SNS pages, proactive contributions such as creating content or participating in conversations, and online recommendations. Public engagement matters for organizations' success because it improves perceptions of corporate transparency and authenticity, nurtures quality organization–public relationships, and fosters public advocacy. In terms of boosting public social engagement, organizations need to understand publics are primarily motivated by needs and gratifications of information, entertainment, and remuneration when liking or following an organization on SNSs (Men & Tsai, 2013; Tsai & Men, 2013). Moreover, the key antecedents driving public engagement include individual variables such as users' social media dependency, usage, and personality match with the corporate social media site; corporate communication variables such as an agreeable corporate character, two-way, open, interactive, transparent, authentic, and responsive communication strategies, as well as conversational messaging tactics; and finally, relational factors including parasocial interaction and communication identification. This integrated model provides important guidelines for organizations' best practices of social media engagement.

Best practices of organization–public social media engagement

To capitalize on the potential of social media to engage publics in a dialogical, interactive, personal, authentic, and genuine manner, organizations must understand the mechanisms underlying publics' social engagement, and implement effective measures to assess the effects of such engagement. Based upon a literature review of corporate social media engagement and an examination of best-in-class practices of corporate social media communication, the following guidelines are provided as a starting point for organizations to gear toward excellence in corporate social media communications.

1   *Understand publics' motivations of engagement and develop customized messages that tailor to publics' needs and interests.* Since access to information is a key reason for users to engage with companies on social media, it is important for organizations to frequently disseminate updated, complete, and useful information and respond to publics' inquiries in a timely manner. Additionally, companies should satisfy publics' needs for entertainment and incorporate a variety of entertaining and enjoyable content (e.g., videos, pictures, jokes, stories, games) and human interest stories. To satisfy publics' need for remuneration, organizations could offer incentives such as

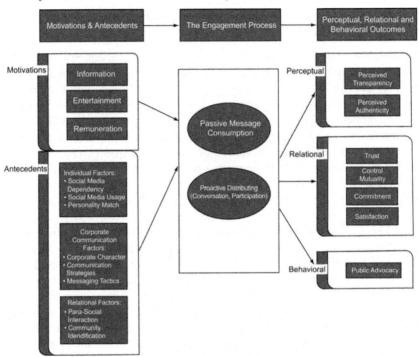

Figure 9.1 An integrated model of public–organization social media engagement: motivations, antecedents, and outcomes.

coupons, free samples, sweep stakes, and publicize their offline promotional campaigns on social media.

2   *Segment social media publics utilizing big data analytics and understand publics' demographic, psychographic, and personal traits.* In the social media landscape, publics can be segmented for better-targeted communication. Big data analytics such as cluster analysis and microsegmentation (Paharia, 2013) can be utilized to different groups of publics based not only on demographic and psychographic factors, but also on patterns of social media usage, social media dependency, match of personality traits with the corporate social media page. Precise and accurate understanding of varied stakeholder groups lead to effective tailored communications.

3   *Adopt interactive, open, transparent, and authentic communication strategies and conversational and personal messaging tactics.* Research shows that offline communication strategies such as symmetrical communication, openness, transparent, authentic, and responsive communication still hold true in the social media context. Therefore, companies should adopt the symmetrical communication worldview, open to publics' inquiries, comments, or even complaints and criticisms on social media, proactively provide accurate,

truthful, complete, and unbiased information, and stay interactive and responsive to publics' comments and needs. Organizations should also act as a corporate person, be authentic and genuine in their communications, be consistent in what they believe, say, and do, and communicate in a conversational, friendly, and personal tone.

4   *Build a unique corporate character that is congruent with organizational culture, values, and goals.* Given the significant effects of corporate character on public engagement, organizations should strive to personify themselves and project an agreeable, honest, sincere, empathetic, pleasant, supportive, and responsible character on social media. Since corporate character defines who a company is and plays a vital role in dictating corporate actions and individual behaviors within a corporation, it is imperative the corporate character reflects the organizational values, goals, culture, and purposes and its offline image. A consistent corporate character reinforces organizational identity and culture, distinguishing the organization from its competitors.

5   *Foster para-social interaction and community identification.* Relational factors such as para-social interaction and community identification drive public engagement and build quality organization–public relationships. Therefore, companies should act as a caring friend, communicate in a personal and friendly tone, and build identifiable personalities to induce intimate para-social interactions. Further, companies should strengthen the communal and relational atmosphere and boost member identification with the corporate SNS community. For instance, companies can take advantage of the popularity of personalized badges to recognize loyal fans and boost their feelings of community belonging and identification. Companies can also initiate social media campaigns that stimulate "peer linking," sharing, member-to-member interactions, and collaboration (Men & Tsai, 2013). Gamification ideas and techniques such as "leveling up" and "points" could not only could mark users' achievement, status, expertise, or loyalty, but also boost a sense of community belonging (Paharia, 2013).

6   *Develop research and metrics to assess the effectiveness of social media engagement.* No evaluation, no improvement. Although a standard measurement for social media communications remains absent, companies should go beyond just evaluating descriptive and superficial outputs (e.g., number of followers, likes, posts/comments) or focusing on the sentiment of posts. Effective social media metrics should be able to gauge the influence of engagement activities on publics' perception, attitudes, and behavior and on organizational business objectives such as sales, revenue, and ROI. With the development of big-data technologies for managing enormous quantities of unstructured data, it has become possible to connect social media engagement efforts to the organization's bottom line.

In sum, the interactive, communal, relational, and participatory characteristics of social media have provided organizations enormous opportunities to engage publics used at a more personal and intimate level. However, like any other technology, social media are simply tools and eventually fall on the people who utilize it to realize its value. Organizations today should be open-minded, embrace the trend, and adopt the new technology to transform their communication landscape. Efforts should focus on developing and retaining social media talents who understand effective communication principles and theories in the globally connected cyberspace, develop big data competencies and technology base that could offer analytical insights, and listen closely to the digital-savvy publics. In this ever-changing business world, "it is not the strongest of the species that survive, but the one most responsive to change." Darwin's rule still applies to both organizations and communication professionals in the social media era.

References

Albert, S., & Whetten, D. A. (1985). Organizational identity. In L. L. Cummings & B. I. M. Staw (Eds.), *Research in organizational behavior* (pp. 263–295). Greenwich, CT: Jai Press.

Boyd, D. (2008). Why youth (heart) social network sites: The role of networked publics in teenage social life. In David Buckingham (Ed.), *Youth, identity, and digital media* (pp. 119–142). Cambridge, MA: MIT Press.

Bruce, P., & Shelley, R. (2010). Assessing stakeholder engagement. *Communication Journal of New Zealand*, 11, 30–48.

Chun, R., & Davies, G. (2006). The influence of corporate character on customers and employees: Exploring similarities and differences. *Journal of the Academy of Marketing Science*, 34(2), 138–146.

Cotterrell, R. (2000). Transparency, mass media, ideology and community. *Cultural Values*, 3, 414–426.

Davies, G., Chun, R., Silva, R. V., & Roper, S. (2004). A corporate character scale to assess employee and customer views of organization reputation. *Corporate Reputation Review*, 7(2), 125–146.

Dei Worldwide (2008). Engaging consumers online: The impact of social media on purchasing behaviour. http://www.deiworldwide.com/files/DEIStudy-Engaging%20ConsumersOnline-Summary.pdf (accessed April 3, 2012).

Edelman, R. (2008). Public engagement: The evolution of public relations. The First Grunig Lecture, University of Maryland, College Park.

Enrique, B. A., Bias, S. S., & Tortes, F. T. (2006). Dependency in consumer media relations: An application to the case of teleshopping. *Journal of Consumer Behavior*, 5(5), 397–410.

Fox, Z. (2013). 10 online activities that dominate Americans' days. http://mashable.com/2013/08/15/popular-online-activities/ (accessed October 29, 2013).

Fuscaldo, D. (2011). More consumers turn to social media for health care information. *Fox Business*. http://www.foxbusiness.com/personal-finance/2011/08/09/more-consumers-turn-to-social-media-for-health-care-information/#ixzz2ABZRM44G (accessed November 4, 2015).

Georg, N., & Jackob, E. (2010). No alternatives? The relationship between perceived media dependency, use of alternative information sources, and general trust in mass media. *International Journal of Communication*, 4, 589–606.

Goodfellow, C. (2014), Can social media platforms replace a business website?http://www.theguardian.com/small-business-network/2014/oct/06/social-media-platform s-replace-small-business-websites (accessed November 4, 2015).

Grunig, L. A., Grunig, J. E., & Dozier, D. (2002). *Excellent public relations and effective organizations: A study of communication management in three countries.* Mahwah, NJ: Lawrence Erlbaum Associates.

Gummerus, J., Liljander, V., Weman, E., & Pihlstrom, M. (2012). Customer engagement in a Facebook brand community. *Management Research Review*, 35, 857–877.

Himelboim, I., Golan, G., Moon, B., & Suto, R. A. (2014). Social networks approach to public relations on Twitter: Social mediators and mediated public relations. *Journal of Public Relations Research*, 26, 359–379.

Kelleher, T. (2009). Conversational voice, communicated commitment, and public relations outcomes in interactive online communication. *Journal of Communication*, 59, 172–188.

Kelleher, T., & Miller, B. M. (2006). Organizational blogs and the human voice: Relational strategies and relational outcomes. *Journal of Computer-Mediated Communication*, 11(2). 395–414.

Lee, D., Kim, H. S., & Kim, J. K. (2011). The impact of online brand community type on consumer's community engagement behaviors: Consumer-created vs. marketer-created online brand community in online social-networking web sites. *Cyberpsychology, Behavior, and Social Networking*, 14, 59–63.

Levenshus, A. (2010). Online relationship management in a presidential campaign: A case study of the Obama campaign's management of its Internet-integrated grassroots effort. *Journal of Public Relations Research*, 22, 313–335.

Men, L. R., & Stacks, D. W. (2014). The effects of authentic leadership on strategic internal communication and employee–organization relationships. *Journal of Public Relations Research*, 26(4), 301–324.

Men, L. R., & Tsai, W. S. (2012). How companies cultivate relationships with publics on social network sites: Evidence from China and the United States. *Public Relations Review*, 38, 723–730.

Men, L. R., & Tsai, W. S. (2013). Beyond liking or following: Understanding public engagement on corporate social media in China. *Public Relations Review*, 39, 13–22.

Men, L. R., & Tsai, W. S. (2014). Perceptual, attitudinal, and behavioral outcomes of organization–public engagement on corporate social networking sites. *Journal of Public Relations Research*, 26(5), 417–435.

Men, L. R., & Tsai, W. S. (2015). Infusing social media with humanity: Corporate character, public engagement, and relational outcomes. *Public Relations Review*, 41(3), 395–403.

Molleda, J., & Roberts, M. (2008). The value of authenticity in global strategic communication: The new Juan Valdez campaign. *International Journal of Strategic Communication*, 2, 154–174.

Muntinga, D. G., Moorman, M., & Smit, E. G. (2011). Introducing COBR as exploring motivations for brand-related social media use. *International Journal of Advertising*, 30, 13–46.

Özdemir, B. P. (2012). Social media as a tool for online advocacy campaigns: Greenpeace Mediterranean's anti genetically engineered food campaign in Turkey. *Global Media Journal: Canadian Edition*, 5, 23–39.

Paharia, R. (2013). *How to revolutionize customer and employee engagement with big data and gamification.* New York: McGraw Hill Education.

Pentina, I., Zhang, L., & Basmanova, O. (2014). Antecedents and consequences of trust in a social media brand: A cross-cultural study of Twitter. *Computers in Human Behavior*, 29, 1546–1555.

Phillips, D. (2008). The psychology of social media. *Journal of New Communications Research*, 3, 79–85.

Pronschinske, M., Groza, M. D., & Walker, M. (2012). Attracting Facebook 'fans': The importance of authenticity and engagement as a social networking strategy for professional sport teams. *Sport Marketing Quarterly*, 21, 221–231.

Rawlins, B. (2009). Give the emperor a mirror: Toward developing a stakeholder measurement of organizational transparency. *Journal of Public Relations Research*, 21, 71–99.

Rubin, A. M., & Step, M. M. (1997). Viewing television talk shows. *Communication Research Reports*, 14(1), 106–115.

Russell, C. A., & Stern, B. B. (2006). Consumers, characters, and products: A balance model of sitcom product placement effects. *Journal of Advertising*, 35, 7–22.

Sedereviciute, K., & Valentini, C. (2011). Towards a more holistic stakeholder analysis approach: Mapping known and undiscovered stakeholders from social media. *International Journal of Strategic Communication*, 5, 221–239.

Shen, H., & Kim, J.-N. (2012). The authentic enterprise: Another buzz word, or a true driver of quality relationships? *Journal of Public Relations Research*, 24, 371–389.

Sung, K. & Kim, S. (2014). I want to be your friend: The effects of organizations' interpersonal approaches on social networking sites, *Journal of Public Relations Research*, 26, 235–255.

Sweetser, K. D., Kelleher, T. (2011). A survey of social media use, motivation and leadership among public relations practitioners. *Public Relations Review*, 37, 425–428.

Sweetser, K. D., & Metzgar, E. (2007). Communicating during crisis: Use of blogs as a relationship management tool. *Public Relations Review*, 33, 340–342.

Tsai, W. S., & Men, L. R. (2013). Motivations and antecedents of consumer engagement with brand pages on social networking sites. *Journal of Interactive Advertising*, 13, 76–87.

Vogt, C., & Knapman, S. (2008), The anatomy of social networks. *Market Leader* (Spring), 46–51.

Walz, A. M., & Celuch, K. G. (2010). Customer advocacy: The moderating role of trust. *Journal of Consumer Satisfaction, Dissatisfaction & Complaining Behavior*, 23, 95–110.

Waters, R. D., Burnett, E., Lamm, A., & Lucas, J. (2009). Engaging stakeholders through social networking: How nonprofit organizations are using Facebook. *Public Relations Review*, 35, 102–106.

Zeng, F., Huang, L., & Dou, W. (2009). Social factors in user perceptions and responses to advertising in online social networking communities. *Journal of Interactive Advertising*, 10, 1–13.

10 New media, new media relations

Building relationships with bloggers, citizen journalists and engaged publics

Amber L. Hutchins and Natalie T. J. Tindall

The Internet has impacted news media outlets and trade publications. Some print publications and broadcasts have either moved entirely online or created a companion website. Individual writers, staff, and contributors, as well as the publications themselves, interact with readers and publish content via social media. Sometimes social media platforms, like blogs, are the exclusive publishing platform used by a publication or writer. In other cases, media outlets have developed entirely online, without affiliation to a traditional or offline media outlet.

The impact of the Internet on traditional news outlets has been widely discussed and analyzed, especially the sustainability of print news media. The constant need for content creation on a 24/7 publication cycle, information overload and fatigue, and the audience's ability to prioritize information have been cited as concerns. Reaching readers in a saturated environment and cutting through the clutter are other problems that affect online media outlets, as well as public relations practitioners looking to gain earned content via placement in online media outlets. The accessibility and affordability of online content delivery platforms has contributed to a diminishing distinction between professional and amateur media outlets. Online publishing and design have become easier and more accessible, giving individuals with a range of experience and backgrounds the opportunity to create online publications and sites that are virtually indistinguishable from professional sites.

As more broadcast and print media outlets develop an online presence, activities like pitching stories to reporters, developing and distributing press releases, and measurement and evaluation of media coverage, have been updated, optimized, or reinvented. As the media landscape and the definition of media continues to evolve, public relations practitioners have worked to adapt traditional approaches and techniques to the new online media environment. However, traditional media outlets are only one segment of the online media landscape. In this unprecedented time of self-publication, top news outlets are sometimes user-created blogs, and the creators of news coverage can be citizen journalists, "accidental amateurs," or fans. Engaged publics are creating, publishing, and distributing their own content and news via social media and in some cases redefining the concept of media outlets. There are many new opportunities for generating earned content, but the process, practices, and assumptions about traditional media relations must evolve, too. Using mass media theories and the Accredited in Public Relations' (APR) Knowledge, Skills, and Abilities (KSAs) for media relations, this chapter will examine "new" media relations for social media, participatory culture, and engaged publics. Relevant issues and techniques will be analyzed and discussed, and examples of successful efforts will be presented.

Participatory culture and engaged publics: prosumers, fans, and influencers

Public relations scholars Phillips and Brabham (2012) acknowledged the new, active roles of publics as a result of social media, including community building, and content creation. These engaged publics, whose level of activity and engagement supersedes current descriptions of "active" publics, are demonstrative of participatory culture, a concept that is typically used to describe behavior and activities of fans of entertainment media but has applications for public relations scholars and practitioners seeking to better understand publics in social media.

According to Jenkins (2006), participatory culture "contrasts with older notions of passive media spectatorship. Rather than talking about media producers and consumers as occupying separate roles, we might now see them as participants who interact with each other" as well as corporations, and that "some consumers have greater abilities to participate than others." These active media consumers are sometimes referred to as "prosumers" (Toffler, 1980, p. 265), a portmanteau of producer and consumer. Fans, defined by fan studies scholar Mark Duffett (2013) as "a self-identified enthusiast, devotee or follower of a particular media genre, text person or activity" (p. 293), are also active in content creation and community building. Some fans act as citizen journalists, reporting news on topics of interest to fellow fans (Batsell, 2015) and can facilitate public relations communication between external publics and the community, for example crisis communication (Brown & Billings, 2013).

These engaged publics can serve as influencers or opinion leaders to individual followers or within a broader community. Their popularity can be the result of either organic or entrepreneurial efforts, and the quality can vary from that of a casual user, to high quality multimedia and writing that would be indistinguishable from professional work. Their work can either be paid, unpaid, or some combination thereof via opportunities like sponsored or syndicated posts, freelance writing and guest blogging, or affiliation with a blogging network for click-through advertising (Griffith, 2011). Beyond popularity (amassing followers on social networks), influencers inspire or encourage sharing of their posts and content (influence) (Cha, Haddadi, Benevenuto, & Gummadi, 2010).

The engaged publics described here serve as gatekeepers, content producers, news reporters, and other roles that resemble traditional conceptions of media outlets or channels in the media relations process. They can serve as a valuable resource for practitioners, but media relations activities must evolve in order to build relationships with engaged publics in participatory culture.

Media relations

Public relations serves a variety of strategic communication functions, but for those outside the field, the terms "public relations" and "media relations" are often used interchangeably to describe the field as a whole. For some, media relations is the defining characteristic of public relations that sets it apart from marketing, advertising, and other communication professions. In the age of participatory culture, media relations continues to be a primary focus of public relations, but practitioners can no longer rely solely on traditional approaches to media relations.

Few topics generate as much interest, discussion, and ink in both the academic and practitioner communities as the issue of media relations does. One of many aspects of public relations, the media relations component of the profession is one of the topics studied and dissected by both the ivory tower and practitioner factions of the public relations discipline. Supa and Zoch (2009) defined media relations as "the systematic, planned, purposeful, and mutually beneficially relationship between journalists in the mass media and public relations practitioners" (p. 2).

Luttrell (2014) in her volume on social media dissected the role of public relations into four quadrants: media, community, government, and business. Of the media element, she wrote "In practice, public relations professionals work closely with the media to distribute their messages to the public. Traditionally, public relations practitioners manage their media relations responsibilities by sending press releases, pitch emails, arranging interviews, organizing press conferences, and responding to media inquiries" (pp. 5–6).

Traditional media relations theory rests upon the theoretical concepts of gatekeepers (Lewin, 1947; Shoemaker, 1991, 1996). Gatekeeping, defined by Shoemaker, Eichholz, Kim, and Wrigley (2001), is "the overall process through which the social reality transmitted by the news media is constructed" (p. 233). In journalism, editors keep watch of the "gates" of the news hole – the space in a newspaper or news site or time slots for a broadcast segment – thus dictating what stories will be allowed through the gate and be covered. The "influences on content" and the decision to run or air certain stories are rooted in multiple factors, including the editor's or journalist's own subjective desires, whims, fancies, political attitudes, organizational orientation, and socialization (Shoemaker & Reese, 2011). Gardner (2012) called the key media gatekeepers of television criticism "key tastemakers."

Gatekeeping created the system of media pitching, where publicists and media relations professionals toss (hopefully) well-crafted queries and stories to journalists and hope for an article or placement. The reverse of media pitching is what Waters, Tindall, and Morton (2010) considered "media catching," when the journalists toss out their needs and wants for stories and sources and hope that publicists can deliver. Either way, the gatekeeper is still in control of who is invited into the article, who is allowed to be featured, and what the frame will be.

Online media relations

Zoch and Supa (2014) noted:

> Changes in the traditional media from network television, newswires, and newspapers to cable, blogs, the Web and social media present media relations practitioners with new challenges, but the importance of making a point clearly and presenting an organization well remains the same.
>
> (p. 3)

To put it succinctly, "as go media, so go media relations" (Bajkiewicz, Kraus, & Hong, 2011, p. 329). The changes afoot in the media industries now allow for organizations and institutions to sidestep the once-dominant influencers of content – the gatekeeping editors and journalists – and communicate directly with online influencers and audiences.

The social web has shifted the ground. Rather than pitching and hopefully flowing ideas through media "to opinion leaders and from these to the less active sections of the population" (Katz, 1957), practitioners are able to disseminate messages directly on their own platforms, through their social media presences, or through online influences. Stansberry (2015) introduced the radial model of information flow. Instead of journalists and editors serving as the conduits of information, online influencers serve as the "dominant meaning-makers in online, interest-based communities" (p. 14). These persons seek out information, collate and curate content, serve as key reference points for those in the community, and act as "l[i]nchpins for information flow within [their] communities" (p. 16); in online environments with the seat of information flow and influencing power shifted away from journalists, the media relations practice has to pivot and adjust to the new gatekeepers.

Online journalists and participatory journalists

Journalists' functions and roles (or perceptions of their roles) have evolved as a result of the Internet. Gate-keeping, for example, is a traditional function of journalists that is considered in flux. According to Singer (1998), given the user's unlimited access to information, self-selection, and ability to retrieve information directly from sources, perhaps gatekeeping is no longer necessary, but the author also posits the opposite: that perhaps gatekeeping is more necessary than ever for the same reasons. As Carpenter (2008, p. 540) notes, "The objectivity norm is a dominating principal guiding journalist behavior in the United States." Carpenter's study found that newspaper journalists were more likely to rely on external sources, while online citizen journalists are more likely to rely on unofficial sources, press releases, and opinion.

Whether there is a difference between journalists and online journalists is also a matter for public debate (Friend and Singer, 2007). The First Amendment protection extended to journalists comes without a definition of "journalist" and discourages credentialing, licensing, or any other system that would impede the freedom of the press. Who is a journalist remains a philosophical rather than legal question, and the operational definition is that anyone who considers themselves to be a journalist is one. Some, who functionally serve as reporters but do not necessarily self-identify as journalists, might use a title that modifies their status, such as opinion journalists, citizen journalists, or online journalists. They might be unaware of or reject the rights and responsibilities of journalists (Hutchins, 2008), including ethical standards like refusing gifts or special treatment in exchange for coverage ("pay for play") or maintaining impartiality (SPJ, 2015). Efforts have been made to address situations concerning non-journalists who receive cash or gifts in exchange for product reviews or endorsements (FTC, 2009).

Because of mobile technology and social media, many can report news or contribute content to a news story, even in a temporary, limited capacity. This includes "accidental journalists" who report news by virtue of being at the right place at the right time, as demonstrated by the Twitter users who were first to report the Osama Bin Laden capture (Mirvajová, 2015), and "participatory journalists," who participate in the editorial process through crowdsourcing and other methods of engagement.

Analysis of media relations practices with participatory journalists

The Public Relations Society of America (PRSA), as a member of the Universal Accrediting Board, has developed standards and criteria to assist practitioners with bettering the practice of public relations. Practitioners attempting to earn the APR credential and become certified, accredited practitioners must be knowledgeable about the following areas:

- **Media relations:** Understands the relationships among public relations professionals, journalists, and media organizations as well as needs of each. Builds effective relations with mass and specialized media based on mutual respect and trust.
- **News sensibility:** Analyzes current events and trends for opportunities and threats. Relates current events and market trends to employers and clients.
- **Understands media:** Considers strengths and weaknesses, needs, and lead times of media. Identifies appropriate media channels for delivering messages to internal and external audiences. Identifies influencers.

- **Distribution methods:** Understands distribution systems (e.g. wire services, electronic news conferences, special events, face-to-face communication, word-of-mouth and third-party communication).

(PRSA, 2015)

The PRSA Knowledge, Skills, and Abilities (KSAs) represent standards of skill mastery for a variety of functions of public relations. The media relations KSAs are consistent with standards across the discipline. These standards will be used to analyze current practices and interpretations of media relations in participatory culture.

KSA 1: media relations

Public relations practitioners can use social media to establish and maintain relationships with journalists and media organizations with customized pitches, and respond directly to journalists' requests for sources and information via services like Help a Reporter Out and ProfNet. These services recognize the shift in the traditional model from media pitching to catching.

Mass and specialized media no longer translates to print and broadcast mainstream, trade, and niche publications. Mass media can include outlets like BuzzFeed.com, which juxtaposes crowd-sourced, community-created content alongside news stories created by editorial staff with previous experience at traditional news organizations (Mullin, 2015). The site claims that its reach, especially among Millennials, has surpassed major broadcast networks like MTV and Fox (Buzzfeed, 2014).

Specialized media now includes engaged publics, both as individuals and communities. Individual influencers, with or without profit model or external sponsorship, can reach the same audience in quality and/or quantity as a niche publication, but with two-step flow influence, third-party credibility, and authenticity. Their influence, reach, and motivation to create content (whether it is to develop status within the community, maintain relationships, pursue entrepreneurial goals, show devotion to a brand or text, or personal expression/ gratifications), can result in significant and measureable impact.

An example is Leslie Kalbfleisch, a Toronto area Disney fan who created Disneybound.Tumblr.com to share her Disney-inspired everyday fashion – a practice now commonly referred to as "Disneybounding." Kalbfleisch's site garnered 1.5 million page views in three months (Desmond, 2011) and generated coverage in *Time Magazine, Huffington Post, OC Weekly, The Orlando Sentinel, The Detroit Free Press*, and MTV (http://disneybound.tumblr.com/m edia). Disney has featured Kalbfleisch in their branded content channel "DisneyStyle" and has invited her to media events designed to target Millennials and fashion bloggers (one recent event coincided with the Coachella Valley Music Festival). Kalbfleisch is an authentic voice of brand advocacy for Disney, and offers a valuable opportunity to reach a niche audience not usually associated with the brand.

As scholars and experts have noted, pitching stories to bloggers expands the definition of relationships in media outreach activities. Forming a relationship with engaged publics goes beyond the pre-Internet model of journalist–practitioner relationship. Exclusives and customized pitches are more important than ever. Relationships must be established long before the pitch (and the "pitch" must be an offer that benefits the recipient more than the client). To establish a long-term relationship with engaged publics, PR practitioners need to become a fan of the influencer, demonstrating genuine interest in and respect for the influencer's interests and follower community.

The balance of power between practitioner and journalist differs from that between practitioner and influencers. Journalists might have more access to information and sources, both official and unofficial via social media and organizations' websites, but at some point, many greatly benefit from or sometimes cannot complete stories without the assistance of a PR practitioner or PR collateral (press releases, media kits, etc.). However, fans and engaged publics can generate content and function without the interference of PR practitioners. In fact, interacting with a PR practitioner, while it might yield exclusives or access to valuable information behind the corporate firewall, can also put the influencer at risk: when the primary capitol in the community is trust and authenticity, the influencer can lose status by appearing to have succumbed to outside (paid) influence.

It is the practitioner's new job to understand that "mutual respect and trust" extends beyond a quid-pro-quo business exchange. Influencers or prosumers exist in a participatory culture that includes co-creation and shared ownership of content. At the same time, their work (fan labor) should not be exploited.

KSA 2: news sensibility

Environmental scanning has expanded to include social media listening. This has become such a significant part of PR efforts that some organizations have created elaborate "command centers" or "listening stations" with multiple computers and screens dedicated to finding news and opportunities for "real-time" engagement. Staff can monitor broadcast news, conduct general web searches, or use sophisticated monitoring software like Radian6 to track social media conversations via keywords, sentiment, and other indicators of activity and engagement. International agency Golin developed The Bridge, a "global network of media and digital experts … [who] collaborate and curate to discover actionable opportunities and execute ideas at the speed of culture" (Golin, 2015) with installations the physical spaces (software and hardware) at offices worldwide (Elliot, 2011). Constant, extensive scanning of all media and online communication for placement or engagement is sometimes integrated with other (or all) roles within the agency or public relations department, rather than centralized within one space or team.

The content created and distributed as a result of social media monitoring is often called strategic content or "real-time" content. One of the most notable examples of real-time content was Oreo's "Dunk in the Dark" graphic deployed during a blackout at the Super Bowl. By shifting their approach to environmental scanning to real-time social media listening, Oreo was able to produce and share content that garnered immediate results.

The description of Edelman's Creative Newsroom concept encapsulates many of the new approaches to news sensibilities:

> Edelman's Creative Newsroom approach works – either as an event-specific storytelling vehicle or an ongoing social content solution – because it deeply integrates the critical disciplines of community management, creative production, analytics and content strategy to provide real-time data, audience insights, design excellence and media amplification.
>
> (Creative Newsroom – Edelman, n.d.)

For social media and participatory culture, *news sensibility* means creating shareable stories with longevity, driven by community conversation, communicated immediately using visual, creative, and multimedia elements as per the "language" of the platform or publics, and with immediate, measurable results that can be tracked in real time.

KSA 3: understands media

Identifying and evaluating appropriate media channels means consideration of all media in the "PESO" model (Paid, Earned, Shared, and Owned media) (Iliff, 2014). Paid placement, which has raised ethical concerns, is becoming more prevalent as more organizations struggle for placement. When Facebook changed its algorithm to favor organizations who had paid for advertising in the site, it left brands and organizations with few options to achieve organic, earned results.

Practitioners are turning to sponsored content, including sponsored influencer outreach campaigns – paid content that strives for authentic news value. Companies like Starbucks and Kraft pay to sponsor content on the @food Instagram account, reaching 380,000 followers (England, 2015). Influencers who have a smaller, but dedicated, following can also be effective media channels for public relations efforts. Erika House, a fitness and lifestyle influencer with a comparatively smaller following of 54,000 Twitter followers, 365,000 YouTube followers, and 9,700 Instagram followers (Erikadhouse.com/mediakit, 2015), has created sponsored content for high profile brands like Walgreens, Old Navy, and Reebok. She provides a media kit, not unlike those produced by traditional media outlets, outlining fees and results of previous partnerships, to contextualize her reach and influence for potential sponsors.

The involvement of traditional news outlets in placement of paid content, like *The New York Times'* T Brand Studio, gives the practice legitimacy and credibility. T Brand Studio's sponsored content for Netflix's series *Orange is the New Black* featured multimedia elements, data visualization, and newsworthy facts alongside first person narratives that unfold in an interactive post. This content represents the integration of several elements of the PESO model: originating with paid placement, the content was shared by key influencers (including personnel affiliated with the show who had significant social media following) and resulted in earned favorable media coverage from mainstream and trade press (Castillo, 2014).

Earned media best reflects the traditional model of media placement, and pitching directly to reporters and editors and generating news and media coverage. There are many opportunities for practitioners to generate third-party credibility online, but as discussed above, practitioners must expand their definition of media outlets to include influencers, fan-created media, community-created and crowdsourced media, and participatory journalists.

Owned media content is created and published by the organization. Public relations expert Richard Edelman's assertion that "every company is a media company" captures the reality that, for most organizations, creating content for their own website, social media outlets, and other online venues creates a workload and process that resembles a newsroom and operates on the same 24/7 schedule as most media outlets. With new opportunities for leap-frogging gatekeepers and control of the message are responsibilities to create newsworthy content on a variety of topics, publish frequently, and liaise directly with target publics – who are now audiences. Some organizations hire "brand journalists" who toggle between advocacy and objectivity, depending on their professional experience and outlook. Owned news stories appear in search engine results alongside independent reporting and personal blogs, sometimes removed from its original context. Engaging multiple PESO media opportunities can create longevity for the campaign by extending the reach of the brand narrative.

KSA 4: distribution methods

Online public relations distribution includes using wire services like PR Newswire to reach media and influencers with enhanced, multimedia press releases (social media press releases, or SMPRs) that are also available to the public and often optimized for search engines so they can be easily found by average users and media alike. Direct access and shareability means that engaged publics have a much larger role in the distribution process.

Attendees at media events and press conferences now also include engaged publics. NASA Social events invite fans and social media influencers to apply for access to a rocket launch, facility tour, and press conference (Eididin, 2013). Attendees are members of relevant communities (such as engineers, photographers, tourism professionals, science fiction writers, and educators). During the event, Fans capture photo and video alongside traditional media attendees, but are also provided access and opportunities to capture multimedia and stories that help influencers provide social media content to share with their own communities and fans. NASA staff interacts with attendees on social media and share their posts, and the fan-created media becomes part of the official communication of the event.

In the Reddit community, where users vote on content and create communities for discussion on specific topics, the AMA or "Ask Me Anything" event has become a media opportunity that provides access to the site's hundreds of millions of unique monthly visitors and 3.5 million active members, and can often generate media coverage from traditional outlets. One of AMA's most notable guests was President Barack Obama, whose interview took place during his re-election campaign (Mendoza, 2012). The live interview reached a real-time audience and inspired user-created memes, motivating campaign staff to create a meme to be used in official promotions, extending the life of the effort.

During Woody Harrelson's AMA, the actor refused to answer questions and said that he was only interested in promoting his current film. Failure to demonstrate understanding of the community resulted in negative feedback from the community and unfavorable coverage by third-party media outlets like Mashable and Forbes (Hill, 2012). When using events like the Reddit AMA to leverage community, practitioners must understand that they and their clients will be expected to meet the standards of its members, like respect and authenticity.

Conclusion

The PRSA KSAs in media relations offer guidelines for proficiency in key areas in the practice of public relations, and can be applied to online or offline PR efforts. Effective media relations activities can generate media coverage that provides value to PR campaigns. Media relations continues to be part of the PR practitioner's toolkit in the social media and participatory culture era, but new definitions of media outlets, journalists, influencers, and publics mean that practitioners need to consider media relations in a new light. Understanding of the community, openness, authenticity, and providing value for fans, engaged publics, and influencers is essential for effective and ethical media relations in participatory culture. Reassessing the approaches, tactics, and techniques is necessary in order to continue provide this key function of public relations and to advance the profession.

References

Bajkiewicz, T. E., Kraus, J. J., & Hong, S. Y. (2011). The impact of newsroom changes and the rise of social media on the practice of media relations. *Public Relations Review*, 37(3), 329–331.

Batsell, J. (2015). *Engaged journalism: Connecting with digitally empowered news audience.* New York: Columbia University Press.

Brown, N. A., & Billings, A. C. (2013). Sports fans as crisis communicators on social media websites. *Public Relations Review*, 39(1), 74–81.

Buzzfeed. (2014, November). How technology is changing media. Retrieved July 9, 2015, from http://insights.buzzfeed.com/industry-trends-2014/.

Carpenter, S. (2008). How online citizen journalism publications and online newspapers utilize the objectivity standard and rely on external sources. *Journalism & Mass Communication Quarterly*, 85(3), 531–548.

Castillo, M. (2014, June 16). Netflix looking to pursue more native advertising. Retrieved July 10, 2015, from http://www.adweek.com/news/technology/net flix-looking-pursue-more-native-advertising-158367.

Cha, M., Haddadi, H., Benevenuto, F., & Gummadi, K. P. (2010). Measuring user influence on Twitter: The million follower fallacy. Paper presented at the 4th International Association for the Advancement of Artificial Intelligence Conference on Weblogs and Social Media, Washington, DC.

Creative Newsroom – Edelman. (n.d.). Retrieved July 1, 2015, from http://www. edelman.com/expertise/creative-newsroom-4/

Desmond, P. (2011, July 12). Disney designer. *Waterloo Chronicle.CA*. Retrieved July 9, 2015, from: http://www.waterloochronicle.ca/news/disney-designer/.

Duffet, M. (2013). *Understanding fandom*. New York: Bloomsbury.

Ehrlich, B. (2012, April 12). How journalists are using social media for real results. Retrieved July 9, 2015, from http://mashable.com/2010/04/12/journalists-gist/.

Eididin, R. (2013). Inside a NASA meetup, where science fans become space ambassadors. Retrieved July 1, 2015, from http://www.wired.com/2013/11/nasa-socials/.

Elliott, S. (2011, June 14). Account executive is antiquated. Consider yourself a catalyst. Retrieved July 1, 2015, from http://www.nytimes.com/2011/06/15/business/m edia/15adco.html?_r=3.

England, L. (2015, June 26). This woman was one of the first people to use Instagram for business – now she's cutting huge deals with Starbucks and Kraft. Retrieved July 9, 2015, from http://www.businessinsider.com/sarah-phillips-is-the-instagram-user-behind-food-and-baking-2015-6.

Federal Trade Commission (FTC). (2009, October 5). FTC publishes final guides governing endorsements, testimonials. Retrieved July 9, 2015, from https://www.ftc. gov/news-events/press-releases/2009/10/ftc-publishes-final-guides-governing-endors ements-testimonials.

Friend, C., & Singer, J. (2007). *Online journalism ethics: Traditions and transitions*. New York: M.E. Sharpe.

Gardner, D. H. (2012). Abracadabra: Key agents of mediation that define, create, and maintain TV fandom. Thesis, Georgia State University, 2012. http://scholarworks. gsu.edu/communication_theses/95.

Griffith, E. (2011, May 11). Mommy bloggers, meet ad-supported video. Retrieved July 9, 2015 from http://www.adweek.com/news/technology/mommy-bloggers-meet-a d-supported-video-131307.

Hill, K. (2012, February 6). Woody Harrelson's attempt to promote new movie on Reddit goes horribly wrong. Retrieved July 9, 2015, from http://www.forbes.com/ sites/kashmirhill/2012/02/06/woody-harrelsons-attempt-to-promote-new-movie-on -reddit-goes-horribly-wrong/.

Hutchins, A. L. (2008). Roles, responsibilities, and responses: The intersection of journalism and public relations in the Armstrong Williams, McManus and Gallagher, and "El Nuevo Herald" ethics controversies (Doctoral dissertation). Retrieved from ProQuest Databases (Accession number 3340524).

Iliff, R. (2014, December 5). Why PR is embracing the PESO model. Retrieved July 10, 2015, from http:// mashable.com/2014/12/05/public-relations-industry/.

Jenkins, H. (2006). *Convergence culture: Where old and new media collide.* New York: New York University Press.

Katz, E. (1957). The two-step flow of communication: An up-to-date report on an hypothesis. *Public Opinion Quarterly,* 21(1), 61–78.

Lewin, K. (1947). Frontiers in group dynamics: Channels of group life; social planning and action research. *Human Relations,* 1–2, 5–41.

Luttrell, R. (2014). *Social media: How to engage, share, and connect.* New York: Rowman & Littlefield.

Mendoza, D. (2012, August 31). President Barack Obama gets upvoted – CNNPolitics. com. Retrieved July 9, 2015, from http://www.cnn.com/2012/08/29/politics/obama-on-reddit/.

Mirvajová, V. (2015, January 14). The golden age of citizen journalism: Annales UMCS, Politologia. Retrieved July 9, 2015, from http://www.degruyter.com/view/j/curie.2013.21.issue-1/curie-2013-0010/curie-2013-0010.xml.

Mullin, B. (2015, June 15). The BuzzFeed news app, out today, was built for social interactions. Retrieved July 9, 2015, from http://www.poynter.org/news/media wire/351841/the-buzzfeed-news-app-out-today-was-built-for-social-interactions/.

Phillips, L. M., & Brabham, D. C. (2012). How today's digital landscape redefines the notion of power in public relations. *PRism,* 9(2): http://www.prismjournal.org/hom epage.html.

PRSA. (2015). Accreditation readiness review guide and materials. Retrieved July 1, 2015, from http://www.praccreditation.org/resources/documents/apr-rr-candida te-instructions.pdf.

Reddit. (n.d.). We power awesome communities. Retrieved July 9, 2015, from https:// www.reddit.com/about.

Shoemaker, P. J. (1991). *Gatekeeping.* Newbury Park, CA: Sage.

Shoemaker, P. J. (1996). Media gatekeeping. In M. B. Salwen & D. W. Stacks (Eds.), *An integrated approach to communication theory and research* (pp. 79–91). Mahwah, NJ: Lawrence Erlbaum.

Shoemaker, P. J., Eichholz, M., Kim, E., & Wrigley, B. (2001). Individual and routine forces in gatekeeping. *Journalism & Mass Communication Quarterly,* 78(2), 233–246.

Shoemaker, P., & Reese, S. D. (2011). *Mediating the message.* London: Routledge.

Singer, J. B. (1998). Online journalists: Foundations for research into their changing roles. *Journal of Computer-Mediated Communication,* 4(1). doi: 10.1111/j.1083-6101.1998.tb00088.x.

Society of Professional Journalists (SPJ). (2014). Code of ethics. Retrieved July 1, 2015, from http://www.spj.org/ethicscode.asp.

Stansberry, K. (2015). Identifying and engaging online influencers through the social web. *PRism* 12(1): http://www.prismjournal.org/homepage.html.

Supa, D. W., & Zoch, L. M. (2009). Maximizing media relations through a better understanding of the public relations–journalist relationship: A quantitative analysis of changes over the past 23 years. *Public Relations Journal,* 3(4), 1–28.

The Bridge – Golin. (n.d.). Retrieved July 9, 2015, from http://golin.com/thebridge/.

Tink and Minnie Festival Style Roundup | Disney Style. (2015, April 13). Retrieved July 9, 2015, from http://blogs.disney.com/disney-style/fashion/2015/04/13/tink-a nd-minnie-festival-style-roundup/.

Toffler, A. (1980). *The third wave.* New York: William Morrow.

Waters, R. D., Tindall, N. T., & Morton, T. S. (2010). Media catching and the journalist–public relations practitioner relationship: How social media are changing the practice of media relations. *Journal of Public Relations Research*, 22(3), 241–264.

Zoch, L. M., & Supa, D. W. (2014). Dictating the news: Understanding newsworthiness from the journalistic perspective. *Public Relations Journal*, 8(1).

Part III

Brand perspectives: applying theories of public relations and fandom in corporate, government, and nonprofit spaces

11 General Mills

[Re]manufacturing the gluten-free consumer community

Patricia A. Curtin

> "Everything we do starts with the consumer in mind."
>
> Ken Powell, CEO, General Mills
> (July 7, 2014, Taste of General Mills blog)

Introduction

In 2008, General Mills moved the niche gluten-free market into the mainstream by launching Gluten-Free Rice Chex®. Market analysts considered it a risky undertaking: total gluten-free food sales were less than $1 billion annually, and GM had to retool its entire production chain (Hughlett, 2011). Seven years later, GM is one of the largest players in a rapidly growing U.S. market expected to reach $15 billion in sales in 2016 (Strom, 2014a). The company's more than 600 gluten-free products include Betty Crocker® cake mixes, Bisquick®, and Pillsbury® cookie dough.

Helping fuel GM's success was its in-depth research of consumer preferences and its decision to market products almost totally digitally through creation of a company-sponsored online community. In March 2011, GM launched GlutenFreely.com, a one-stop gluten-free shop with product sales, recipes, nutrition and medical advice, and blog posts. The site allowed GM to gather consumer data to guide new product development and drive marketing strategy, but it was short-lived. GM discontinued it in January 2013 as gluten-free diets gained general popularity.

This study uses the cultural-economic model (CEM) of public relations (Curtin, Gaither, & Ciszek, 2015) as a lens through which to examine the discursive strategies GM used to manufacture, define, and then disband its online consumer community. The results provide an in-depth look at how corporations create identities for, and ostensibly empower, niche consumers through online communities while simultaneously using these sites to achieve marketing goals and objectives.

Gluten disorders and gluten-free diets

For some individuals, gluten, a complex array of proteins in wheat, rye, and barley, causes a severe autoimmune reaction known as celiac disease, which prevents proper absorption of nutrients. Celiac disease was seldom recognized in the United States until 2003, when a study determined that 1 of every 133 Americans (about 1%) suffer from it (Fasano, et al., 2003). To be medically diagnosed with celiac disease requires an intestinal biopsy and blood work.

In 2011 the U.S. medical community officially recognized a related condition, gluten sensitivity, which affects another 6% to 10% of Americans (Moore, 2014). Although gluten-sensitive individuals do not experience a full-blown autoimmune reaction, they suffer similar symptoms to celiacs; some believe the conditions are points on a spectrum from slight sensitivity to celiac disease. No decisive medical test exists for gluten sensitivity; diagnosis is accomplished by seeing whether symptoms abate when gluten is excluded from the diet.

Doctors originally associated gluten-related disorders only with gastro-intestinal symptoms, but they now tie them to more than 200 signs and symptoms, including infertility, stunted growth, mental health and neurological disorders, and some cancers. About 83% of Americans with gluten-related disorders are either undiagnosed or misdiagnosed (Celiac Disease, n.d.); given that the only treatment is a gluten-free diet, people often self-diagnose and try the diet without medical supervision.

Achieving a gluten-free diet, however, is more difficult than it sounds. Gluten is found not just in bread products but also in such foods as soy sauce, malt vinegar, salad dressings, and soup broths; modified food starch; and some drug capsules. Adhering to a gluten-free diet is difficult from a taste standpoint as well. The texture and taste of many early gluten-free foods gave rise to the joke that the packaging tasted better than the product (Jiménez, 2009). Gluten-free products are also expensive, often running about 2.5 times more than their gluten-filled counterparts (Strom, 2014a).

Online communities and Internet affinity portals

When GM entered the nascent gluten-free marketplace it created an e-commerce website and supporting social media channels to provide consumers an online gathering place. Companies sponsor online community sites as strategic invest-ments (Gruner, Homburg, & Lukas, 2014; Pai & Tsai, 2011): they support their brands, facilitate new product development and adoption, and provide consumer insight marketing data (Miller, Fabian, & Lin, 2009). In turn, rela-tionship marketing professionals claim a company-sponsored site "show[s] consumers that their feedback is both appreciated and utilised for company improvements" (O'Brien, 2011, p. 34). They can thus strengthen B2C rela-tionships by increasing brand loyalty and consumer trust, satisfaction, and commitment. The result, according to some, is the emergence of the "social media empowered consumer," which has switched the balance of power from companies to consumers (O'Brien, p. 36).

When these sites are targeted toward a specific market segment, such as celiac sufferers, they are termed *affinity portals* and offer entry points to communities that form around a common issue or cause (Rainer & Cegielski, 2010). Although these portals can empower otherwise marginalized consumers by making them feel part of a larger community, the benefits a corporation reaps from connecting with a desirable demographic cannot be ignored. Affinity portals allow corporations to gather market data through online registration requirements, surveys, use of cookies, and tracking onsite product sales and site use, "render[ing] online communities into profitable communities" (Campbell, 2005, p. 669). Affinity portals thus form sites of contested meanings characterized by fluid power flows that defy easy categorization of companies and consumers into empowered or disempowered, requiring a more nuanced theoretical approach to their study than relationship marketing or management allows.

The cultural–economic model of public relations

The cultural–economic model (CEM) of public relations is built on the circuit of culture, developed by Open University scholars to demonstrate how meaning is constructed through discursive practice (du Gay, Hall, Janes, Mackay, & Negus, 1997). The model comprises five interconnected moments that constrain the possible range of meanings, but their articulation is sensitive to situational particulars and not predetermined. The model incorporates Foucault's notion of power as potentially empowering or disempowering, arising from the interplay of contextual nuance and structural constraints (Curtin, et al., 2015).

The moment of regulation encompasses social norms, law, and policy, such as food-labeling regulations and public attitudes toward gluten-free diets. Representation comprises how meaning is presented, including how gluten-free diets were characterized in GM's materials. How supply-chain retooling, marketing budgets, and similar considerations shape meaning falls within the moment of production. Identity consists of the fluid and conflicting categories that producers apply to consumers and products and that consumers adopt, adapt, or reject. The meanings that consumers make of products and issues in their everyday lives is the focus of the moment of consumption.

The GlutenFreely.com affinity portal provides a case study through which to examine how companies create a community around an issue, control membership, and weigh the costs and benefits of their investment. In particular, this study examines how GM's discourses created the identity of the gluten-free consumer and constructed social norms around that identity, as well as how production and regulatory factors determined the community's strategic value and ultimate viability.

Deconstructing discourses

The CEM is predicated on the notion that meaning arises through discursive practices, making discourse analysis the method of choice. Analysis begins by problematizing texts to determine their underlying values, such as what is normal, who is allowed to define an issue, how institutional practices embody these values, and which voices are silenced (Hall, 1997). The approach is not a systematic content analysis but an immersion in the texts to uncover the underlying relational webs of meaning.

Because GM's GlutenFreely.com site was active only from March 2011 through early January 2013, the Wayback Machine Internet Archive was used to access it. Additional texts analyzed include all tweets from @GlutenFreely from 2011 through early 2013, which are available through Twitter's search engine. GlutenFreely also had a dedicated Facebook page, YouTube channel, and Pinterest account, although only pieces of these channels remain. The author is familiar with them through past use – she has two gluten-intolerant family members and was a community member almost from the moment of its inception. Memory can be unreliable, however, so only impressions that can be reinforced by screen captures, archived links, and other supporting materials are included in the analysis.

The GM website provided news releases and annual reports from this time period. Additionally, more than 100 articles from a Google news alert for "General Mills" and "gluten-free" and a general library search using those terms yielded many studies. The most apt from these sources provide analytic depth.

General Mills manufactures the online gluten-free community

Stories vary as to why GM ventured into the niche gluten-free market when only full-blown celiac disease was recognized as necessitating a gluten-free diet. According to some company sources, several GM employees or their relatives were celiacs, calling company attention to the issue (Rinella, 2010). According to others, questions about gluten led the topics on the GM consumer-information hotline from 2005 (Newman, 2008).

In either event (or quite possibly both), GM research in 2008 found that 12% of U.S. households wanted gluten-free products and that the market had grown 28% over four years (White-Sax, 2009). That same year GM launched gluten-free Rice Chex® with no standard advertising plan (Newman, 2008); instead, GM marketed its gluten-free products almost totally digitally (York, 2009). GM does not reveal how much it spends on social media marketing (McGuire, 2010), but as GM's cereal president observed, "In this new era of marketing, you can try a lot of ideas for very little money and really experiment with them, and we're doing it with them quite effectively" (Webb, 2013, para. 8).

In 2009, GM's website included a liveglutenfreely.com section, which listed its gluten-free products and a few recipes. GM targeted bloggers, sending them samples, hosting tasting suites at BlogHer conferences, and inviting them to company headquarters (McGuire, 2010). In November 2010, GM held a bloggers' summit, asking well-known opinion leaders, such as The Savvy Celiac Amy Leger (2011), for their feedback. Based on their input, GM rebranded its gluten-free web site into the affinity portal GlutenFreely.com. GM's (2012, para. 2) stated mission was "to make GlutenFreely.com a dynamic and useful resource for the gluten-free community through great food products, lifestyle tips, new recipes and the latest information about living gluten-free." The community was built on a Microsoft cloud-based platform, allowing GM to minimally invest in its set-up and maintenance (Hatch, 2012).

When the site debuted, the only homepage mention of GM occurred at the bottom of the partner listing: the Bell Institute for Health and Nutrition/General Mills. Although company materials defined the site as a one-stop shop to meet all community needs, the site's design emphasized sales. The first of six top buttons led consumers to *Our Store*; a second, lower button invited consumers to *Shop Our Store*, and a checkout cart appeared prominently in the top-right corner. In its second year, the top button changed to *Shop Now*, a more active call to action, and the homepage's midsection changed from a mainly graphic design to new product links. GM used Twitter and Facebook to drive traffic to the site, encouraging product reviews, asking consumers to report their favorite brands and ingredients, and offering coupons as incentives. The store stocked complementary and competing products from partnering manufacturers. By selling competitors' products, GM was able to collect what would have otherwise been expensive marketing research data, such as identifying weaknesses in competitors' products, acquiring data for new product development, and determining optimal price points.

The second button, *Living Freely*, provided fact sheets and backgrounders on issues such as *Dining Out* and a *Gluten-Free Kitchen*. It included a *Real Life Stories* section that for most of the site's life ran the same anonymous story of unknown origin, even though the site promised "Soon you'll be able to share your stories. Stay tuned for more!" Twitter was used to drive traffic to the *Recipes* section, the third button, as well as collect recipe ideas, with tweets such as "How do you make GF stuffing?" and "What's your favorite gluten-free recipe?" The Pinterest page also posted recipes. Community feedback led to new recipe development.

The Tools button contained the most GM-centric materials: a GM product list, a GM product locator, a preprinted request sheet for your local grocer to carry gluten-free GM products, and a link to a coupon site. The fifth button, *Medical Insight*, linked to fairly technical celiac disease data from two GM partner organizations and one additional medical source. Midway through 2012, the site began providing more consumer-friendly medical information through its *Ask a Doc* video series, which appeared under the *Community* button as well as on GlutenFreely's YouTube channel.

The *Community* section also contained blog posts and an *Ask Danna* section in which community members could query the author of *Living Gluten Free for*

Dummies. The same 12 questions and answers appeared in this section for most of the site's life. GlutenFreely had its own blog, but the site also featured between two and four other bloggers over the course of its lifespan, all of whom were celiacs themselves and/or had children with celiac disease.

The site featured little interactive material that could foster community dialogue and engagement. Instead, the site aggregated content for easy viewing – and purchasing. Its wide selection of gluten-free products was a luxury in 2011. Most gluten-free brands were local, with localized distributions (Strom, 2014a). GlutenFreely brought together brands such as Udi's from Colorado, Dr. Schärs from Italy, Pamela's from California, and Barkat from England all in one easily browsed location, with products delivered to consumers' doors.

On its first day, the site received orders from 25 states; a year later a company spokesperson said, "While we can't share specific sales or traffic numbers, we are very pleased with the results of the site ... it is meeting our expectations for a start-up business" (Hatch, 2012, para. 8). Two months after its launch, GlutenFreely boasted 75,000+ members; six months later, approximately 110,000 people had joined. Using the cloud, GM had tapped a large test market eager to share its buying habits, concerns, recipes, tips, and preferences.

June Cleaver and Better Crocker

From the website pictures, to the blog stories, to GM officials' quotes, a clear picture of the normalized community member emerges: she's white, married to a white man, and mom to a child with celiac disease. Admittedly, gluten disorders are more common in those of Northern European descent, but they are also found in people from Asia, Africa, and the Caribbean (Jiménez, 2009). A glance at GlutenFreely.com, however, shows Caucasian faces, the majority of them women of child-bearing age. Blog posts addressed gluten-free back-to-school breakfasts, packing a gluten-free lunch box, and ensuring safe snacks for after-school sports. @GlutenFreely hosted a Back 2 School chat and pointed parents to the website for advice on parenting a celiac child and kid-approved recipes, among other child-centered topics.

The site also constructed community members as solidly middle class – their children aren't on reduced- or free-lunch programs but can afford school meals. These moms have time and money for their children's numerous extracurricular activities, and they own two sets of everyday appliances to ensure that one set remains gluten-free. After all, as the *Ask Danna* column noted, using a breadmaker and gluten-free bread mix "is quick and easy, and you'll feel just like June Cleaver when the house fills up with that awesome aroma of fresh-baked bread!" The expense of gluten-free packaged foods is almost never mentioned, although one blogger opined that GM "is making a good effort to provide naturally great gluten-free foods at a reasonable price." *Reasonable* isn't defined. GM's gluten-free mixes are about twice the cost of its regular formulations, putting them beyond reach of a number of families.

While not materially lacking, these moms are psychologically unfulfilled. "Baking is important to mom and she wants to experience that with her family" (GM, 2013, para. 3), but having a child with celiac disease means mom is excluded from the:

> sweet moments of life – family moments sharing a cake, being able to reward your son with a cookie when he gets off the bus. Those are the things we take for granted, but it's emotional to have those things taken away from you.
>
> (GM marketing manager in Rinella, 2010, para. 6)

Bloggers write of the pain of having to deny their children their favorite foods: "When my daughter Emma was diagnosed with celiac disease, I made it my personal mission to recreate each and every gluten-filled treat she ever liked into a gluten-free version ... . my 'mama bear' instinct was in full force." As a *Fortune* magazine story noted: "They're selling the gluten-free story, targeting that mom who's watched her celiac child's face after another birthday party where they couldn't eat the cake" (Barack, 2011, para. 13).

The site equates food with love, and GM positioned Betty Crocker as the means by which to assuage maternal guilt and return the family to a loving balance. Now moms of celiac children could "share everyday moments with loved ones. Whether enjoying a slice of banana bread for breakfast, splitting a plate of cookies after dinner, or sharing a birthday cake to celebrate someone special, Betty Crocker allows families to feel normal again" (GM, 2013, para. 6). Regaining normality was a frequent blog topic because, as *Ask Danna* observed, the children of these white, hetero-normative, middle-class families shouldn't have to "feel 'different'."

Selling your soul to the company store

GM has used Betty Crocker since the 1920s as the trusted face of the company (McGuire, 2010). According to GM, Betty Crocker's ability to erase difference and ease guilt was based in large part on trust: "Gluten-free moms already trust the great taste of Betty Crocker Gluten Free Brownie, Cookie and Cake mixes – and enjoy them with their entire family" (GM, 2013, para. 2). This trust, however, stemmed not from transparency but was necessitated by a consistent lack of it. A typical GM response to requests for information is "We don't share information ... so that's our total response ... . We have the highest possible standards and our consumers know us and trust us" (Schmidt, 2008, p. C3).

In fact, at the time consumers had to trust that GM's products were indeed gluten-free because no U.S. regulatory standard for gluten existed until 2014. For those with gluten disorders, however, knowing what products contain gluten is a medical necessity. A 2008 investigative report found that gluten-free dinosaur-shaped chicken nuggets actually contained up to 2,200 ppm of gluten.

Several children were hospitalized as a result. The manufacturer never recalled the product, however, because with no federal standard in place no law had been violated (Roe, 2008a, 2008b). Some studies estimate that prior to 2006, one in five products labeled gluten-free actually contained large amounts of gluten (Derr, 2006).

Concurrently, lawyers who had prosecuted tobacco companies began filing cases against large food manufacturers, including two against GM, for mis-labeled product ingredients (Strom, 2012, 2014b). This regulatory environment may help explain why GlutenFreely.com contained almost as much legal language as it did marketing effort, including a 2,208-word privacy policy, a 533-word community rules section, and a 1,658-word terms-of-use section. The legal discourse made plain that all user-submitted materials became GM's property, which it could – and did – use to its benefit. For example, an @GlutenFreely tweet asking, "What are your favorite GF mobile apps?" was followed by the launch of the Betty Crocker app, with a gluten-free section, about two years later. A tweet asking community members for their favorite pie crust ingredients was followed by the introduction of Pillsbury® gluten-free pie and pastry dough about two years later. A survey about oat consumption and concerns in 2012 was followed by the 2015 announcement that soon five flavors of gluten-free Cheerios®, all made from oats, would be available. GM holds the patents for all these products.

While consumers were handing over their legal and intellectual property rights, GM retained the right to use web cookies, beacons, and transparent GIFs to collect user data for marketing purposes. Users were warned that disabling cookies would block them from accessing parts of the community; to retain full community membership, users were required to surrender personal data for corporate gain.

Losing community affinity

As noted earlier, the dominant identity GM created for a community member was that of a celiac sufferer or the close relative of one. Site bloggers stressed the importance of medical diagnosis – possible only for celiacs. The medical information provided was technical data on celiac disease. Two of the three site partners were university celiac research centers; the site also linked to two nonprofits: the Celiac Sprue Association and the Celiac Disease Foundation. GM used Twitter and Facebook to reinforce the priority of celiac disease and medical diagnosis as badges of community membership, with @GlutenFreely retweeting cautions against adopting a gluten-free diet without medical testing.

Medical diagnosis is a contested procedure, however. It's invasive, and for those with gluten sensitivity, it's inconclusive. Because "you don't need a pre-scription to go gluten-free" (Copelton & Valle, 2009, p. 627), many self-diagnose, which "opens space for non-medically diagnosed individuals to take on the identity of a person in need of a gluten-free diet" (Worosz & Wilson, 2012, p. 294). This audience-adopted identity was at odds with the primary identity

GM imposed on community members, and the lack of site interactivity and spaces for community dialogue left community members with little recourse or ability to adopt their own on-site identities.

Many relationship marketing and management scholars have credited affinity portals and supporting social media with shifting power from businesses to consumers, turning what was formerly customer relationship management into customer-managed relationships (e.g., O'Brien, 2011). Conversely, critical scholars, citing Foucault, point to the ability of companies to use these same channels for consumer surveillance, ultimately disempowering consumers relative to corporate interests (e.g., Marx, 2004). Taking a more balanced view, scholars such as Campbell (2005) point to the promise these sites hold for validating the concerns of disenfranchised audiences but caution that their surveillance potential cannot be ignored.

The results of this case study support this latter, more nuanced, perspective. While these results are not generalizable, they provide insight into the contours of online corporate-sponsored community interactions and their relative power flows. For example, while these sites can promote trust and long-term brand affinities (Pai & Tsai, 2011), they don't necessarily do so, and providing consumer fulfillment does not preclude corporate gain. Company-sponsored online communities may co-opt consumers, but it may be equally true that consumers allow themselves to be co-opted (Johnston, 2008) when it suits their needs.

For GM, GlutenFreely.com provided a minimal-investment, low-involvement testing laboratory for the gluten-free market. Existing in the cloud, it occupied a nebulous, liminal space – neither of the company nor entirely separate from it. It was a community ostensibly built around a medical issue, but in fact it was a community built on an exchange of goods. Consumers turned over their money and intellectual property rights in exchange for the convenience of packaged products. In turn, GM collected proprietary market research data for little cost through the use of web surveillance devices and legal strictures, and it continues to profit from those measures today.

Throughout, GM defined its role in the community as the trusted supplier of family nutritional and emotional needs: "It's about trust ... families around the world trust our brands to nourish and delight the most important people in their lives" (GM, 2012, p. 3). But its lack of transparency, dominant legalistic discourse, and strict control of site content made consumer trust a necessity for membership, not an inherent characteristic of the community itself. This need for blind trust made GlutenFreely.com a community more in terms of shared consumption than in terms of reciprocity.

Although this analysis concentrated on company efforts, it appears the portal occupied an ambiguous space for consumers as well. People join affinity portals because they "provide not only utilitarian support for online buying but also social support through learning and fellowship experiences" (Pai & Tsai, 2011, p. 605). Numerous studies have documented the isolation experienced by those with gluten disorders. While sufferers look like everyone else, they can't eat normally, making travel and dining out stressful (Lee & Newman, 2003; Olsson, Lyon, Hörnell, Ivarsson, & Sydner, 2009). The psychological trauma incurred by celiacs is more than that caused by disease symptoms alone because of the impact on their social and family lives (Veen, te Molder, Gremmen, & van Woerkum, 2010). At the time, GlutenFreely.com provided one of the very few community spaces for gluten sufferers, and it offered at least some validation of their lived realities. It may have been far from the "fun" and "interactive" site GM (2011, para.4) promised, but it's also not surprising that community numbers quickly soared. Ironically, in some sense site consumers were empowered inasmuch as they had more freedom of consumption; rather than buy naturally gluten-free foods they could now buy processed foods, similar to other consumers, achieving a degree of normality through consumption.

Affinity portals are constructed on the notion of specifically appealing to a single demographic/psychographic identity (Campbell, 2005), and the lack of site space for community interaction did not allow consumers to explore other identities to come to terms with their medical condition (Worosz & Wilson, 2012). The articulations GM made between gluten-free and celiacs, celiacs and maternal guilt, and Betty Crocker as the route to redemption, however, wrote nonceliacs out of consideration, ignoring the majority of the audience who were gluten-sensitive. This same discourse wrote out of consideration the many audience members who didn't self-identify as white, middle class, hetero-normative, and child bearing.

As celebrities such as Gwyneth Paltrow, Lady Gaga, and Novak Djokovic endorsed a gluten-free lifestyle, gluten-free went from medical necessity for some to trendy for many. GM's materials occasionally recognized these other identities: for example, the news release announcing the site said it was for those "who need or desire to live a gluten-free lifestyle" (GM, 2011, para. 1). Similarly, @GlutenFreely tweeted, "If you're celiac, gluten sensitive, or just want to live a gluten free life then our community is the place for you" (November 28, 2011). But GM's dominant discourse was celiac-centered, and a relatively static community built around 1% of the population made little sense as gluten-free diets gained in mainstream popularity.

GlutenFreely.com's not quite two-year lifespan ended not with a bang, but a whimper. In early 2013 the company announced it was shutting down the site because "more retailers carry a wider assortment of gluten-free products, there is less of a need for a specific gluten-free store" (Leger, 2013, para. 3). Unstated was that gathering market data on a small segment of the population was unnecessary in the face of widespread product adoption. GM stressed, however, that it "remain[ed] committed to the gluten-free community by continuing to offer more than 300 gluten-free products" (Ratner, 2012, para. 3), and it directed consumers to its in-house sites, BettyCrocker.com and LivingBetter-America.com, where gluten-free options appeared among other products. GM received some blowback from those who claimed gluten-free products were unavailable locally, but it was notably the lack of shopping options that drew the most comment – not the lack of an affinity portal for what had once been a marginalized group.

As this case demonstrates, affinity portals provide contested spaces for meaning that operate within a complex interplay of corporate production constraints, consumer needs, cultural norms, and competing identities. We enhance our understanding of how consumer engagement unfolds in digital spaces when we approach the study of it from theoretical standpoints and using methodological tools that do not reduce power relations to simplistic binaries and thus impede our understanding of the complex interplay between producers and consumers these sites enable or the competing and conflicting narratives they engender and promote.

References

Barack, L. (2011, August 19). Food giants mine the gluten-free gold rush. *Fortune*. Retrieved from http://fortune.com/2011/08/19/food-giants-mine-the-gluten-free-gold-rush/.

Campbell, J. E. (2005). Outing PlanetOut: surveillance, gay marketing and internet affinity portals. *New Media and Society*, 7(5), 663–683. doi: 10.1177/1461444805056011.

Celiac Disease (n.d.). *Celiac disease and gluten-free fast facts*. National Foundation for Celiac Awareness. Retrieved from http://www.celiaccentral.org/celiac-disease/facts-and-fi gures/.

Copelton, D. A., & Valle, G. (2009). "You don't need a prescription to go gluten-free": The scientific self-diagnosis of celiac disease. *Social Science and Medicine*, 69, 623–631. doi: 10.1016/j.socscimed.2009.05.012.

Curtin, P. A., Gaither, T. K., & Ciszek, E. (2015). Articulating public relations practice and critical/cultural theory through a cultural-economic lens. In J. L'Etang, D. McKie, N. Snow, & J. Xifra (Eds.), *The Routledge handbook of critical public relations* (pp. 41–53). London: Routledge.

Derr, L. E. (2006). When food is poison: The history, consequences, and limitations of the Food Allergen Labeling and Consumer Protection Act of 2004. *Food and Drug Law Journal*, 61(1), 65–166.

du Gay, P., Hall, S., Janes, L., Mackay, H., & Negus, K. (1997). *Doing cultural studies: The story of the Sony Walkman*. Thousand Oaks, CA: Sage.

Fasano, A., Berti, I., Gerarduzzi, T., Not, T., Colletti, R. B., Drago, S., & Horvath, K. (2003). Prevalence of celiac disease in at-risk and not-at-risk groups in the United States: A large multicenter study. *Archives of Internal Medicine*, 163(3), 286–292. doi: 10.1001/archinte.163.3.286.

GM (2011, May 12). GlutenFreely.com serves as one-stop shop for gluten-free community. General Mills news release. Retrieved from http://www.reuters.com/article/2011/05/12/idUS254278+12-May-2011+BW20110512.

GM (2012, September 12). Gluten-free advocate Elisabeth Hasselbeck joins gluten-Freely.com. General Mills news release. Retrieved from http://www.businesswire.com/news/home/20120912005521/en/Gluten-Free-Advocate-Elisabeth-Hasselbeck-Joins-GlutenFreely.com#.VOYeZS4fdpk.

GM (2013, July 18). Betty Crocker expands gluten-free offerings, giving households more reasons to bake family favorites. General Mills news release. Retrieved from http://www.prnewswire.com/news-releases/betty-crocker-expands-gluten-free-offerings-giving-households-more-reasons-to-bake-family-favorites-216023301.html.

Gruner, R. L., Homburg, C., & Lukas, B. A. (2014). Firm-hosted online brand communities and new product success. *Journal of the Academy of Market Sciences*, 42, 29–48. doi:10.1007/s11747–11013–0334–0339.

Hall, S. (1997). The work of representation. In S. Hall (Ed.), *Representation: Cultural representations and signifying practices* (pp. 13–64). Thousand Oaks, CA: Sage.

Hatch, D. (2012, May 15). General Mills tries gluten-free sales in the cloud. *USNews. com*. Retrieved from http://money.usnews.com/money/business-economy/articles/2012/05/15/general-mills-tries-gluten-free-sales-in-the-cloud.

Hughlett, M. (2011, March 8). Demonized gluten means major dough. *Star Tribune*. Retrieved from http://www.startribune.com/business/121444784.html.

Jaffee, D., & Howard, P. (2010). Corporate cooptation of organic and fair trade standards. *Agriculture and Human Values*, 27(4), 387–399. doi: 10.1007/s10460–10009–9231–9238.

Jiménez, M. (2009, July 9). Celiacs surge to one in one hundred. *The Globe and Mail*, p. L1.

Johnston, J. (2008). The citizen–consumer hybrid: Ideological tensions and the case of Whole Foods Market. *Theory and Society*, 37, 220–270.

Lee, A., & Newman, J. M. (2003). Celiac diet: Its impact on quality of life. *Journal of the American Dietetic Association*, 103(11), 1533–1535. doi:10.1016/S0002-8223(03)01233-1.

Leger, A. (2011, March 2). Improved "Gluten Freely" solidifies General Mills in the gluten free market. *The Savvy Celiac*. Retrieved from http://www.thesavvyceliac.com/2011/03/02/improved-gluten-freely-solidifies-general-mills-in-the-gluten-free-market/.

Leger, A. (2013, January 8). Today is the final day for GlutenFreely.com as we know it. *The Savvy Celiac*. Retrieved from http://www.thesavvyceliac.com/2013/01/08/today-is-the-final-day-for-glutenfreely-com-as-we-know-it/.

Marx, G. T. (2004). What's new about the new surveillance?: Classifying for change and continuity. *Knowledge, Technology & Policy*, 17(1), 18–37.

McGuire, K. (2010, November 14). A new recipe for the Web. *Star Tribune*, p. D1.

Miller, K. D., Fabian, F., & Lin, S. J. (2009). Strategies for online communities. *Strategic Management Journal*, 30(3), 305–322. doi: 10.1002/smj.735.

Moore, L. R. (2014). "But we're not hypochondriacs": The changing shape of gluten-free dieting and the contested illness experience. *Social Science & Medicine*, 105, 76–83. doi: 10.1016/j.socscimed.2014.01.009.

Newman, E. (2008, May 5). Giant General Mills goes after gluten-free market. *Brandweek*, 49(18), 18–19.

O'Brien, C. (2011). The emergence of the social media empowered consumer. *Irish Marketing Review*, 21(1&2), 32–40.

Olsson, C., Lyon, P., Hörnell, A., Ivarsson, A., & Sydner, Y. M. (2009). Food that makes you different: The stigma experienced by adolescents with celiac disease. *Qualitative Health Research*, 19(7), 976–984. doi: 10.1177/1049732309338722.

Pai, P.-Y., & Tsai, H.-T. (2011). How virtual community participation influences consumer loyalty intentions in online shopping contexts: An investigation of mediating factors. *Business and Information Technology*, 30(5), 603–615. doi.org/10.1080/0144929X.2011.553742.

Rainer, R. K., & Cegielski, C. G. (2010). *Introduction to information systems: Enabling and transforming business* (3rd Ed.). Hoboken, NJ: Wiley.

Ratner, A. (2012, December 13). General Mills closing gluten free online story. *Gluten-Free Living blog*. Retrieved from http://gluten-freeliving.blogspot.com/2012/12/general-mills-closing-gluten-free.html.

Rinella, H. K. (2010, January 13). Gluten-free zone. *Las Vegas Review-Journal*. Retrieved from http://www.reviewjournal.com/life/food-and-cooking/gluten-free-zone.

Roe, S. (2008a, November 21). Children at risk in food roulette. *Chicago Tribune*. Retrieved from http://articles.chicagotribune.com/2008-12-31/news/chi-whole_foodsdec31_1_foods-market-whole-foods-libba-letton.

Roe, S. (2008b, December 31). Whole Foods pulls "gluten-free" products from shelves after Tribune story. *Chicago Tribune*. Retrieved from http://www.chicagotribune.com/news/nationworld/chi-whole_foodsdec31,0,4055580.story.

Schmidt, S. (2008, October 27). Sources of food problems; manufacturers' secrecy pushed consumers toward local markets. *Times Colonist*, p. C3.

Strom, S. (2012, August 19). After tobacco, lawyers set their sights on food industry. *The New York Times*, p. A1.

Strom, S. (2014a, February 18). Big bet on gluten-free. *The New York Times*, p. B1.

Strom, S. (2014b, April 17). When "liking" a brand online voids the right to sue. *The New York Times*, p. B1.

Veen, M., te Molder, H., Gremmen, B., & van Woerkum, C. (2010). Quitting is not an option: An analysis of online diet talk between celiac disease patients. *Health*, 14 (1), 23–40. doi: 10.1177/1363459309347478.

Webb, T. (2013, September 17). General Mills crunches the numbers on better cereal sales. *St. Paul Pioneer Press*. Retrieved from http://www.twincities.com/ci_24120663/general-mills-1q-sales-rise-acquisitions.

White-Sax, B. (2009, September 14). Gluten-free takes the cake in snack food products. *Drug Store News*, p. 125.

Worosz, M. R., & Wilson, N. L. W. (2012). A cautionary tale of purity, labeling and product literacy in the gluten-free market. *The Journal of Consumer Affairs*, 46(2), 288–318. doi: 10.1111/j.1745–6606.2012.01230.x.

York, E. B. (2009, July 13). Social media allows giants to exploit niche markets. *Ad Age*, 80(25), pp. 3, 25.

12 Boosters, idealized citizens, and cranks

City communicators share and moderate information in social media, but real engagement is messy and time-consuming

Jacqueline Lambiase and Laura F. Bright

Introduction

Cities work hard to foster engagement with their residents, with many groups urging local government to increase transparency and exchange among citizens, elected officials, and city staffers. The National Civic League, the International City/County Management Association and the City-County Communications and Marketing Association, among others, have all recently emphasized the importance of building better stakeholder connections. Former San Francisco Mayor Gavin Newsom has long promoted online participatory budgeting and digital platforms that collect the "wisdom of people outside of government" to transform government itself into what he calls Government 2.0 (Newsom, 2013). Academic scholarship points to the importance of social media engagement in the reinvigoration of democratic ideals through public participation models (Gil de Zúñiga & Valenzuela, 2011; Gil de Zúñiga, Jung, & Valenzuela, 2012; Hilbert, 2009).

This study focuses on the front-line communicators responsible for messaging and strategies of engagement in cities' main social media channels. Using depth interviews and a brief survey, the researchers interviewed and analyzed responses from 40 public information officers (PIOs) or directors of marketing for cities in Texas, Minnesota, and Georgia. Researchers analyzed social media policies for these cities to determine how citizens were classified, described, and situated within the context of participatory government. The broad research questions delve into how PIOs monitor and moderate social media channels through policy, confront conflict and encourage healthy debate, and battle social media fatigue compounded by the intensity of channel monitoring. This chapter will shed light on how PIOs operate within a digital participatory culture that is part marketing, part citizen engagement, part complaint department, and part town square. This study is needed because the "forms of communication afforded by Web. 2.0" for citizen engagement and political conversations have been neglected by academic inquiry (Ellison & Hardey, 2013).

Literature review

Many levels of government have been exploring technology-based citizen engagement for the last two decades trying to leverage the web's power of facilitating collective intelligence, crowdsourcing, and participatory governing. Social media have provided newer, more personal communication platforms for interaction between government agencies and their stakeholders. In a 2013 survey, the International City-County Management Association found that 80% of local governments in its database used official social media platforms as part of their public outreach (ICMA, 2013); most of the respondents were in the US, and smaller towns were less likely than larger cities to be utilizing social media platforms. The four social platforms with the highest use were LinkedIn, YouTube, Facebook, and Twitter.

While most local governments in the European Union use social media tools, according to Bonsón, Torres, Royo, and Floresc (2012), the concept of "corporate dialog" or non-hierarchical distribution of viewpoints from both local officials and individual citizens in a single digital forum, as a mechanism to promote participation, is not well developed. Other scholars also recognize the problem of "opportunities for active citizen collaboration and participation (being) underdeveloped" online (Wojtczak & Morner, 2014, p. 2). Related to these concerns are more serious issues about social networking sites and citizenship, including shallow dialogue, distractions, and political disengagement (Gil de Zúñiga, et al., 2012).

These social networking sites may lessen a citizen's reliance on local connections by diversifying overall ties to others beyond a geographic location (Hampton, Lee & Her, 2011). While these long-term worries are difficult to address, research has shown social networking sites to provide "adequate and relevant information to reinvigorate the democratic process" (Gil de Zúñiga, et al., 2012, p. 329).

The web and social media can be seen as providing important tools to help cities meet goals of improving public-sector transparency, policy-making, public services, and knowledge management (Bonsón, et al., 2012); yet these authors found much communication is uni-directional rather than interactive. One roadblock to building a non-hierarchical model for viewpoint sharing could be intimidating, inflammatory, and emotional responses that sometimes become "normative communication behaviors for many participants" (Lambiase, 2010; see also Herring, 1999). When topics get hijacked by dominant users, egalitarian participatory discourse becomes difficult or impossible (Lambiase, 2010).

Political consumerism and social media

Experienced users of social media expect full-bodied exchanges among participants when so-called political consumerism is associated with general digital media use (Gil de Zúñiga, Copeland, & Bimber, 2013). These scholars assert "that social media use mediates the relationship between general Internet use and political consumerism ... (and) the relationship of digital media to participation and engagement" (Gil de Zúñiga, et al., 2013, p. 501). Young citizens, especially, identify with other political consumers, giving them the opportunity to develop "civic competencies necessary for engagement in the formal political sphere" (Gotlieb & Wells, 2012).

In addition to political consumerism, motivation may be related to a citizen's ability to process messages when engaged in online political discussions, since interpersonal communication is mixed with computer-mediated platforms (Valenzuela, Kim & Gil de Zúñiga, 2012).

In a study of online political discussions, researchers discovered that online networks are effective ways for citizens to share public petitions and political messages, when compared to in-person conversations (Valenzuela, et al., 2012). Other motivational strategies include government's articulation of coproduction, in which citizens are encouraged to become partners with government (Linders, 2012; Thomas, 2013). One way that citizens can partner with government is to be engaged in creating guidelines governing online interactions, with the ability to share, tag, and flag messages. Social media policies that govern both citizen engagement and best practices for PIOs can be powerful tools to help mediate conversations as well as combat the social media fatigue associated with constant monitoring.

Citizen engagement and social media

While Thomas' framework (2013) for classifying public audiences in three ways – citizens, customers, and partners – is useful and acknowledges the complexity of working with the public at large, it sidesteps the important work that communicators must do to imagine such diverse audiences and create messages to reach them effectively. To some scholars, the audience is a fiction invented by a speech or composition writer (Long, 1980; Ong, 1975), while others believe both writers and speakers create their compositions to closely align with the needs of a "real" audience (Mitchell & Taylor, 1979). Ede and Lunsford (1985/1999) take a different approach and avoid this either/or dichotomy of "fictional" or "real" audiences, by demonstrating the density of every writer's rhetorical strategies. They developed an approach to audience in terms of "audience addressed/audience invoked." The audience addressed "refers to those actual or real-life people who read a discourse, while the 'invoked' audience refers to the audience called up or imagined by the writer" (p. 157). Ede and Lunsford problematize their own audience addressed/audience invoked dichotomy throughout their work, pointing out that the term "audience" perhaps should give way to "public" or "discourse community"; they also recommend the need to understand the complexity of audience awareness, collaboration, and participation in new media (Lunsford & Ede, 2009, p. 47), which is particularly apt for this study. These insights into the difficulty of literally calling an intangible public into being (Ryder, 2009) – and then activating those publics in their various roles as citizens, customers, or partners – show the challenges faced by PIOs on a daily basis.

Social media fatigue

While we have considered both the audience involvement and message strategies for engaging citizens in social media, we must also consider the impact social media management has on the PIOs who manage these channels. A recent study shows that time spent on social networking sites accounts for one in every six minutes spent online (Lipsman, 2011) – this no doubt increases for those managing social media for government organizations. This level of engagement could produce fatigue whereby PIOs tire of their responsibilities related to social media management, leading to mistakes or faux pas.

Social media fatigue is defined as "social media users' tendency to back away from social media usage when they become overwhelmed with too many sites, too many pieces of content, too many friends and contacts and too much time spent keeping up with these connections" (Technopedia, 2011; Goasduff & Pettey, 2011). Technology leaders are beginning to recognize that users have reached a point where there is simply no more time. "We are definitely at a point where the supply of things to do online is at a dramatic overcapacity relative to what we can actually do in our lives as human beings. When you have technology that has an infinite supply of possibility and you have finite time, at a certain point, people shut down. They simply cannot handle anything else," said Ning co-founder, Gina Bianchini (Boskers, 2011).

Despite this clear evidence of fatigue, Facebook and Twitter are boasting their highest numbers ever – the trend continues to show increased social media usage for US Internet users (Facebook, 2014; Sullivan, 2011). This increased usage has been linked to the "fear of missing out" (Przybylski, Murayama, DeHaan, & Gladwell, 2013) as well as anxiety (McCord, Rodebaugh, & Levinson, 2014). Lee, Moore, Park, and Park (2012) found that the social compensation hypothesis could be an explanation for increased usage amongst those with lower self-esteem (e.g., Lee, et al., 2012, p. 1037). In addition, increased social media usage has been linked to stress in the workplace (Bucher, Ficseler, & Suphan, 2013). Recent research by Bright, Kleiser, and Grau (2015) found that social media fatigue can be caused by a variety of factors including level of confidence and privacy concerns – both of which are factors related to the management of social media.

Research questions

To understand and describe the daily routines, policies, protocols, and working environments of PIOs, both close-ended and open-ended questions were used to gather information. The authors used a mixed-methods approach to answer these research questions:

- How do city communicators monitor and moderate social media channels?
- What policies are in place, and how do these policies describe idealized interactions and discourage negative interactions?
- How do city communicators describe residents who interact on social media sites? How are fans and influencers described and encouraged? How do city communicators describe residents who are not fans of the city? How are outsiders (nonresidents) who interact on social media sites described by these communicators?
- Do communicators recognize the possibilities of social media fatigue in themselves and their residents and its potential impact on communication?
- How do communicators describe and reflect on the most difficult interactions with their cities' citizens?

Methodology

Participants include PIOs for cities across the country, but primarily drawn from Texas. Researchers used a two-pronged approach to reach out to public-sector communicators. First, links to a survey were sent to members of a statewide municipal communication organization. Next, a snowball method of gathering participants was used, starting with people enrolled in a public-sector communication certificate program at the authors' institution. Some of these latter participants were asked questions during interviews which occurred in the week prior to completion of the online survey. Researchers then reviewed responses, classifying them through an iterative process of theme analysis. A total of 40 response sets were analyzed including data from 25 surveys and 15 interviews.

In the second phase of this study, social media policies were collected from participants and analyzed by the researchers. The policies were analyzed and compared with one another, to discover the similarities among them, particularly in the ways they refer to external stakeholders outside of the city's own employees. The researchers analyzed each policy to see how its guiding principles related to each participant's description of his or her social media environment. The policies were then analyzed for themes related to conflict, stress, and fatigue to determine if, and how, cities are coming to grips with the realities of social media management.

Findings

While "citizen engagement" is currently a buzzword in government communication circles, practicing engagement and fostering participatory culture have proven to be difficult. Descriptions of the ways PIOs monitor and moderate discussion, apply social media policies, and handle dynamics show that local discussion communities may be as difficult to maintain as huge, largely anonymous online forums. While this study's participants expressed confidence and satisfaction with their abilities in social media spaces, their responses in open-ended interviews and questions were more mixed, with frustration expressed especially concerning their roles as bridges between external audiences and internal decision-makers.

Monitoring, moderating, and policies

A city's community engagement usually means only one city employee – usually the director of communication or PIO – often serves as the voice, eyes, and ears of a city's digital channels. "I am the only person in our Communication Department," said one respondent. "I check social media throughout the day, including weekends. I have it up on my desktop computer and available on my tablet and iPhone when I'm not at my desk." Half of participants left an open field blank or answered "no one" when asked who else monitors channels. A few people used automated digital dashboards such as Hootsuite or web archiving software such as PageFreezer. One participant said her city did not monitor channels at all. A few participants did have informal backup monitoring, ranging from a librarian to "other employees."

In terms of moderating, PIOs use their policies to remove inappropriate, irrelevant, or profane postings, if comments from outsiders are allowed. "One of our assistant city managers did not want to enable comments," said one participant, yet when comments were finally enabled on Facebook, "we haven't had any real issue with negative comments." Other challenges include getting internal approvals when timely responses are needed in a crisis. One participant said her city "took a beating on not being open" when a zoning controversy raged without a city statement. "In a perfect world, 'I' would provide as much information as possible as early as possible and I am working on getting manager buy-in," she said. More than 10 participants related that their internal challenges take up as much time as communicating to external stakeholders when there is a crisis.

This social media policy about interactions was typical for the participants of this study:

> The City of [name removed] Public and Media Relations Office reserves the right to delete any comment or posting that is deemed inappropriate, malicious, offensive, threatening, profane or insulting. Content that promotes, fosters or perpetuates discrimination on the basis of race, creed, color, age, religion, gender, marital status, disability, national origin or sexual orientation will not be permitted. Users who violate these guidelines may be blocked from posting commentary to City of [name removed] social media sites/pages.

Another policy from a different city includes more positive language about participatory culture: "[the city] encourages online conversation with residents, guests, visitors and online community," and then gives guidance about those interactions.

Most social media policies analyzed included guidelines not only for residents or citizens, but also for city employees. One of the largest cities included in the study had the most liberal statement about social media practice for its own employees:

> Where appropriate, the City [name removed] encourages the use of social media to further the goals of the City and the missions of its departments. Social media tools provide an excellent resource for communicating the City's various messages and promoting City services, programs and initiatives. They also allow real-time interaction with citizens, which enables the City to better serve the needs of citizens.

While "citizen" or "citizens" was used in a few policies, most referred to external audiences as "users." When participants were asked to describe some of the types of people who regularly interact within their cities' social media spaces, they generated many rich terms for these social media "users": attendees from events, animal lovers, executive leadership staff, angry residents, people asking questions about the city, political activists, neighborhood leaders, everyday residents seeking information, potential visitors, community members, 50+-year-old residents, chronic complainers, fans, academics, those who feel they have a voice in social media, city employees, busy bodies, new residents, complainers and malcontents, posters, local media, crazies, and actively engaged members of the community.

Not one social media policy included time limits (such as "no more than 40 hours per week" or "during normal business hours only") for communicators tasked with monitoring and interacting within social media spaces. Like most media relations professionals, city communicators must be ready for emergencies and crisis in a moment's notice. In a follow-up question to survey participants, two specified that on paper, monitoring of social media sites is supposed to occur during normal business hours, but that in reality, they monitor social media during all waking hours. One participant described setting an alarm at 2 a.m. in order to check her smart phone, to be sure that something hadn't happened during the first half of overnight hours.

Interaction dynamics

PIOs identified these groups as the most engaged audience members (with most frequently mentioned listed first):

- "Residents"
- "Businesses"
- "HOA (home owners' associations) groups"
- "Media outlets"
- "Mostly women 25–44" and "most engaged with full-time female residents on Facebook"

- "Citizens needing information"
- "Ourselves" (meaning a city's own employees)
- "Angry/negative citizen: when people are happy for the most part they do not engage much. It is the upset citizen ..."

Not mentioned here is the word "customer," or the word "partner."

These same groups from the "most engaged" community members also appear on the list of "least engaged," and the list of "least engaged" has more variety (most frequently mentioned are listed first):

- "Actual consumers," "our residents," "the general public," and "average citizen"
- "Seniors, non computer users, teens" and "Seniors, the elderly"
- "Businesses" and "merchants"
- "College students"
- "The media"

One respondent said "I believe we are least engaged with the average citizen. We have just under 2,000 Facebook fans and almost 2,800 Twitter followers but we tend to hear from the same handful of people." Another said the least engaged groups are "those who have no interest in how their community is governed ... or in their community."

The most difficult interactions involve criticisms, apologies, "establishing social media practices," the volume of comments in a time of controversy, and content related to unpopular public projects. Six PIOs mentioned elected officials or other city staffers as being the source or cause of difficult interactions. "Not within our social media but rather a separate Facebook group born out of controversy ... (when) council members try to be helpful and informational [and] actually ended up in the thick of it and caused issues with a key upcoming vote," said one participant. Another said "elected officials believe these sites exist to aid their election effort, so we have to gingerly explain that we are not allowed to take sides on issues."

Controlling conversation on sites was a source of conflict as well, "with people who just want to vent rather than listen or learn. On social media it's common to speculate; our organization likes for things to be tied down." One city's policy was to leave posts online, even when comments are negative, because following policies meant that "we could not adequately justify removing it." No study participants reported any programs or strategies for supporting positive influencers.

Sometimes simple informational posts from PIOs erupted into unanticipated problems, such as one city's update on street construction. "It can cause a full-blown hate-filled conversation from our residents," one participant explained. His strategy for handling these negative comments is to leave them online, but to offer contact information or web links for more information. "Many times the residents won't call and they continue to blast their opinions online," he said.

Online survey results

The survey was completed by 25 PIOs from three different states: Georgia, Minnesota, and Texas. Most of the sample has a job as a PIO where they are in charge of the social media channels and are expected to monitor those channels, at minimum, on a daily basis. The majority of the sample accesses social media on their computer (92%, N=23), tablet (80%, N=20), or phone (88%, N=22) with the most used social media channels including Facebook (88%, N=22), Twitter (80%, N=20), and YouTube (68%, N=17). Respondents indicated that they found social media easy to use (M=5.71, SD=1.01), clear and understandable (M=5.33, SD=1.28), and that they were confident using the technology (M=5.68, SD=1.06). Most respondents indicated that they were confident in their abilities to deal with the large amounts of information available on social media websites (M=5.05, SD=1.39); however, they also indicated that they were likely to receive too much information from these websites (M=4.58, SD=1.17) and that they were frequently overwhelmed by the amount of content available on these websites (M=4.26, SD=1.45) – both of which can lead to social media fatigue.

Sixty percent of the sample (N=15) checks Facebook daily while 20% checks it hourly (N=5) and roughly the same holds true for Twitter with 60% checking it daily (N=15) and 12% checking it hourly (N=3). Seventy-two percent of the sample (N=18) spends less than one hour per day monitoring and engaging with citizens on Twitter while 52% (N=13) spends one or more hours per day doing the same activities on Facebook. A total of 19 respondents (76%) indicated that checking social media sites is one of the first things they do each morning; however, few indicated having a lack of control over their social media usage (M=2.28, SD=0.86) or a feeling of loss when they could not access their social media sites (M=2.84, SD=1.34). In fact, many respondents reported that their work-related interactions on social media sites were overall pleasant, valuable, beneficial, and useful – however, those interactions could happen at all hours of the day. Only 48% (N=12) of respondents has a social media policy in place and only eight respondents indicated that they have a backup in place for social media monitoring – all others are one-person shops. Forty-four percent (N=11) of the respondents agreed that social media monitoring had caused challenges within their organization.

Discussion and conclusions

Survey results indicate most cities have the apparatus of social media, which matches national and international figures on local government usage of social media. Yet in the qualitative findings, some responses show that interaction is limited or nonexistent, such as: "We don't interact with anyone on social media." This means that social media sites serve as one-way channels, rather than a channel for exchange and listening. True citizen engagement, then, becomes impossible. Real innovation and participatory governing will "require substantial changes to the status quo and it may take some time for local government 2.0 in the EU to really make a difference, or even remain an illusion" (Bonsón, et al., 2012, p. 29). Real engagement and participatory culture must be more than one person sending outbound messages, or one person from a city listening to channels and interacting in those channels. Yet city policies have a chilling effect on organic interactions involving employees beyond the communications office, such as this statement: "Employees bear full responsibility for the material they post on social media sites. Inappropriate usage of social media can be grounds for disciplinary action, up to and including termination."

While single PIOs may be listening to online discussion, others are not clued in, but may be too focused on what they deem to be important, ignoring their community's organic conversation. "I notice on Twitter people will try to ask questions or make comments, especially about fracking, but I don't think anyone acknowledges this," said one PIO. Since social media have no boundaries, trouble related to a city can erupt in other social spaces and on sites not controlled by or related to official sites, yet conversation there reflects on the city. "I get calls from reporters about a post on another public safety [Facebook] page or Twitter account," said one participant. "It's a bit of a surprise to get a call about our event as posted by someone else."

The ways that cities, communicators, and policies frame citizens or residents – the ways that they invoke an audience, to use Lunsford and Ede's terms – may also influence how interactions occur. Within the qualitative responses, the variety of nomenclature suggests that social media are used in a non-targeted way, that the community outside the city is framed mostly as an amorphous mass of uninterested or unreachable people, less frequently as activated citizens, or as single-issue cranks. One important framework employed by the authors was based on Thomas (2013) and his three primary roles of citizen, partner, and customer. While citizen was used commonly in open-ended responses (and even in some social media policies), the terms partners and customers were never used. User was a common term in the policies. Yet terms such as partner and customer would reframe interactions and relationships in a way that might foster better outreach and engagement.

These findings support the earlier mentioned studies on social media fatigue (Bright et al., 2015); while social media are often considered helpful and easy to use it can also lead to fatigue. Survey results show that participants are confident using social media and use it frequently as part of their job functions; however, they also become wary of the responsibilities associated with it and overloaded from the amount of information they are expected to process. It is clear from this push and pull between social media usefulness and social media fatigue that policies need to be in place for the proper management and monitoring of social media channels. More importantly, communicators must be allowed to provide leadership within their cities in order to foster robust engagement and participation in local government through social channels.

Acknowledgement

The authors thank TCU graduate research assistant Callie Cunyus for her assistance.

References

Bonsón, E., Torres, L., Royo, S., & Floresc, F. (2012). Local e-government 2.0: Social media and corporate transparency in municipalities. *Government Information Quarterly*, 29(2), 123–132. doi: 10.1016/j.giq.2011.10.001.

Boskers, B. (2011). Gina Bianchini, co-founder of Ning on what's next for social media. http://www.huffingtonpost.com/2011/10/11/gina-bianchini-ning-social-media_n_1005676.html.

Bright, Laura F., Kleiser, Susan Bardi, & Grau, Stacy Landreth. (2015). Too much Facebook?: An exploratory examination of social media fatigue. *Computers in Human Behavior*, 44, 148–155. http://www.sciencedirect.com/science/article/pii/S0747563214006566.

Bucher, E., Fieseler, C., & Suphan, A. (2013). The stress potential of social media in the workplace. *Information, Communication & Society*, 31(10), 1639–1667.

Ede, L. & Lunsford, A. (1985/1999). Audience addressed/audience invoked: The role of audience in composition theory and pedagogy. In L. Ede (Ed.) *On writing research: The Braddock essays, 1975–1998* (pp. 156–171). Boston: Bedford Books of St. Martin's Press.

Ellison, N., & Hardey, M. (2013). Developing political conversations? *Information, Communication & Society*, 16(6), 878–898. doi: 10.1080/1369118X.2012.740495

Facebook. (2014). Facebook statistics. https://www.facebook.com/press/info.php?statistics.

Gil de Zúñiga, H. G., Copeland, L., & Bimber, B. (2013). Political consumerism: Civic engagement and the social media connection. *New Media & Society* 16(3), 488–506.

Gil de Zúñiga, H., Jung, N. & Valenzuela, S. (2012). Social media use for news and individuals' social capital, civic engagement and political participation. *Journal of Computer-Mediated Communication*, 17(3), 319–336.

Gil de Zúñiga, H., & Valenzuela, S. (2011). The mediating path to a strong citizenship: Online and offline networks, weak ties and civic engagement. *Communication Research*, 38(3), 397–421.

Goasduff, L., & Pettey, C. (2011). Gartner survey highlights consumer fatigue with social media. http://www.gartner.com/it/page.jsp?id=1766814

Gotlieb, M. R., & Wells, C. (2012). From concerned shopper to dutiful citizen: Implications of individual and collective orientations toward political consumerism. *Annals Of The American Academy Of Political And Social Science*, 644(1), 207–219. doi: 10.1177/0002716212453265.

Hampton, Keith N., Lee, Chul-joo, & Her, Eun Ja. (2011). How new media affords network diversity: Direct and mediated access to social capital through participation in local social settings. *New Media and Society*, 13(7), 1031–1049. http://nms.sagepub.com/content/early/2011/02/09/1461444810390342.

Herring, S. (1999). Interactional coherence in CMC. *Journal of Computer-Mediated Communication*, 4(4). http://jcmc.indiana.edu/vol4/issue4/herring.html.

Hilbert, M. (2009). The maturing concept of e-democracy: From e-voting to online consultations to democratic value out of jumbled online chatter. *Journal of Information Technology & Politics*, 6, 87–110.

International City-County Management Association (2013, October 17). Eighty-four percent of local governments have a social media presence. http://icma.org/en/icma/newsroom/highlights/Article/103830/Eightyfour_Percent_of_Local_Governments_Have_a_Social_Media_Presence.

Lambiase, J. (2010). Hanging by a thread: Topic development and death in an online discussion of breaking news. *Language@Internet*, 7(9). http://www.languageatinternet.org/articles/2010/2814.

Lee, J.-E., Moore, D.C., Park, E-A., & Park, S.G. (2012). Who wants to be "friend-rich"? Social compensatory friending on Facebook and the moderating role of public self-consciousness. *Computers in Human Behavior*, 28, 1036–1043.

Linders, D. (2012). From e-government to we-government: Defining a typology for citizen coproduction in the age of social media. *Government Information Quarterly*, 29 (4), 446–454.

Lipsman, A. (2011). The network effect: Facebook, Linkedin, Twitter & Tumblr reach new heights in May. comScore. http://blog.comscore.com/2011/06/facebook_linkedin_twitter_tumblr.html.

Long, R. (1980, May). Writer–audience relationships: Analysis or invention. *College Composition and Communication*, 31: 223–225.

Lunsford, A., & Ede, L. (2009). Among the audience: On audience in an age of new literacies. In M. E. Weiser, B. M. Fehler, & A. M. Gonzalez (Eds.) *Engaging audience: Writing in an age of new literacies* (pp. 42–69). Urbana, IL: NCTE.

McCord, B., Rodebaugh, T., & Levinson, C. (2014). Facebook: Social uses and anxiety. *Computers in Human Behavior*, 34, 23–27.

Mitchell, R., & Taylor, M. (1979). The integrating perspective: An audience-response model for writing. *College English*, 41(3), 247–271.

Newsom, G. (2013). *Citizenville: How to take the town square digital and reinvent government.* New York: Penguin Press.

Ong, W. J. (1975, January). The writer's audience is always a fiction. *Publications of the Modern Language Association*, 90, 9–21.

Przybylski, A., Murayama, K., DeHann, C., & Gladwell, V. (2013). Motivational, emotional, and behavioral correlates of fear of missing out. *Computers in Human Behavior*, 29, 1841–1848.

Ryder, P. M. (2009). The stranger question of audience: Service learning and public rhetoric. In M. E. Weiser, B. M. Fehler, & A. M. Gonzalez (Eds.) *Engaging audience: Writing in an age of new literacies* (pp. 207–228). Urbana, IL: NCTE.

Sullivan, D. (2011). Twitter CEO Dick Costolo's State of the Union address. http://searchengineland.com/live-blog-twitter-cco-dick-costolos-informal-business-address.htm.

Technopedia. (2011). Definition of social media fatigue. http://www.techopedia.com/definition/27372/social-media-fatigue.

Thomas, J. C. (2013). Citizen, customer, partner: Rethinking the place of the public in public management. *Public Administration Review*, 73(6), 786–796.

Valenzuela, S., Kim, Y., & de Zúñiga, H. G. (2012). Social networks that matter: Exploring the role of political discussion for online political participation. *International Journal of Public Opinion Research*, 24(2), 163–184.

Wojtczak, M., & Morner, M. (2014). Bringing the citizen back in: Motivational aspects of citizen-administration collaboration. Permanent Study Group I: E-Government (ICT in PA); EGPA, 2014.

13 Brand community management via Google+

Michael North, Cong Li, Fan Yang and Jiangmeng Liu

Businesses initially resisted social media, but after witnessing the number of users skyrocket, companies incorporated social media within branding efforts. Facebook started the social media trend in 2004 and now boasts almost 1.2 billion users. YouTube followed in 2005 and has also eclipsed the billion user mark. A year later in 2006, Twitter launched and has steadily attracted users amounting to more than 500 million. Not to be outdone, Google created Google+ in 2011, a social networking site resembling Facebook that has seen its membership increase from 25 million in its first month to more than 2 billion four years later.

These statistics have not gone unnoticed in the corporate world as businesses now use social media for public relations, advertising, customer service, and for brand awareness. This research centers on branding and specifically how Fortune 500 companies use Google+ to differentiate, remain relevant, foster esteem, and impart knowledge to stakeholders, thereby creating brand strength and emotional capital. Based on the results of this research, conclusions and suggestions will be made on how organizations should foster a participatory culture on Google+.

Literature review

Google+ background

Google+ began as an invitation only launch in 2011 (Kaste, 2011), and grew quickly from 25 million users to more than 2 billion just four years later (Barrie, 2015). This user base surpasses all social media platforms (Noyes, 2015). Google initially positioned its social media foray as an attempt to compete with Facebook including similar functions allowing users to post, comment, and share pictures with others (Efrati, 2012). However, the impressive growth and substantial user total can be attributed to Google requiring a Google+ account to sign up for other Google-operated entities such as Gmail, a requirement that has been rescinded (Kim, 2014).

Even with more than 2 billion users, Google+ has been characterized as a disappointment. Only about 5 million users actually posted or engaged with other users on Google+ in 2015, which is less than 0.4% of all users (Barrie, 2015). Over the course of the platform's existence, only about 9% of users have posted any content on Google+, and about half of these users admit that the most recent activity was commenting on YouTube or changing a profile photo (Barrie, 2015). Users, on non-mobile devices, spend three minutes on average each month on Google+ (Efrati, 2012). This pales in comparison to the almost seven hours per month users spend on Facebook on non-mobile devices (Efrati, 2012). Companies investing in a social media presence that included Google+ have noticed the disappointing lack of activity. Removing the requirement to join Google+ when signing up for Gmail or YouTube was seen by many as a red flag, along with Google's decision to allow non-members to join Google Hangouts (Kim, 2014). *The Financial Brand*, a digital publication that focuses on financial institutions, described Google+ as "by far the lamest major social media network around today" (Passman, 2013, p. 58), and advised financial institutions to focus on one social media entity and hope for average performance on another. Google+, then, is late to Facebook and Twitter's party.

While Google+ may have failed as a direct competitor to Facebook when positioned as a network of people, Google+ is showing signs of life as a network of ideas. The new head of social networking at Google, Dave Besbris, is positioning the site as a network of interests and passions (Elgan, 2014). With Twitter cornering breaking news and Facebook grabbing personal connections, Google+ has transitioned to a "social search engine that you can add things to directly … For anyone interested in anything, there's no better place to explore and connect around that interest than Google+" (Elgan, 2014). Rather than organizing around people, Google+ is grouped by specific interests such as photography, music, baking, tattoos, or whatever else and conversations are initiated around these subjects (Elgan, 2014).

From a functionality perspective, Google+ is strikingly similar to Facebook. Users have a profile that serves as a space to differentiate themselves from others by including information such as employment, places lived, relationship status, education, contact information, and interests (Anderson, & Still, 2011). The similarities with Facebook continue as users can create posts, comment on other's posts, and add pictures along with sharing content in much the same way as a retweet (Anderson, & Still, 2011). Borrowing from Twitter, Google+ users can find information and group their posts by using hashtags or view their information on a stream similar to Facebook's newsfeed (Anderson, & Still, 2011). Google+ integrates the picture functionality seamlessly and many believe it is the best social media platform for visual elements (Elgan, 2014).

Message strategy and generating engagement

The overall intent of most companies on social media is to increase brand awareness and not to overtly advertise (Lohtia, Donthu, & Hershberger, 2003).

Social media allow for frequent communication that mimics informal conversation. This humanizes the communication between companies and publics more than with traditional media while increasing the chances for replies from users seeking to respond to dialogue (Schultz, Utz, & Göritz, 2011). By fostering conversation, social media aligns with public relations theory by becoming a "pursuit of reconciliation, an endeavor that lasts as long as practitioners can keep the humane conversation going" (Maier, 2015, p. 36).

To sustain the conversation, four main strategies are used most often by organizations: informative, facilitative, persuasive, and cooperative problem-solving (Page, & Hazleton, 1999). Informative displays facts using rational appeals while persuasive creates action by using emotional appeals (Werder, 2005). Facilitative presents options for publics to achieve a task while cooperative aligns the organization and public together to find a solution (Werder, 2005). However, these strategies fall flat without the support of dialogic communication, which requires respecting and listening to publics along with demonstrating a willingness to improve (Shin, Pang, & Kim, 2015).

However, conversations are difficult to measure. Public relations demands measurement and evaluation for all communication endeavors so social media is often characterized by frequencies of clicks, views, follows, friends, and plusses. Neiger et al. (2012) refers to low engagement as Likes on Facebook or Favorites on Twitter so the +1 on Google would fall into this category. Medium engagement includes tweets and retweets along with comments (Neiger, et al., 2012), so Google+'s share and comment functions would fall into this category. High engagement is physical action and not relevant for this research. While conversations are the goal for public relations, measuring the amount of Likes or Favorites is easier and often the method used to gauge engagement.

This study examines Google+ messages and the engagement generated from a public relations perspective. Specifically, we propose the first research question as follows:

RQ1: What basic message strategy do Fortune 500 companies use on Google+ to generate engagement?

Customer relations

Customer service is not a public relations function but when it is conducted on a social media platform with hundreds of millions of users, the customer service outcome shapes organizational reputation instantly while generating word-of-mouth communication among users (Creamer, 2010). Customer service through social media empowers users to not only help themselves but also to share the information thereby reducing the workload for the company (Creamer, 2010). Users are motivated to share their experiences with companies online as happy customers wish to brag about the positive experience and dissatisfied customers seek a platform to "vent their frustration" (Wu, 2013, p. 977).

Previous research points to the fact that negative information not only captures users' attention but also is deemed to be more important than positive information. Customers tend to seek out negative word-of-mouth when information is scarce about products or services (Wu, 2013). Businesses may want to ignore online negativity (Chen, & Lurie, 2013), but interacting and engaging with the public humanizes the company. By allowing some negativity into the conversation, companies are able to increase credibility when championing the benefits of products and services or when trying to strengthen the brand (Roering, & Paul, 1976).

When faced with a negative experience, customers can choose an alternative or post a near permanent message complaining about the offending company in a public social media forum for the world to see (Boon, 2013). In a recent study, more than 80% of Internet users believe that complaining on social media can influence companies to change and the primary reason for users' complaints is to protect other users from enduring a similar negative experience (Barnes, 2008). The pressure on companies to respond on social media is increasing so companies are devoting more manpower to digital platforms. AT&T, a company receiving more than 10,000 mentions on social media per day, has increased its team from five to 19 employees and created a specific Twitter handle to address customer complaints (Patel, 2010).

Customer service on social media is an example of a brand community solving users' problems. Brand communities come together to "discuss, critique and celebrate" (Guschwan, 2012, p. 24). For this to work, a culture of participation needs to be present that includes low barriers, support for user generated content, and a sense that contributions matter (Jenkins, 2009). Users become deeply engaged when they are involved in remedying problems and this high level of engagement, coupled with a successful outcome, may lead to a sense of fandom or a phenomenon involving only the most passionately engaged users (Hutchins, & Tindall, 2015).

Lastly, companies respond to users' online replies with either emotional or information support. Emotional support attempts to fix the problem by helping the user feel better about the situation while informational support supplies the user with needed facts (Knight, & Carpenter, 2012). Dialogic communication is two-way so it is important to also analyze the companies' responses to users.

To understand how companies handle user comments, especially when they are negative, this study proposes the second and third research questions:

RQ2: What type of comments do publics provide to Fortune 500 companies' Google+ posts?

RQ3: How do Fortune 500 companies respond to users' comments on Google+, especially when the comments are negative?

Social media from a global perspective

The worldwide Web pushes social media across borders and with Google's ubiquity and translate feature, Google+ should also be examined with a global perspective as companies try to shape reputations abroad. Social media is an effective means to reach an international audience because penetration rates are often higher than traditional media platforms in developing countries. For instance, there are 30 mobile phones per 100 people in sub-Saharan Africa but only three landlines per 100 people in the same region (Owiny, Mehta, & Maretzki, 2014), and during Arab Spring, about half a million Twitter accounts were created each day in March 2011 in a region without much Internet access (Uysal, Schroeder, & Taylor, 2012).

Concerning Google+, almost 70% of users reside outside of the U.S. (Mcloughlin, 2014), giving companies important access abroad. Engagement appears to be intense among international users. Google+ caps comments at 500 for each post and the 20 users who average 500 comments per post are all from Asia (Elgan, 2014). The user who generates the most engagement on Google+ is Namita Pawaskar, who is from India, and she averages almost two thousand shares and almost 10 thousand +1s per post (Elgan, 2014). Importantly, Google+ offers a "Translate" button for any post or comment. This means that Google+ users can craft posts in their native language and be instantly understood by everyone in the world. To further examine companies' relational strategies on Google+ from a global perspective, the fourth research question is proposed:

RQ4: Do Fortune 500 companies change strategy on Google+ if users are international or comments are in a foreign language?

Method

Data collection

One post was randomly selected for each company per month (as long as the company had at least one post that month) within the time frame of November 2011 to December 2013. Once a post was selected, it was immediately saved. The number of "comment," "plus," and "share" associated with the post were also recorded. If the post had generated comments from other users, the last two comments were saved as well. This data collection method lasted about six weeks from mid-May to the end of June in 2014 and yielded a total of 2,852 posts and 1,505 comments.

Coding scheme

For each post, the number of hyperlinks, photos, videos, and hashtags were coded to analyze companies' basic message strategies.

Comments on the posts were classified into one of two categories – "English only" and "not English only" – based on the language used in the comments. In terms of valence, each comment was coded into one of the following three categories: (1) positive comments, such as providing compliments to the company (e.g. "I'm losing more than I may think of cos [sic] my nike sneaker [sic] does the magic when I'm running"); (2) negative comments, such as complaining about an issue (e.g. "I had a terrible online and store experience thanks to Walmart! Don't recommend using their website or visiting their Muncie Clara Lane location."); (3) neutral comments, such as asking questions, or delivering self-promotion information (e.g. "Hello, I would like detailed information to participate in the selection of the Nike Academy. If there are age groups, such as where the program takes place, where to register and all that goes with it.").

To investigate how the companies handle the users' comments, company responses were coded into one of the following categories based on the content: (1) emotional support (e.g. "Thanks for entering, good luck!" by Staples); (2) informational support (e.g. "Please send us an email at socialteam@lowes.com and We'll send you some plans for a chicken coop" by Lowe's).

Coding procedure

Two English-speaking graduate students served as coders for this study. Posts from Fortune 500 companies' Google+ accounts that were not in the sample data were adopted as training materials, and refinements to the initial code book were made during the one-week training and extensive practice. Then, 5% of the actual sample was used to test inter-coder reliability. Measured by percent agreement, the overall reliability is high (92.7%). Once reliability was established, the two coders reconciled differences, split the rest of the sample, and coded independently.

Results

RQ1: what basic message strategy do Fortune 500 companies use on Google+ to generate engagement?

Photos and hyperlinks, when compared to videos and hashtags, were the more frequently used message strategies by Fortune 500 companies on Google+. Among the 2,852 collected posts, more than half (56.6%, n=1,641) utilized photos. Most of the posts (n=1,531) contained one photo and 83 posts used two or more photos including one post which used six photos. Hyperlinks were a less common strategy used by Fortune 500 companies on Google+ as 55.3% (n=1,578) of the posts did not include any hyperlinks. About 44.7 % (n=1,274) of the posts utilized at least one and at most four hyperlinks. Similarly, the majority of the posts (71.5%, n=2,038) did not include any hashtags. Only 11.2 % (n=319) of the posts contained a video.

Additionally, three regression analyses were conducted separately on three engagement measures – number of plusses, number of comments, and number of shares – to test the effectiveness of these message strategies. The results of the regression analyses found that the number of photos was a significant and positive predictor for all engagement measures ($p < .001$). It demonstrated that using more photos was significantly associated with receiving more plusses ($\beta = .13$), more comments ($\beta = .08$), and more shares ($\beta = .09$). Similarly, the number of hyperlinks was statistically significant on number of plusses ($p < .01$, $\beta = -.06$), number of comments ($p < .001$, $\beta = -.08$), and number of shares ($p < .05$, $\beta = -.05$). However, the negative coefficients indicated that including hyperlinks was not an effective strategy for attracting user engagement on Google+. Increasing the number of hyperlinks led to fewer plusses, comments, and shares. The number of videos was a significant and positive predictor for two engagement measures – number of plusses ($p < .01$, $\beta = .06$) and number of shares ($p < .01$, $\beta = .06$). The number of hashtags, however, was not significant for any engagement measures. These results suggest that photos and videos are successful message strategies that could generate engagement on Google+ (see Table 13.1).

RQ2: what type of comments do publics provide to Fortune 500 companies' Google+ posts?

In total, there were 15,371 comments made by Google+ users relating to the 2,852 posts, ranging from 0 to 500 comments per post. On average, a post from Fortune 500 companies received 5.39 comments ($SD = 28.60$). In this study, we collected 1,505 comments coding for purpose and valence. In terms of purpose, 40.7% of these comments (n=612) were compliments, 12.2% (n=184) were complaints, and the rest was somewhat neutral.

Table 13.1 Results of regression analyses

Predictors	Regression 1 (Number of Plusses)			Regression 2 (Number of Comments)			Regression 3 (Number of Shares)		
	β	t	p	β	t	p	β	t	p
Number of Hyperlinks	-.06	-3.17	.002	-.08	-4.15	.000	-.05	-2.49	.013
Number of Photos	.13	6.62	.000	.08	3.89	.000	.09	4.63	.000
Number of Videos	.06	3.15	.002	.02	.87	.383	.06	3.08	.002
Number of Hashtags	.01	.63	.529	-.02	-1.3	.197	-.00	-.21	.835
R^2	.019			.011			.011		

RQ3: how do Fortune 500 companies respond to users' comments on Google+, especially when the comments are negative?

Generally, Fortune 500 companies prefer not to respond to users' comments. For the 1,505 collected comments, only 5% (n=75) received replies from the corresponding company. There was no statistically significant difference between the valence of comments and companies' responses (χ^2 (2, N=1,505) = 4.73, p = .094). Generally speaking, Fortune 500 companies do not treat negative comments differently from other comments, and no special attention is paid to negative comments.

Of the 75 replies from Fortune 500 companies, 58.7% (n=44) were to users' neutral comments, followed by positive comments (29.3%), and negative comments (12.0%). In terms of response strategy, 54.7% (n=41) of these replies provided emotional support, while the remainder (45.3%, n=34) provided informational support. To investigate the relationship between the valence of comments and companies' response strategies regarding emotional or informational support, a chi-square test was conducted and a significant association was observed, χ^2 (2, N=75) = 16.67, p < .001. As seen in Table 13.2, emotional support appears most often when companies respond to positive comments (n=20, 90.9%). Informational support is used infrequently when companies respond to positive comments (n=2, 9.1%), assuming that the observed frequencies are random departures from a model of independence. In other words, Fortune 500 companies tend to reply to positive comments by providing emotional support, yet no significant difference was observed for replying to neutral and negative comments.

RQ4: do Fortune 500 companies change strategy on Google+ if users are international or comments are in a foreign language?

Most comments (91.7%, n=1,380) were written in English, whereas 8.3% of comments (n=125) used a language other than English. In terms of comment valence, 45.8% (n=632) of the English-only comments were neutral, followed by positive (n=568, 41.2%) and negative (n=180, 13.0%). On the other hand, 61.6% (n=77) of the non-English comments were neutral, also followed by positive (35.2%, n=44) and negative (3.2%, n=4). A significant association was observed (χ^2 (2, N=1,505) = 16.16, p < .001, see Table 13.3) between comment valence and language used in comments. An examination of the residuals

Table 13.2 Association between comment valence and company responses

	Negative	Neutral	Positive	Total
Emotional support	3 (33.3%)	18 (40.9%)	20 (90.9%)	41
Informational support	6 (66.7%)	26 (59.1%)	2 (9.1%)	34
Total	9 (100%)	44 (100%)	22 (100%)	75

χ^2 (2, N=75) = 16.67, p < .001

indicates that the relatively high frequency of neutral comments and relatively low frequency of negative comments among the non-English comments suggest the rejection of the independence assumption. In terms of response rates, 5.3% (n=74) of the English-only comments received replies from the corresponding companies while only 0.8% (n=1) of the non-English comments received replies, which indicates Fortune 500 companies paid less attention to comments written in a foreign language.

Discussion

This research examined 2,852 Google+ posts from the Fortune 500 from 2011 to 2013. While Google+ can still be characterized as being in its infant stage when compared to Facebook or Twitter, the results lead to some interesting conclusions. First, the majority of posts from the Fortune 500 included a photo. Using a photo on Google+ is a positive predictor to generate more engagement in the form of plusses, comments, and shares. This is supported in the literature as visual elements have been found to increase engagement and credibility (Martin & Johnson, 2010), in addition to the fact that Google+ is considered to be one of the best social media platforms for posting and sharing images (Elgan, 2014). Including videos also generated more plusses and shares. Using hyperlinks in posts decreased engagement leading to the conclusion that linking to outside destinations such as official documents is best reserved for Twitter, which is characterized as a pure information platform. Google+ hashtags had no effect on engagement, meaning the hashtag, a function developed by Twitter, could be avoided on Google+. Google+ appears to be effective at building the brand through visual elements, but poor at disseminating text-heavy information.

In terms of user comments, users tend to post positive messages. Importantly, only 12.2% of user comments were complaints leading to the conclusion that Google+ is not used as a customer service forum such as how the public uses Twitter. Diers and Donohue (2013) found that companies tend to use Twitter to disseminate short messages and Facebook to address lengthier topics and questions. Facebook has the first mover advantage over Google+ and users have most likely been conditioned to use Facebook or Twitter to complain

Table 13.3 Association between comment valence and comment language

	Negative	Neutral	Positive	Total
English-only	180 (13.0%)	632 (45.8%)	568 (41.2%)	1,380 (100%)
Not English-only	4 (3.2%)	77 (61.6%)	44 (35.2%)	125 (100%)
Total	184	709	612	1,505

χ^2 (2, N=1,505) = 16.16, $p < .001$

about a negative experience. Also, with Google+ emerging as a network of passions and a platform for pictures, the negativity surrounding customer service seems like something neither company nor user would embrace on Google+.

Regardless of user comment valence, Fortune 500 companies do not interact very often with users as only 5% of user comments received a response from a company on Google+, demonstrating a lack of interactivity. This is common in public relations research and while dialogic communication is recommended, companies rarely incorporate it into social media messages. The point of dialogic communication is to generate lasting relationships through understanding and conversation (McAllister-Spooner & Kent, 2009). Responding to publics online, generating return visits, providing simplistic interfaces, and keeping users on the site are all additional aspects of dialogic communication (McAllister-Spooner, & Kent, 2009), and are somewhat present in corporate Google+ accounts. Companies did not interact often, but Google+'s interface allows for content to be posted easily and users can navigate with little trouble. Creative social media teams can post content to generate return visits that also keep users on the specific page by presenting large amounts of information. The potential for dialogic communication is present for Google+, but not realized.

Regarding customer service, negative comments do not receive special attention from companies. Literature does recommend that responding to negativity only worsens the situation (Chen, & Lurie, 2013). But more and more potential customers are researching products and services on social media and a substantial amount of customers are addressing their concerns post-purchase on social media (Barnes, 2008). Responding to every complaint may be unrealistic, but demonstrating good customer service on a public forum boasting more than 2 billion users can potentially serve as valuable public relations. No significant relationship existed for company responses to negative or neutral comments, but a significant relationship existed for company replies to positive comments as these receive emotional support from companies 90.9% of the time.

From a global communication perspective, Google+ offers a translate feature for all posts and comments so communication can occur between users anywhere in the world. However, 91.7% of user comments were in English. Interestingly, the English and non-English user comments followed the pattern of the majority being neutral, followed by positive, and the smallest percentage being negative. However, English user comments received a response rate from companies of 5.3% while non-English user comments only received a company response 0.8% of the time. So while Google+ may be designed to accommodate international connections, the Fortune 500 does not seem to employ social media teams capable of addressing users posting in a foreign language. Even with the translate feature, only one of the 125 non-English user comments received a reply from a company leading to the conclusion that Fortune 500 social media teams either do not make the effort to translate the comment or they do not place a great deal of emphasis on users living abroad.

This all builds toward Google+'s ability to foster an online brand community defined as a group of users unrestricted by location who share positive feelings toward a specific brand on the Web (Kwon, Kim, Sung, & Yoo, 2014). These online brand communities allow consumers to share experiences and for companies to monitor the communication (Adjei, Noble, & Noble, 2010). The relationship is anything but transient as effective interaction between company and user can lead to deep-rooted loyalty (Kilambi, Laroche, & Richard, 2013). With this in mind, Google+ does not appear to be a viable forum for brand community building. While some companies can boast numerous followers and comments on each post, overall activity on Google+ is decreasing significantly. In this research, the most common number of comments for each post was zero. User participation is imperative for an online brand community to exist, and without it, the situation becomes traditional one-way communication (Casaló, Flavián, & Guinalíu, 2008). While Google+ may have enjoyed initial popularity, online brand communities are by no means eternal (Kilambi, et al., 2013). Companies enjoy a large audience on Google+, but without the user participation, the platform is not a place for brand community management.

Conclusion

This research revealed how the Fortune 500 used Google+ over the past few years and the information allows for some recommendations. Firstly, companies should rely heavily on visual elements and refrain from too much text. Secondly, companies need to interact and display more dialogic communication on Google+. Thirdly, users rarely complain or ask questions on Google+ so the Fortune 500 should try to establish Google+ as a sphere of positivity or a place for creativity and innovation, not a customer service forum. Lastly, the Fortune 500 should embrace posts in different languages. Google+ could help companies stretch their influence across the globe. But with engagement decreasing, companies should assess the efficacy of Google+ and either maximize the value or delete the account altogether.

References

Adjei, M., Noble, S., & Noble, C. (2010). The influence of C2C communications in online brand communities on customer purchase behavior. *Journal of the Academy of Marketing Science*, 38(5), 634–653. doi: 10.1007/s11747–009–0178–5.

Anderson, K., & Still, J. (2011). An introduction to Google Plus. *Library Hi Tech News*, 28(8), 7–10. doi: 10.1108/07419051111187842.

Barnes, N. (2008). Society for new communications research study: Exploring the link between customer care and brand reputation in the age of social media. *Journal of New Communication Research*, 3(1), 86–91.

Barrie, J. (2015, January 20). Nobody is using Google. *Business Insider*. Retrieved from http://www.businessinsider.com/google-active-users-2015-1.

Boon, E. (2013). A qualitative study of consumer-generated videos about daily deal web sites. *Psychology & Marketing*, 30(10), 843–849. doi: 10.1002/mar.20649.

Casaló, L., Flavián, C., & Guinalíu, M. (2008). Promoting consumer's participation in virtual brand communities: A new paradigm in branding strategy. *Journal of Marketing Communications*, 14(1), 19–36. doi: 10.1080/13527260701535236.

Chen, Z., & Lurie, N. (2013). Temporal contiguity and negativity bias in the impact of online word of mouth. *Journal of Marketing Research*, 50(4), 463–476. doi: 10.1509/jmr.12.0063.

Creamer, M. (2010, October 11). Offline vs. online, service is game of telephone. *Advertising Age*. Retrieved from http://adage.com/article/news/marketing-consum ers-experience-offline-online-gap/146392/.

Diers, A., & Donohue, J. (2013). Synchronizing crisis responses after a transgression: An analysis of BP's enacted crisis response to the Deepwater Horizon crisis in 2010. *Journal of Communication Management*, 17(3), 252–269. doi: 10.1108/JCOM-04-2012-0030.

Efrati, A. (2012, February 28). The mounting minuses at Google+. *The Wall Street Journal*. Retrieved from http://www.wsj.com/articles/SB10001424052970204653604 577249341403742390.

Elgan, M. (2014, October 11). Why Google+ is the place for passions. *ComputerWorld*. Retrieved from http://www.computerworld.com/article/2824613/why-google-is-the-place-for-passions.html.

Guschwan, M. (2012). Fandom, brandom and the limits of participatory culture. *Journal of Consumer Culture*, 12(1), 19–40.

Hutchins, A., & Tindall, N. (2015). "Things that don't go together?": Considering fandom and re-thinking public relations. Retrieved from http://www.prismjournal.org/fandom_ed.html.

Jenkins, H. (2009). *Confronting the challenges of participatory culture: Media education for the 21st century*. Cambridge, MA: Massachusetts Institute of Technology Press.

Kaste, M. (2011, June 29). Facebook's newest challenger: Google Plus. National Public Radio. Retrieved from http://www.npr.org/2011/06/29/137507567/facebooks-ne west-challenger-google-plus.

Kilambi, A., Laroche, M., & Richard, M. (2013). Constitutive marketing: Towards understanding brand community formation. *International Journal of Advertising*, 32(1), 45–64. doi:10.2501/IJA-32-1-045-064.

Kim, L. (2014, October 14). Google+ is dying. What's your exit strategy? *Inc.* Retrieved from http://www.inc.com/larry-kim/google-is-dying-what-s-your-ex it-strategy.html.

Knight, M., & Carpenter, S. (2012). Optimal matching model of social support: An examination of how national product and service companies use Twitter to respond to consumers. *Southwestern Mass Communication Journal*, Spring, 21–35.

Kwon, E., Kim, E., Sung, Y., & Yoo, C. (2014). Brand followers: Consumer motivation and attitude towards brand communications on Twitter. *International Journal of Advertising*, 33(4), 657–680. doi: 10.2501/IJA-33-4-657-680.

Lohtia, R., Donthu, N., & Hershberger, E. (2003). The impact of content and design elements on banner advertising click-through rates. *Journal of Advertising Research*, 43 (4), 410–418. doi: 10.1017/S0021849903030459.

Maier, C. (2015). Public relations as humane conversation: Richard Rorty, stakeholder theory, and public relations practice. *Public Relations Inquiry*, 4(1), 25–39.

Martin, K., & Johnson, M. (2010). Digital credibility and digital dynamism. *Visual Communication Quarterly*, 17, 162–174.

McAllister-Spooner, S., & Kent, M. (2009). Dialogic public relations and resource dependency: New Jersey community colleges as models for web site effectiveness. *Atlantic Journal of Communication*, 17(4), 220–239. doi: 10.1080/15456870903210113

Mcloughlin, A. (2014, February 14). Infographics – The latest global, US & UK Google+ user statistics. Web log post. Retrieved from https://www.tone.co.uk/infographic-google-plus-user-statistics-2014/.

Neiger, B., Thackeray, R., Wagenen, S., Hanson, C., West, J., Barnes, M., & Fagen, M. (2012). Use of social media in health promotion: Purposes, key performance indicators, and evaluation metrics. *Health Promotion Practice*, 13(2), 159–164.

Noyes, D. (2015, February 10). The Top 20 Facebook statistics – Updated February 2015. Retrieved from https://zephoria.com/social-media/top-15-valuable-facebook-statistics/.

Owiny, S., Mehta, K., & Maretzki, A. (2014). The use of social media technologies to create, preserve, and disseminate indigenous knowledge and skills to communities in East Africa. *International Journal of Communication*, 8(14), 234–247. Retrieved from http://ijoc.org/index.php/ijoc/article/view/1667.

Page, K. G., & Hazleton, V. (1999). An empirical analysis of factors influencing public relation strategy usage and effectiveness. Paper presented at the annual meeting of the International Communication Association, San Francisco, CA.

Passman, A. (2013). Google+ proves to be a big minus for most credit unions. Retrieved from http://www.cujournal.com/issues/17_8/google-plus-proves-to-be-a-big-minus-for-credit-unions-1017962-1.html.

Patel, K. (2010, June 21). How AT&T plans to lift its image via social-media customer care. *Advertising Age*. Retrieved from http://adage.com/article/digital/t-plans-lift-image-social-media/144561/.

Roering, K., & Paul, R. (1976). The effect of the consistency of product claims on the credibility of persuasive messages. *Journal of Advertising*, 5(2), 32–36. doi: 10.1080/00913367.1976.10672634.

Schultz, F., Utz, S., & Göritz, A. (2011). Is the medium the message? Perceptions of and reactions to crisis communication via twitter, blogs and traditional media. *Public Relations Review*, 37, 20–27.

Shin, W., Pang, A., & Kim, H. (2015). Building relationships through integrated online media: Global organizations' use of brand Web sites, Facebook, and Twitter. *Journal of Business and Technical Communication*, 29(2), 184–220.

Uysal, N., Schroeder, J., & Taylor, M. (2012). Social media and soft power: Positioning Turkey's image on Twitter. *Middle East Journal of Culture and Communication*, 5(3), 338–359. doi: 10.1163/18739865–00503013.

Werder, K. (2005). An empirical analysis of the influence of perceived attributes of publics on public relations strategy use and effectiveness. *Journal of Public Relations Research*, 17(3), 217–266. doi: 10.1207/s1532754xjprr1703_2.

Wu, P. (2013). In search of negativity bias: An empirical study of perceived helpfulness of online reviews. *Psychology and Marketing*, 30(11), 971–984. doi: 10.1002/mar.20660.

14 What's at stake in the fan sphere?

Crisis communication, Skittles and how the Trayvon Martin case mobilized a fan-brand community

Amanda K. Kehrberg and Meta G. Carstarphen

Introduction: a taste of the rainbow

Skittles is a product phenomenon. With its iconic ads and social media sites, this candy has built a fandom like no other. Its image is fun, youthful, and hip, cultivated through a careful strategy of quirky messaging, an intentionally exuberant use of color, and a corporate policy to stay clear of controversy. Industry experts suggested that the product's intentional use of a multicolored brand logo and the emblem of a rainbow had a built-in, if only accidental, resonance with consumers concerned about race, human equality, and unity across racial (and gender identity) lines (Ghosh, 2013; Steel, 2009). But the product's embrace by African American youth might be linked to two external factors: one, the proliferation of social media use by youth of color, and two, the eating habits of this same population.

While policy makers expressed great concern about the "digital divide" in the late 1990s, more recent analyses showed that African American youth were closing the gap through access to mobile media and a dominant presence in social media (Carstarphen, 2013; Krogstad, 2015).

In social media, the Skittles brand has emerged as a leader in cultivating a dynamic, interactive brand community – or rather, a fandom. Currently, the candy brand has more than 26 million Facebook fans and 200,000 Twitter followers. In 2014, StatSocial rated it the most influential candy brand on Twitter (Goldstein, 2014). Public relations practitioners have consistently praised Skittles for its authentic interaction with fans, citing it as a brand that embraces the value of user-generated content and is unafraid to participate in conversations (Goldstein, 2014; PR News, 2010; Van Camp, 2012). On its social media accounts, Skittles pushes out daily updates, including humorous content with often no direct relationship to the candy, reposts user content, and provides opportunities for fans to both participate and be celebrated for their participation, such as their "Greatest Fan in the World" contest (Van Camp, 2012).

Skittles' celebration as an authentic, interactive brand is precipitated on a website relaunch that was dubbed both groundbreaking and foolhardy (O'Brien, 2009). In the 2009 redesign, Skittles replaced its traditional home-page content with a continuously updating feed of all the brand's mentions on Twitter, as well its Wikipedia page (Markowicz, 2009). Zerillo (2009) descri-bed this experiment, in which "brand communications are ceded to consumers, sans filter," as decidedly "brave." Yet while Skittles was forced to ultimately roll back the changes, this temporary cession of messaging power and its con-sequences symbolized an early example of both the opportunities and dangers to be encountered in the interactive public sphere of social media.

Fandom: the new public sphere

Though the public sphere has its origins in the physical reality of spaces for debate – such as the Greek philosophers' salons and Roman forums – Habermas's (1989) definition of the public sphere as public *debate* allows the metaphor to extend easily to online deliberative spaces. Here, the sense of community or shared space can be entirely constructed in the minds of each individual. On Twitter (and increasingly other social networks, like Facebook and Instagram), the hashtag serves as an apt example of the artificial creation of public boundaries.

Black Twitter, for example, is a counterpublic entirely formed by the con-nective tissue of hashtags, whether critiquing public or private institutions in activist campaigns (#justicefortrayvon) or stereotypical and/or revolutionary representations in media (#empire). Conceptually, we can understand this through Burke's (1969) work on how individuals connect with each other and communities through internal identification, and not just external persuasion. According to Burke, we act to persuade ourselves to connect as we perceive the motives and goals of others as like our own. Because identity in the digital age is increasingly understood as fluid and multidimensional (Turkle, 1996; Tracy, 2002; Tsetsura, 2011), individuals may actively identify with – and par-ticipate in – multiple communities at any given time, with definite opportu-nities for overlap. Hermans, Kempen, and Van Loon (1992) described this process as dialogic self theory (DST), which argues that the self has a multi-plicity of positions that may be activated at different times to fit each unique situation. This potential for activation of multiple identifiers is all the more salient in online spaces (Hermans, 2004).

The Internet (and particularly social media) has become an increasingly important tool and context for advocacy and activism (Dozier, & Lauzen, 2000; PR News, 2012; Sommerfeldt, Kent, & Taylor, 2012). For instance, in reac-tion to the Ferguson police chief's announcement that he would step down, Goldstein (2012) writes that "2012 will be remembered as the year online activism established itself as a force in redirecting the actions of corporations, nonprofit organizations, and – now – local governments."

Fandom as identification

The history of fandom is rooted in the history of shifting conceptualizations of power dynamics between senders and receivers of communication messages. The "fan" is the child of both the increasingly complex and multidimensional models of communication processing in the twentieth century and the active audience of cultural studies. Today, the fan goes by many names: prosumer, inspirational consumer, brand advocate, creative audience, and so on, each born of a paradigm shift in recognizing the power of these interactive consumers to practice multi-directional and continuous communication as producers of their own poached, remixed, and decontextualized messages (Castells, 2009; Jenkins, 1992, 2006). In Castells' (2009) model of the creative audience, there is no separation between message sender and addressee; codes bubble up from below as much as they are transmitted down from above.

Grossberg (1992) explains that fandom is *inherently* an act of identification, which is what ties it to consumerism: "It is in consumer culture that the transition from consumer to fan is accomplished. It is here, increasingly, that we seek actively to construct our own identities, partly because there seems to be no other space available" (p. 63). Grossberg's point is all the more valid in the digital age, when identity construction is organized by likes and dislikes, associations with brands, and reviews of favorite products.

Within audience and fandom studies, these trends are unsurprisingly heralded for their seeming democratization of meaning-making; yet one need only interrogate Jenkins' (1992) use of the phrase "textual poachers" to describe fans to perceive how they may be seen by organizations as a threat. In analogizing fans to "poachers," Jenkins suggests that they are like the poachers of old, stealing into the king's forests to illegally hunt, an act both criminal and facilitated by severe inequality. This is the rhetoric of fandom that is definitively confrontational, characterized as *resistant* or *oppositional* reading of polysemic texts. In these acts of energy and productivity, the fan reimagines and reshapes the meaning of symbols to reflect his/her own identity, community, and goals.

While this is a process of identification, it is as importantly one of affect; increasingly, brands recognize the potential of loyal consumers and seek to build emotional relationships with them, emotions that can be easily extended to companion brands (Jenkins, 2007). As Grossberg (1992) explains, the affective/emotional investments of fans carry great weight:

> By making certain things and practices matter, the fan "authorizes" them to speak for him or her, not only as a spokesperson but also as surrogate voices (when we sing along to popular songs) ... Fans let them organize their emotional and narrative lives and identities.
>
> (p. 59)

It is not unreasonable, then, to understand how fans may come to see this process as transactional: *You may speak for me, and I may speak for you. I am in crisis, therefore we are in crisis.* This underscores how scholarship on increasingly active/interactive publics from an organizational perspective has so often echoed a narrative of losing control.

While the fan remains a woefully understudied construct in public relations literature, recent research has begun to interrogate the sports fan as a kind of active public within traditional frameworks defining organization-public relationships (Waters, Burke, Jackson, & Buning, 2011). Following the historical trajectory of communications and audience studies research, scholars have begun to acknowledge that active audiences present a challenge (and opportunity) for crisis communication. In a study of how sports fans acted to respond to crises themselves, Brown and Billings (2013) discovered that fans will act in a crisis because their identity is bound up in the organization/brand (in this study, the football team they support). Thus, a crisis for the brand becomes a crisis for both the fan's personal and community identity. These fans will act, then, to remedy a crisis both to restore an equilibrium of self *and* social capital.

A sweet threat? Social media, sugar, and Skittles

A 2009 analysis of the top-selling candy brands in the U.S.A. ranked Skittles as one of "America's 25 Favorite Candies," in which it landed as number 14, and with a reported annual sales of \$150.2 million (Arndt, 2009). However, this privately held candy empire is famously elusive when it comes to revealing specific demographic information about the consumers it attracts, except in broad terms: it is the leading candy on the market "with teens and younger children" (Brodesser-Akner, 2013). Even as Skittles became an emblem of social justice for Trayvon Martin's supporters, some activists wondered aloud about the negative consequences of embracing candy. Sugary products, such as Skittles, could be seen as a contributing factor to "a disproportionately black obesity epidemic" whose implications are "staggering" (Brodesser-Akner, 2013). Studies tracking health issues and food choices have also noted a particularly high preference for certain snacks among youth of color as they search for ways to intervene in chronic health issues, such as obesity and diabetes (Cohen, Sturm, Scott, Farley, & Bluthenthal, 2010; Ford, Ng, & Popkin, 2014).

Maybe the product's vivid colors and "taste the rainbow" slogan became an unwitting emblem of Martin's innocence (Benedictus, 2013). But just as likely, his supporters, who were largely African American, knew the Skittles brand as well as Martin did, after years of seeing its ubiquitous presence in the places where they shopped for food. Coupled with a strong social media presence in environments where youthful users of color dominate, Skittles was perfectly, if unknowingly, positioned for an appropriation of its brand.

Case study: Skittles moves to the center of a crisis

Faces peering from hooded jackets, reflecting the activism of a new generation, have replicated themselves in media depictions across the United States, and even the world. These protesters, ultimately reflecting many generations and identities, became galvanized by news of a seeming legal stalemate over the shooting death of unarmed African American teenager Trayvon Martin by a mixed white and Hispanic citizen, George Zimmerman.

The circumstances of teenager Trayvon Martin's death nearly went unnoticed. On February 26, 2012, 17-year-old Martin went to a 7-Eleven convenience store in Sanford, Florida, while visiting his father. With a can of Arizona Tea and a bag of Skittles candy, Martin began to walk back to the neighborhood at the Retreat at Twin Lakes where he was staying. Zimmerman, a resident and neighborhood watch volunteer, encountered Martin while the youth was walking back to his apartment. An altercation ensued, leaving Martin dying of a gunshot wound and Zimmerman bruised (Memmott, 2012).

Without identification, Martin's body remained unclaimed for two days, even as his father reported to the police that his son was missing. On February 28, police positively identified Martin's body (Fuchs, 2012). Although the teenager carried nothing that had his name, his identity became fused with the items he did have with him at the time of his death: a hoodie, a can of Arizona Tea, and a bag of Skittles.

In an intricate analysis of how traditional media blended with social media, three researchers illustrated that an interplay between local, national, and social media helped catapult Trayvon Martin's death into a *cause celebre* (Graeff, Stempeck, & Zuckerman, 2014). Significantly, a public relations consultant hired by the Martin legal team during March 2012 reached out to traditional media, while an empathetic and concerned male student from Howard University launched the initial Twitter campaign following the first national news conference about the rapidly evolving case.

The campaign for justice for Trayvon Martin exemplified the power of online activism, particularly as amplified through social media. As the #justicefortrayvon hashtag trended on Twitter, the Change.org petition calling for Zimmerman's arrest quickly became the fastest-growing in the site's history (Scott, 2012). While broadcast media coverage was integral to the case taking on national resonance, it was the cohort of online activists "working through participatory media to co-create the news" who helped set the agenda for these important platforms (Graeff, et al., 2014, p. 20).

Perhaps because of the delay in reporting the details about this incident, or setting a trial date, Martin sympathizers seized upon the visual – and media-friendly – symbols of the case. These began with a hoodie, a can of Arizona Tea and a bag of Skittles. As time went on, the hoodie and the candy alone reached near iconic status, standing in by name or by image for the Martin tragedy. After his death, both the Arizona and the Skittles brands attempted to conduct business as usual, much to the disappointment of many critics (Ghosh, 2013; Gianatasio, 2012; Severson, 2012).

Key to understanding the power of Skittles as a resonant symbol for activists is in the symbolic meaning of Trayvon Martin's image and body. This is rooted in a long history of assumptions of black male bodies as dangerous and criminal, echoed in a cacophony of problematic media representations that span both news and entertainment (Oliver, 2003; Yancy, Miller, & Johnson, 2014). With a brand identity of playful, youthful innocence, Skittles became a perfect symbol to contradict this archetypal framing of Martin. As Choi (2012) writes, "That's why the candy became such a vivid detail in the Martin case." The brand's symbolic meaning directly contrasted with the perception of Martin as criminal, reframing him as a child headed home from the store with a bag of candy.

As Zimmerman moved forward to trial, Skittles remained a prominent – and divisive – symbol of the tragedy. Yet within that branded context, it also resonated for what it *was*: a candy treat, of the kind children in costumes scramble to grab on Halloween, purchasable on a child's allowance, and the sort of sugary snack at the center of many a dentist's and parent's scolding. What functioned so forcefully as a symbol of life was now as much one of life cut short.

Skittles is a product produced by Wrigley under Mars Inc., its parent company. As pressure rose for a response, the corporate giant released a short statement on March 22, 2012 – almost a month after the teenager's murder:

> We are deeply saddened by the news of Trayvon Martin's death and express our sincere condolences to his family and friends. We also respect their privacy and feel it inappropriate to get involved or comment further as we would never wish for our actions to be perceived as an attempt of commercial gain following this tragedy.
>
> (*NewsOne*, 2012)

Despite this well-calibrated statement, some observers noted the irony of the candy's increased revenues in the midst of the controversy, and many raised questions about whether the company should make tangible contributions with the candy's additional profits (Ghosh, 2013; Severson, 2012; *NewsOne*, 2012).

Crisis communication, Skittles, and race: a different kind of problem

Responding to the uptick in sales Skittles received, as well as burgeoning dissatisfaction with the company's continued silence, Fleishman-Hillard senior partner Heidi Hovland described the brand as "a candy that was in the wrong place at the wrong time" (quoted in Severson, 2012). Trayvon Martin is a powerful example of the opportunities and challenges for public relations practitioners in an age where messages go viral instantly, and communities are formed through unseen interconnections. While Martin supporters used social media to organize out of a vacuum, the Skittles brand had long established a dominant marketing presence in cyberspace.

Identification with a brand or fandom is important to how individuals organize online and form communities; by connecting users through the salient identity dimension of "fan," these communities facilitate the social capital that allows deliberative spaces to become functioning public spheres. Within these still branded spaces, publics and counterpublics form around issues viewed as relevant to the brand message/meaning; anticipating these issues and the fandom's sensibility of brand meaning is essential to both relationship-building and crisis/risk management.

Increasing research on the role of social media in crisis communication reveals an understanding of crisis that, reflecting its newfound platforms, is increasingly *participatory* and *emotional*. As exemplified in the Trayvon Martin campaign's influence on national broadcast media, social media are increasingly powerful in bringing crises to national (and even international) attention, as journalists use social media for story-mining (Liu, 2012; Austin, Liu, & Jin, 2012). As Liu (2012) explains, "social media provide emotional support for publics after crises occur as well as a way for publics to virtually band together, share information, and demand resolution" (p. 346). In times of crisis, publics' social media use increases, as they rely more and more on these interactive channels for both information and emotional support (Austin, et al., 2012).

As defined by Coombs (2012), a crisis represents an important turning point for an organization – whether negative or positive. Crisis communication research has been criticized for a managerial bias (Baker, 2001; Lee, 2004; Waymer & Heath, 2007), as well as limited work on the role of the pre-crisis stage (Avery, Lariscy, Kim & Hocke, 2010) and race as a complicating factor (Williams & Olaniran, 2002). As Carstarphen (2013) contends, ignoring race in developing public relations theory "asserts a genuine conviction that sound theoretical perspectives and well-executed practices will automatically – and implicitly – forge positive relations among diverse communities and disperse strategic messages evenly" (p. 143). As Williams and Olaniran (2002) point out, race not only significantly increases the volatility of a crisis situation, but many traditional best practices of crisis response prove inappropriate and/or ineffective.

Race remains a key category in constructing both social identity and sense of self, and functions as a lens through which individuals view and process their environment (Carstarphen, 2013). Yet like other fluid dimensions of identity – particularly in online spaces – race can be activated when a situation becomes salient to an individual's identification with a racial community. As Bradley (2012) summarizes, "issues of race will galvanize and unite communities of color like nothing else."

In seeking to define the racially oriented crisis, Liu (2012) identifies several characteristics: heavy media coverage; significant financial damage; alienation of the organization from important stakeholders; and the escalation of racial tensions. Baker (2001) also segments types of racial crises into three categories: action, words, and symbols. According to Baker, organizations should focus on ongoing crisis management, practicing environmental scanning that reveals all potential racially-oriented crises. But when the crisis hits, there is one clear strategy: apologize, as soon as possible (Baker, 2001).

However, part of the complexity of the Skittles crisis was that none of the corporate employees were contributors to the incidents leading up to Martin's death, and had no direct role in the chain of events that transpired since. How would they apologize? To whom? And for what?

Conclusion: fandom, power, and public relations

The formation of increasingly active and interactive fandoms around brand identification offers both significant relationship-building opportunities for organizations and potential for crisis – in much the same way that increasingly emotional relationships carry ever greater risks. Drawing on the literature on fandom, crisis communication, and diverse identities, we argue that organizations must adapt to understanding these fan communities as potentially powerful, inspirational brand advocates, yet also as emotional stakeholders who may expect a return on their affective investment.

As the Martin case illustrates, publics formed within fan contexts provide significant opportunities for social activist campaigns, which may seek to – or quite unexpectedly – activate participants through shared symbols and meanings. In a structural sense, networks formed within fan spaces may, contingent on co-created meanings, bridge easily to social causes. This is where it is important for brands to understand the ever-shifting eco-systems in which they operate, particularly online. Twitter has been an especially important space for digital activism (Lim, 2012), and has cemented itself as a platform for rapid information sharing in times of crisis.

Fandom studies have hinged upon shifting understandings of power dynamics, with fans understood on a spectrum in relationship to the brand/organization from the critical (oppositional/resistant readings) to the useful (inspirational consumers, loyals, advocates). The case of Skittles and Trayvon Martin represents a strange kind of meeting of these two far ends of the spectrum, in which acts of resistance coincided with enthusiastic amplification of the brand. By elevating Martin to celebrity status, the Twitter conversations may have facilitated a fandom ardently seeking "the capturing of goodwill" (Kehrberg, 2015, p. 96) of the community of supporters forged in his name. And the Skittles brand went along for the ride.

And yet, when Skittles remained silent, its fan community expected economic and emotional identification to be returned in kind: "In just one week," writes Scott (2012), "the brand has gone from being a symbol of an innocent victim to one of corporate greed." This is an important reminder of the symbolic nature of brands and reputations: the symbolic is easily hijacked and reimagined in online spaces, where communities likewise exist through symbolic (and not actual, geographical) associations. Ultimately, Skittles' fandom was both a contributing factor for its Trayvon Martin crisis, but also a strength that helped the company to recover, better understand, and interact with its base in the future.

Because, increasingly, target publics may find social media content more credible than traditional media, organizations should consider harnessing user-generated content and interactive engagement with publics directly through social media in performing their information function during a crisis (Austin, et al., 2012). Research trends show that the United States will continue to morph into a country whose citizens are younger, savvy users of technology and more ethnically diverse than ever before (Pew Research Center, 2014). While organizations might cultivate fandom networks for the potential brand loyalty they can engender, public relations strategists must recognize that fans see themselves in identities that are multifaceted, dynamic, and highly meaningful outside of the brand's influence or control.

In managing this intersectionality, Jenkins (2007) cautions us all against merely "co-opting grassroots activities back into the commodity culture" (p. 148). Even as brands harness polysemic opportunities to speak directly to communities, they must avoid the appearance of commercializing activism for their own gains.

References

Arndt, M. (2009). Top-selling sweets: Skittles. *Bloomberg*. Retrieved from http://www. bloomberg.com.

Austin, L., Liu, B. F., & Jin, Y. (2012). How audiences seek out crisis information: Exploring the social-mediated crisis communication model. *Journal of Applied Communication Research*, 40(2), 188–207.

Avery, E. J., Lariscy, R. W., Kim, S., & Hocke, T. (2010). A quantitative review of crisis communication research in public relations from 1991 to 2009. *Public Relations Review*, 36, 190–192.

Baker, G. (2001). Race and reputation: Restoring image beyond the crisis. In R. L. Heath (Ed.), *Handbook of public relations* (pp. 513–520). Thousand Oaks, CA: Sage.

Benedictus, L. (2013). How skittles became a symbol of Trayvon Martin's innocence. The *Guardian*. Retrieved from http://www.theguardian.com/world/shortcuts/2013/jul/15/skittles-trayvon-martin-zimmerman-acquittal

Bradley, T. (2012). What the Trayvon Martin case should teach PR pros. *PR Week*. Retrieved from http://www.prweek.com.

Brodesser-Akner, C. (2013). Skittles, Trayvon Martin, and corporate responsibility: One of the web's biggest social media successes suddenly goes silent. *Time*. Retrieved from http://entertainment.time.com/2013/07/18/strange-fruit-skittles-trayvon-martin-and-corporate-responsibility/.

Brown, N. A., & Billings, A. C. (2013). Sports fans as crisis communicators on social media websites. *Public Relations Review*, 39, 74–81.

Burke, K. (1969). *A rhetoric of motives*. Berkeley: University of California Press.

Carstarphen, M. G. (2013). New media, new challenges: Towards a theory of transactional diversity for public relations. 16th International Public Relations Research Conference, University of Miami: Coral Gables, FL.

Castells, M. (2009). *Communication power*. Oxford/New York: Oxford University Press.

Choi, C. (2012). In Trayvon Martin killing, Skittles joins food brands at the center of tragedy. *The Associated Press*. Retrieved from http://www.masslive.com.

Cohen, D., Sturm, R., Scott, M., Farley, T. A., & Bluthenthal, R. (2010). Not enough fruit and vegetables or too many cookies, candies, salty snacks and soft drinks? *Public Health Reports*, 125(1), 88–95.

Coombs, W. T. (2012). Parameters for crisis communication. In W. T. Coombs & S. J. Holladay (Eds.), *The handbook of crisis communication* (pp. 17–53). Chichester.: Wiley-Blackwell.

Dozier, D. M., & Lauzen, M. M. (2000). Liberating the intellectual domain from the practice: Public relations, activism, and the role of the scholar. *Journal of Public Relations Research*, 12(1), 3–22.

Ford, C. N., Ng, S. W., & Popkin, B. N. (2014). Are food and beverage purchases in households with preschoolers changing? A longitudinal analysis from 2000 to 2011. *Preventive Medicine*, 47(3), 275–282.

Fuchs, E. (2012). The Trayvon Martin shooting: A timeline of the entire ease. *Business Insider–U.S. Edition*. Retrieved from http://www.businessinsider.com/a-minute-by-minute-timeline-of-everything-thats-known-about-the-trayvon-martingeorge-zi mmerman-shooting-2012-6?op=1.

Ghosh, P. (2013). Trayvon Martin's death and Skittles: A peculiar marketing dilemma. *International Business Times*. Retrieved from http://www.ibtimes.com/trayvon-ma rtins-death-skittles-peculiar-marketing-dilemma-1346469.

Gianatasio, D. (2012). Skittles, Arizona iced tea caught in no man's land in the Trayvon Martin case. *AdWeek*, March 28.

Goldstein, S. (2012). Police chief steps down, as Trayvon Martin petition builds steam. *PR News*. Retrieved from http://www.prnewsonline.com.

Goldstein, S. (2014). Re-Halloween infographic: Skittles tops list of most influential candy brands on Twitter. *PR News*. Retrieved from http://www.prnewsonline.com.

Graeff, E., Stempeck, M., & Zuckerman, E. (2014). The battle for "Trayvon Martin": Mapping a media controversy online and off-line. *First Monday*, 19(2), 1–29.

Grossberg, L. (1992). Is there a fan in the house? The affective sensibility of fandom. In L. A. Lewis (Ed.), *The adoring audience: Fan culture and popular media* (pp. 50–68). London and New York: Routledge.

Habermas, J. (1989). *The structural transformation of the public sphere*. Cambridge, MA: MIT Press.

Hermans, H. J. M. (2004). Introduction: The dialogical self in a global and digital age. *Identity: An International Journal of Theory and Research*, 4(4), 297–320.

Hermans, H. J. M., Kempen, H. J. G., & Van Loon, R. J. P. (1992). The dialogical self: Beyond individualism and rationalism. *American Psychologist*, 47, 23–33.

Jenkins, H. (1992). *Textual poachers: Television fans and participatory culture*. New York and London: Routledge.

Jenkins, H. (2006). Interactive audiences? In H. Jenkins (Ed.), *Fans, bloggers, and gamers: Exploring participatory culture* (pp. 134–151). New York: NYU Press.

Jenkins, H. (2007). Afterword: The future of fandom. In J. Gray, C. Sandvoss, & C. L. Harrington (Eds.), *Fandom: Identities and communities in a mediated world* (pp. 357–364). New York: NYU Press.

Kehrberg, A. K. (2015). "I love you, please notice me": The hierarchical rhetoric of twitter fandom. *Celebrity Studies*, 6(1), 85–99.

Krogstad, J. S. (2015). Social media preferences vary by race and ethnicity. Pew Research Center. Retrieved from http://www.pewresearch.org/fact-tank/2015/02/ 03/social-media-preferences-vary-by-race-and-ethnicity/.

Lee, B. K. (2004). Audience-oriented approach to crisis communication: A study of Hong Kong consumers' evaluation of an organizational crisis. *Communication Research*, 31(5), 600–618.

Lim, M. (2012). Clicks, cabs, and coffee houses: Social media and oppositional movements in Egypt, 2004–2011. *Journal of Communication*, 62(2), 231–248.

Liu, B. F. (2012). Effective public relations in racially charges crises: Not black or white. In W. T. Coombs & S. J. Holladay (Eds.), *The handbook of crisis communication* (pp. 335–358). Chichester: Wiley-Blackwell.

Markowicz, C. (2009). Edelman to revamp Krispy Kreme site. *PR Week*. Retrieved from http://www.prweek.com

Memmott, M. (2012). Trayvon Martin was "typical teen," George Zimmerman is hard to categorize. National Public Radio. Retrieved from http://www.npr.org/blogs/thetwo-way/2012/03/23/149206896/trayvon-martin-was-typical-teen-george-zimmerman-is-hard-to-categorize.

NewsOne. (2012). Skittles releases statement on Trayvon Martin's murder. *NewsOne*. Retrieved from http://newsone.com/1951455/skittles-releases-statement-on-trayvon-martins-murder/.

O'Brien, K. (2009). Companies should consider value before jumping into social media. *PR Week*. Retrieved from http://www.prweek.com.

Oliver, M. B. (2003). African American men as "criminal and dangerous": Implications of media portrayals of crime on the "criminalization" of African American men. *Journal of African American Studies*, 7(2), 3–18.

Pew Research Center. (2014). Millennials in adulthood: Detached from institutions, networked with friends. Pew Research Center. Retrieved from http://www.pewsocialtrends.org/2014/03/07/millennials-in-adulthood/.

PR News. (2010). How to deftly manage user content on facebook. *PR News*. Retrieved from http://www.prnewsonline.com.

PR News. (2012). Quick study: Confidence in earned media up while paid plummets; online advocacy soars; smartphones propel web radio. *PR News*. Retrieved from http://www.prnewsonline.com.

Scott, K. (2012). Skittles caught in an unforgiving spotlight. *PR News*. Retrieved from http://www.prnewsonline.com.

Severson, K. (2012). For Skittles, death brings both profit and risk. *The New York Times*. Retrieved from http://www.nytimes.com.

Smith, H. G. (2009). Skittles' experiment ceded too much control of brand. *PR Week*. Retrieved from: http://www.prweek.com.

Sommerfeldt, E. J., Kent, M. L., & Taylor, M. (2012). Activist practitioner perspectives of website public relations: Why aren't activist websites fulfilling the dialogic promise? *Public Relations Review*, 38, 303–312.

Steel, E. (2009). Skittles cozies up to social media; Candy's site is built on consumer-created content from Twitter, Facebook. *The Wall Street Journal*. Retrieved from http://www.wsj.com/articles/SB123604377921415283.

Tracy, K. (2002). *Everyday talk: Building and reflecting identities*. New York: Guilford.

Tsetsura, T. (2011). How understanding multidimensional diversity can benefit global public relations education. *Public Relations Review*, 37, 530–535.

Turkle, S. (1996). Who am we? *Wired*. Retrieved from http://www.wired.com.

Van Camp, S. (2012). Give back component, authenticity keys to reaching powerful millennials. *PR News*. Retrieved from http://www.prnewsonline.com.

Waters, R. D., Burke, K. A., Jackson, Z. H., & Buning, J. D. (2011). Using stewardship to cultivate fandom online: Comparing how national football league teams use their web sites and Facebook to engage their fans. *International Journal of Sport Communication*, 4, 163–177.

Waymer, D., & Heath, R. L. (2007). Emergent agents: The forgotten publics in crisis communication and issues management research. *Journal of Applied Communication Research*, 35(1), 88–108.

Williams, D., & Olaniran, B. (2002). Crisis communication in racial issues. *Journal of Applied Communication Research*, 30(4), 293–313.

Yancy, G., Miller, E. E., & Johnson, C. (2014). Interpretive profiles on Charles Johnson's reflections on Trayvon Martin: A dialogue between George Yancy, E. Ethelbert Miller, and Charles Johnson. *The Western Journal of Black Studies*, 38(1), 1–12.

Zerillo, N. (2009). Skittles' new website showcases social media. *PR Week*. Retrieved from http://www.prweek.com.

15 Riding the wave

How the ALS Ice Bucket Challenge used storytelling and user-generated content to embrace slacktivism[1]

Jamie Ward

"A tweet by itself is just a tweet, but a thousand tweets are a song" (Moore, 2012, para. 5). Recently, several high profile social media campaigns have reignited a discussion surrounding social media's ability to facilitate meaningful contributions to collective activism. Proponents of social activism maintain that for many non-governmental organizations (NGOs) or other advocacy groups, social media has the ability to raise awareness to assist supporters in forming collective identities. Shirky (2008) maintains that "we are living in the middle of a remarkable increase in our ability to share, to cooperate with one another, and to take collective action, all outside the framework of traditional institutions and organizations" (pp. 20–21). Jenkins (2012) expands on this, highlighting the ways in which today's millennials use social media for collective action and have the ability to seamlessly navigate between being socially and culturally active with various types of technology (i.e., Facebook, Twitter, YouTube) to being politically and civically engaged utilizing those same platforms. However, not everyone is convinced that digital activism can lead to increased, meaningful contributions. Many critics argue that digital activism is not nearly as substantial as traditional activism (Ganz, 2014; Gladwell, 2010; Morozov, 2009). A sketch on Saturday Night Live aptly illustrates this sentiment: "Look, if you make a Facebook page, we will 'like' it – it's the least we can do. But it's also the most we can do" (Meyers, 2012).

Individuals who participate in social campaigns are often criticized for participating in campaigns that are fleeting and meaningless. They are accused of providing faux support for a cause simply to raise their own social capital. Terms such as hashtag activism, clicktivism and slacktivism are often associated with online campaigns, and each term views online activism as narcissistic and lacking any substantial social impact. Clicktivism is simply supporting a cause by monitoring likes or "clicks" of a mouse (White, 2010). Slacktivism has been defined as "low-risk, low-cost activity via social media whose purpose is to raise awareness, produce change, or grant satisfaction to the person engaged in the activity" (Rotman, et. al., 2011, p. 821). Kristofferson, White, and Peloza (2014). expand on this definition citing slacktivism as "a willingness to perform a relatively costless, token display of support for a social cause, with an accompanying lack of willingness to devote significant effort to enact meaningful change" (p. 1149). This ideology completely dismisses the meto-nymic adage of "the pen is mightier than the sword." In fact, it would offer the complete reverse, "the sword is mightier than the pen," implying that communication is not nearly as effective as direct participation.

Despite this criticism, a number of nonprofit organizations have found ways to effectively connect with audiences in the digital realm. Research shows that nonprofit organizations perceive significant benefits from social media cam-paigns and believe that increased awareness of their cause is the initial step to increasing donations and public support. Essentially, they believe that one of the key components of slacktivism, raising awareness, is crucial to building support and engaging an audience. One example looks to research that sur-veyed 53 advocacy groups in the United States and found a prevalent belief that the use of social media strengthens outreach efforts by "facilitating civic engagement and collective action" (Obar, Zube, & Lampe, 2012, p. 20). In their book, *Social change anytime everywhere*, Kapin and Ward (2013) echo this sentiment:

> The emphasis and effort spent on spreading information and raising awareness has always resulted in people doing what organizations ask, even if it's considered slacktivism. Liking a Page, liking a post, and all the rest are not the actions and real impact you're looking for, ultimately, but those actions are important! Why? Because, through them, people are telling you that they will do what you ask to support the cause.
>
> (p. 29–30)

Streight (2013) expands on the benefits of slacktivism. When a person engages online with the nonprofit by liking the nonprofit's page, "that person is far closer to donating money, or volunteering, than a person who does not inter-act with the non-profit organization. So we should not dismiss social media interactions as being of no value" (para. 14). Therefore, instead of completely dismissing slacktivism as being apathetic, aimless, and essentially alienating individuals who are indeed helping a cause by increasing awareness, this research argues for a change in the lexicon and a move toward focusing on social championing through both high and low levels of participation. The question then becomes, how can advocacy groups embrace a slacktivist ideol-ogy and assist potential supporters in moving from token support to meaningful contributions? One answer lies in participatory media.

Participatory media is a form of social media whose primary value "derives from the active participation of many people" (Rheingold, 2008, p. 100). A participatory medium is a largely digital platform where the audience can play an active role in the process of collecting, reporting, evaluating, and distributing content through social media (Bowman, & Willis, 2003). A primary compo-nent of participatory media is that end-users are "active participants in value creation" (European Institute for Participatory Media, 2009, para. 12). Advo-cacy groups can combat the traditional notion of slacktivism by altering the way campaigns are constructed and thinking more in terms of a peer-produced or user-generated system. Through social media, campaigns are able to become almost living, breathing, and changing beings. With commons-based peer production (Benkler, 2002), the public controls the campaign and through the use of storytelling provides an authentic voice and unique relationship with both the social problem and the publicity related to its solution. By creating a campaign that grows with its audience, user involvement and engagement are in their most authentic forms creating content that a wider subsection of the public can identify with. According to digital marketing analyst Brian Solis, "monologue has changed to dialogue" in this new era of public relations (2009, p. 2). Commons-based peer production offers the platform for this type of authentic, audience-centered connection. Combine this with a system designed specifically to harness the power of social media and advocacy organizations have a way of reaching out to the public that is not only diverse but also multifaceted and engaged.

This research examines the role of slacktivism in digital advocacy campaigns. Guided in part by the theory of network-enabled commons-based peer production, this research posits that by crafting a digital advocacy campaign completely reliant on user-generated content and embracing traditional notions of slacktivism, advocacy organizations can empower individuals to become active participants in digital campaigns, thus creating unique, individual connections with their publics and essentially empowering others to use their voices to help these campaigns reach critical mass. The *ALS Ice Bucket Challenge* is provided as a successful case study. This model not only offers a remarkable medium for social change and support of humanitarian causes, but also serves as a roadmap for advocacy organizations looking to integrate social media strategies to enhance their outreach efforts.

Peer production

The concept of peer production was first introduced by John Dewey in his 1927 book, *The public and its problems*. Dewey states that a public arises "when a group of people: (1) face a similar indeterminant situation; (2) recognize what is problematic in the situation; (3) organize to do something about the problem" (p. 109). While the definition has shifted within discourses over time to include the utilization of advanced digital technologies, Dewey highlights the act of publics working together to solve a communal problem. Modern day references to peer production are generally divided into two categories: crowdsourcing and commons-based peer production. The distinction between the two is significant due to the way the latter is utilized throughout this manuscript.

Crowdsourcing is a term that was first introduced in the June 2006 issue of *Wired* magazine (Howe, 2006a). The definition is as follows:

> Simply defined, crowdsourcing represents the act of a company or institution taking a function once performed by employees and outsourcing it

to an undefined (and generally large) network of people in the form of an open call. This can take the form of peer-production (when the job is performed collaboratively), but is also often undertaken by sole individuals. The crucial prerequisite is the use of the open call format and the large network of potential laborers.

(p. 5)

Howe views crowdsourcing as a type of directed labor where laborers try to complete tasks with a specific set of solution parameters. Businesses solicit peer produced ideas or solutions for the purposes of eventually taking control of those ideas and utilizing them to propel the business. "It's only crowdsourcing once a company takes that design, fabricates [it] in mass quantity and sell[s] it" (Howe, as cited in Brabham, 2008, p. 76). A company solicits ideas or solutions to a problem from the general public via some type of online medium. The call is answered with varying responses. The company ultimately selects the idea that best fits their ideology and pays a typically modest sum to the producer. The company then utilizes the idea for its own monetary gain.

Motivations for crowdsourcing are wide ranging and reasons for participating include everything from developing creative skills to building a portfolio, benefiting the common good, and simply alleviating boredom (Brabham, 2011). While crowdsourcing has proven to be effective in commercial arenas such as software design, Web 2.0 technologies, and even social media and has launched several thriving business models utilized by the likes of eBay and Facebook, it has not been used effectively in advocacy work. Practitioners designing advocacy campaigns are typically not in positions to extend monetary compensation. Therefore, participants need to be motivated by alternate desires such as social-psychological rewards, that is, a desire for cultural change. Research suggests that individuals are more successful when working to solve problems for others verses solving problems for themselves (Polman, & Emich, 2011). While crowdsourcing is a common approach for businesses to garner a multitude of problem solving options, commons-based peer production tends to be a more practical option for most advocacy organizations.

Commons-based peer production, a term first elucidated by Yochai Benkler in 2002, was originally applied to peer production of free software projects. Benkler discusses the proliferation of communal collaborations taking place in the absence of traditional hierarchies. The most notable example of this type of online collaboration in use today is Wikipedia. According to Benkler, the advantages of peer production are "improved identification and allocation of human creativity" (2002, p. 377). Commons-based peer production systems are not monetarily based. Participation in such systems provides other intrinsic rewards such as the ability to contribute to social change.

Benkler highlights three characteristics necessary for commons-based peer production to thrive. The first characteristic is that the project needs to be "modular" (Benkler, 2002, p. 378). Individuals need to be able to contribute independently produced components based on their own timetables. The second characteristic is that "the modules should be predominantly fine-grained, or small in size" (p. 379). In other words, participants will have varying interests and ways of augmenting content. Contributions will come in various sizes and the system needs to be designed to support this variety. Benkler believes "this allows the project to capture contributions from large numbers of contributors whose motivation levels will not sustain anything more than small efforts toward the project" (p. 379). The third characteristic in "a successful peer production enterprise must have low-cost integration, which includes both quality control over the modules and a mechanism for integrating the contributions into the finished product" (p. 379). Participants must be able to add to the project without significant effort or expense. They also must be able to maintain ownership of their contribution and be able to actually see how their contribution fits into the overall project. The Internet allows such a system to thrive. Without the use of digital technologies or the advent of social media platforms, commons-based peer production could not successfully exist.

Slacktivism

Slacktivism is a combination of the words "slacker" and "activism." According to Davis (2011), the term slacktivism "describe[s] the act of passively supporting causes in order to tap into the satisfaction that accompanies philanthropy, without having to do any heavy-lifting (or heavy spending)" (para. 9). Slacktivist activities include signing an e-petition, changing a Facebook profile picture to highlight a cause, clicking "like" on a Facebook post, retweeting content, or joining an online group. A number of scholars argue that to advance activism and effect real change, one needs to do more than simply passively participate online. They need to physically participate and engage in traditional advocacy tactics (Bimber, 2001; Gladwell, 2010; Morozov, 2011; Scheufele & Nisbet, 2002).

The etymology of the term comes from a shortened version of slacker activism. Credited to Fred Clark, the term references "the bottom up activities by young people to affect society on a small personal scale" (Christensen, 2011, n. p.). The initial usage of the term in 1995 had positive connotations. As previously mentioned, the term has acquired negative connotations associated with being lazy and narcissistic. In order to allow advocacy groups to take control of this term, shift the lexicon and embrace the ideas behind simple, well-intentioned actions, one needs to view the benefits of slacktivism. A study conducted by Georgetown University and Ogilvy Worldwide (2010) shows that people who engaged in "promotional social activity were three times as likely to solicit donations on behalf of their cause and four times as likely to encourage others to sign a petition or contact a political representative" (p. 6). Andresen (2011) further highlights the positive elements of slacktivism:

> The message here isn't that all slacktivists are diehard activists. They may be willing to join a Facebook cause for one non-profit, but run a

marathon and raise a fortune for another. It's up to the non-profit to see slacktivist action as a sign of interest, and then to deepen that interest with strong engagement.

(para. 13)

The *ALS Ice Bucket Challenge* serves as a solid case study illustrating how an organization can successfully transform slacktivist action into profit.

ALS Ice Bucket Challenge

Amyotrophic lateral sclerosis (ALS), also known as Lou Gehrig's Disease, is a "progressive neurodegenerative disease that affects nerve cells in the brain and the spinal cord" (ALS Association, 2010, n.p.). This degeneration leads to loss of muscle control, paralysis, and death. "Based on U.S. population studies, a little over 5,600 people in the U.S. are diagnosed with ALS each year. (That's 15 new cases a day)" (ALS Association, 2010, n.p.). The *ALS Ice Bucket Challenge* raised $114 million dollars from July 29 to September 22, 2014 (ALS Association, 2010, n.p.). According to data presented by Jeremiah Owyang (2014), by the end of September 2014, approximately 2,330,000 videos related to the Ice Bucket Challenge had been posted to YouTube and Google had named the *ALS Ice Bucket Challenge* one of the most popular searched terms of that year (Google, 2014, n.p.).

According to Alexandra Sifferlin at *TIME Magazine* (2014), The *ALS Ice Bucket Challenge* began with a golfer named Chris Kennedy. Chris was nominated to participate in the Ice Bucket Challenge but at the time, the participant could choose the charity they wanted to support. Chris selected ALS because a relative was suffering from the disease. He nominated a family member who began utilizing the hashtag #strikeoutALS. At this point the challenge was slowly being passed between family and friends. After the campaign reached former Boston College baseball player Peter Frates on July 31, 2014, it became completely affiliated with ALS and it went viral. The challenge was simple. An individual had 24 hours to either dump a bucket of ice water on their heads or donate $100 to ALS. They also needed to challenge three people to further the awareness of the campaign. According to blogger, Beth Kanter (2014), over 50 political figures, 200 notable actors and actresses, 200 athletes and over 220 musicians along with thousands of everyday citizens throughout the world have participated in the challenge.

Dragonfly effect

The *ALS Ice Bucket Challenge* followed a model for driving social change through social media known as the Dragonfly Effect (Aaker, & Smith, 2010). The dragonfly model, named for the fact that a dragonfly can move in any direction as long as its four wings are working in unison, focuses on four key principles. Those principles are focus, grab attention, engage, and take action

(Aaker, & Smith, 2010). According to Aaker and Smith (2010), if a social media campaign contains these principles, it will work to create positive, social change. In the case of the *ALS Ice Bucket Challenge*, the principles can be easily seen and followed.

The first key principle, focus, relies heavily on presenting a single, measurable goal. By making the goal small and reachable – dump water over your head, post a video of it to social media, and nominate three people to do the same within 24 hours or donate $100 and nominate three people within 24 hours – viewers are not overwhelmed by the ask. While the ultimate goals are to raise awareness and funds to combat ALS, by starting small, the outreach remains targeted and manageable.

In addition to having a clear focus, this first principle also calls for the goal to be testable. The *ALS Ice Bucket Challenge* began with a modest goal. The goal was to simply increase awareness and donations over the previous year. Before the Ice Bucket Challenge, the ALS website averaged about 8,000 visitors per day. By mid-August 2014, the average number of visitors per day rose to 630,000. This is an increase of 7,775%. By August 24, 2014, the organization had raised $70.2 million in donations compared to the $2.5 million raised during the same time the year before (Perez, 2014, para. 14). Utilizing commons-based peer production in conjunction with a focused targeted message provided for a highly sharable, compelling story that combined gamification and simplicity to engage viewers.

The second principle in the Dragonfly Effect is to grab attention (Aaker & Smith, 2010). The *ALS Ice Bucket Challenge* uses entertaining, user-generated videos to grab attention. The videos contain laughter, smiles, and the building of a community through the challenge to friends and family. Public relations professionals are keenly aware of the power of a narrative. Kevin Allocca (2012), trends manager at YouTube, states that "tastemakers, creative participating communities, and complete unexpectedness" are three of the qualities that allow videos to capture the attention of a broad audience and go viral (p. 1). Videos posted in response to the *ALS Ice Bucket Challenge* contain each of these elements. In terms of tastemakers, the *ALS Ice Bucket Challenge* largely went viral with the assistance of celebrities participating in the challenge. An article by Sarah Perez (2014) in Tech Crunch boasts that the top five celebrity videos were videos created by Charlie Sheen, Bill Gates, Chris Pratt, Lady Gaga, and Kate Upton. Other popular celebrity videos were created by Homer Simpson, Kermit the Frog, and Cookie Monster.

Using celebrities to publicize a cause is nothing new. Generating enough buzz to have the public make unique, individual connections with the videos already posted, then adding their own videos is certainly something to write about. The campaign is relatable to everyone. The majority of the video clips are less than a minute in length and the vast majority of them not only mention the challenge by name, but also further the cause by nominating at least three people. They reinforce the message in a short and simple way. This assists in keeping the audience engaged.

The third principle in the Dragonfly Effect is to engage the audience (Aaker, & Smith, 2010). According to Aaker and Smith, "you might have brilliant arguments as to why people should get involved, but if you can't engage them emotionally, they won't be swayed" (p. 2). Aaker and Smith highlight four specific design principles that engage an audience. Those principles are tell a story, empathize, be authentic, and match the media (p. 101). The *ALS Ice Bucket Challenge* engages the audience on each of these levels. While there are levels of social currency and vanity associated with the videos, the humor and authenticity of the content make people want to watch and get involved. The reality of each video is highlighted by the way the video is presented. The participants are in plain clothes and have either set up a camera or are being recorded by friends or family. The backdrop is often outside a home, in a backyard or other similarly common location. The task is simple so anyone from children to adults can participate. The speakers show their nervousness and excitement about being doused with water through facial expressions and awkward pausing. The voices are unique and authentic. The campaign also engages its audience by inviting them to make a video of their own and continuing the campaign's outreach.

The fourth principle in the Dragonfly Effect is to develop a call to action that is easy, fun, and open to all. The *ALS Ice Bucket Challenge* asks individuals to post personal videos of themselves getting doused with ice water and to spread awareness by nominating others. Many of the videos also ask that individuals donate in addition to their ice bucket participation. The format allows for creativity, ingenuity, and self-expression. There is very little in terms of specific direction. The campaign is easy to become a part of and easy to share. The message is sharp and strong.

Ultimately, the Dragonfly Effect is an easily replicable model about embracing disruptive technology to make a difference in the world, and, by extension, in one's own life. (Chernov, 2010). When used correctly this model not only allows advocacy organizations to embrace slacktivism but can also bring about engaging and impactful social campaigns, as evidenced by the *ALS Ice Bucket Challenge*. Successful public relations campaigns are generally gauged in terms of return on investment (ROI), increased product, or organizational awareness. The *ALS Ice Bucket Challenge* accomplished their awareness and fundraising goals by successfully harnessing the power of user-generated content.

Embracing slacktivism

The *ALS Ice Bucket Challenge* is unique in that it harnesses the ideas of typical public relations campaigns (clearly defined message and objectives, target audience, method of evaluation), but the control of the campaign remains in the hands of a community rather than a bureaucracy. Thus some control over the overall message is relinquished in order to increase the authenticity of the campaign. With such a simple premise and objective, many critics viewed participation in the *ALS Ice Bucket Challenge* as slacktivism and framed it negatively. They highlighted the idea that dumping water over someone's head was not true activism and that it would not lead to continued relationships with the charity (Hiltzik, 2014; Gladwell, 2010). This research would argue that the definition of "true activism" can take many forms. Activism can mean participating on the front lines of a protest but it can also be reaching out and organizing those protestors on a Facebook page. Activism can mean donating thousands of dollars to support a cause or it can be creating videos that share the reasons that the organization needs help. As long as supporters are working to advance the mission of the advocacy organization, they are serving as activists. Slacktivism, as evidenced by the $115 million dollars raised by the *ALS Ice Bucket Challenge* in just a few months, should not be dismissed as a passing fad or as a way to garner one's 15 seconds of fame. According to social media and content marketer, Leslie Nuccio:

> Nonprofit marketing depends on relationship marketing. Personal giving is personal, after all, and someone's willingness to donate to charity depends pretty solidly on two things: (1) cause affinity, and (2) brand affinity. In the case of the Ice Bucket Challenge, the ALS Association is giving folks a fun, refreshing way to raise awareness and money for their cause, and this allows them to form brand relationships, however briefly, with people who don't have the cause affinity – and to earn exposure to new social communities.
>
> (2014, para. 12)

Slacktivism can provide advocacy organizations with the tools to expand their outreach efforts and to increase brand awareness. Embracing slacktivism can provide nonprofits access to increased numbers of individuals interested in their cause. It can also expose new audiences to the organization. According to Nuccio, increased awareness is the top rung of a purchase funnel followed by consideration, preference, purchase, loyalty and lastly advocacy (2012). The *ALS Ice Bucket Challenge* illustrates that awareness can turn into increased financial donations and advocacy efforts.

Conclusion

"To be successful, you must translate your passion into a powerful story and tell it in a way that generates 'contagious energy,' so that your audience reflects on your tweet, blog post, or email, long after they leave their computers" (Aaker & Smith, 2010, p. xiv). By empowering others to create and share content, the *ALS Ice Bucket Challenge* attempts to raise awareness and increase financial support though the use of technology. "Time and time again, initiatives falter because they're developed with the brand, organization or cause – rather than individuals' needs – foremost in mind" (p. xxiii). The *ALS Ice Bucket Challenge* has been successful because individual needs have remained at the forefront of the campaign. Participation was simple, fun, and the user-generated videos were entertaining to watch. By embracing slacktivism and effectively utilizing commons-based peer production, the *ALS Ice Bucket Challenge* became one of the first truly global video memes (Marshall, 2014).

This research not only highlights an effective viral strategy for advocacy organizations but also provides insight into trends promoting advocacy and social change. Future researchers would benefit from further analysis on campaigns that positively embrace slacktivism and on moving from passive to active advocacy.

Note

1 Portions of this research also appear in "The next dimension in public relations campaigns: A case study of the It Gets Better Project," Diversity in Public Relations, special issue *Public Relations Journal*, 7(2), 157–186.

References

Aaker, J. & Smith, A. (2010). *The dragonfly effect: Quick, effective and powerful ways to use social media to drive social change.* San Francisco, CA: Jossey-Bass.

Allocca, K. (2012, February). Why videos go viral. [video file]. Retrieved from http://www.ted.com/talks/kevin_allocca_why_videos_go_viral/transcript?language=en.

ALS Association. (2010). What is ALS. Retrieved from http://www.alsa.org/about-als/what-is-als.html.

Andresen, K. (2011, October 24). Why slacktivism is underrated. [Web log post]. Retrieved from http://mashable.com/2011/10/24/slactivism-cause-engagement/.

Benkler, Y. (2002, December). Coase's penguin, or, Linux and the nature of the firm. *The Yale Law Journal*, 112(3), 369–446.

Bimber, B. (2001). Information and political engagement in America: The search for effects of information technology at the individual level. *Political Research Quarterly*, 54(1), 53–67. doi: 10.1177/106591290105400103.

Bowman, S., & Willis, C. (2003). We media: How audiences are shaping the future of news and information. The Media Center at the American Press Institute. Retrieved from www.hypergene.net/wemedia/download/we_media.pdf.

Brabham, D. C. (2008). Crowdsourcing as a model for problem solving: An introduction and cases. *The International Journal of Research into New Media Technologies*, 14(1), 75–90. doi: 10.1177/1354856507084420.

Brabham, D. (2010). The potential of vernacular video for queer youth. *Flow*. Retrieved from http://flowtv.org/2010/10/vernacular-video-for-queer-youth/#identifier_3_5663.

Brabham, D. (2011). Motivations for crowdsourcing. Crowdsourcing.org. Retrieved from http://www.crowdsourcing.org/navigate-search?q=motivation.

Chernov, J. (2010, October 22). Book review: *The dragonfly effect* – it's all about revenue. *Eloqua Web Comment*. Retrieved from http://blog.Eloqua.com/dragonfly_effect.

Christensen, H., & Serup, B. (2011). Political activities on the internet: *Slacktivism* or political participation by other means? *First Monday*, 16. Retrieved from http://firstmonday.org/article/view/3336/2767.

Davis, J. (2011, October 27). Cause marketing: Moving beyond corporate slacktivism. [Web log post]. Retrieved from http://evidencebasedmarketing.net/cause-marke ting-moving-beyond-corporate-slacktivism.

Dewey, J. (1927). *The public and its problems*. Chicago: Swallow Press.

European Institute for Participatory Media. (2009). Retrieved from http://eipcm.org/research.html.

Ganz, M. (2014, October 17). Why hasn't "big data" saved democracy? *The Nation*. Retrieved from http://www.thenation.com/article/why-hasnt-big-data-saved-democracy/.

Georgetown University's Center for Social Impact Communication. (2010). Dynamics of cause engagement. Retrieved from http://csic.georgetown.edu/research/digital-p ersuasion/dynamics-of-cause-engagement.

Gladwell, M.. (2010, October 4). Small change: Why the revolution will not be twee-ted. *The New Yorker*. Retrieved from http://www.newyorker.com/reporting/2010/10/04/101004fa_fact_gladwell?currentPage=1.

Google. (2014). Top Charts. Retrieved from https://www.google.com/trends/topcha rts#vm=cat&geo=US&date=2014&cid.

HavasWorldwide. (2011). Millennials: The challenger generation. [Data file]. Retrieved from http://prosumer-report.com/blog/millennials.pdf.

Hiltzik, M. (2014, August 18). A few (impolite) questions about the ice bucket chal-lenge. [Web log post]. Retrieved from http://www.latimes.com/business/hiltzik/la -fi-mh-ice-bucket-challenge-20140818-column.html.

Howe, J. (2006a) "Crowdsourcing: A definition," Crowdsourcing: Why the power of the crowd is driving the future of business [Web log post]. Retrieved from http://www.crowdsourcing.com/cs/2006/06/index.html.

Howe, J. (2006b) The rise of crowdsourcing, *Wired*, 14(6). Retrieved from http://www.wired.com/wired/archive/14.06/crowds.html.

Jenkins, H. (2012). Cultural acupuncture: Fan activism and the Harry Potter Alliance. In H. Jenkins & S. Shresthova (Eds.), *Transformative Works and Cultures*, 10. doi: 10.3983/twc.2012.0305.

Kapin, A., & Ward, A. (2013). *Social change anytime everywhere: How to implement online multichannel strategies to spark advocacy, raise money, and engage your community*. California: Jossey-Bass.

Kanter, B. (2014). Ice bucket challenge: Can other nonprofits reproduce it? [Web log post]. Retrieved from http://www.bethkanter.org/icebucket-2/.

Kleinman, A., & Kleinman, J. (1997). The appeal of experience: The dismay of images: cultural appropriations of suffering in our times. In A. Kleinman, V. Das, and M. Lock (Eds.), *Social suffering* (pp. 17–18). Berkeley: University of California Press.

Kristofferson, K., White, K., & Peloza, J. (2014). The nature of slacktivism: How the social observability of an initial act of token support affects subsequent prosocial action. *Journal of Consumer Research*, 40(6), 1149–1166.

Marshall, C. (2014). 2014 ALS Ice Bucket Challenge results: Biggest social video movement ever? [Web log post]. Retrieved from http://www.reelseo.com/ice-buck et-challenge-video-meme/.

Meyers, S. (2012, September 22). Weekend update, Saturday Night Live (television broadcast). New York: National Broadcasting Company.

Moore, G. (2012, May 3). When clicking counts: In defense of slacktivism and clickti-vism. *ONE*. Retrieved from http://www.one.org/us/2012/05/03/when-click ing-counts-in-defense-of-slacktivism-and-clicktivism/.

Morozov, E.. (2009, May 19). The brave new world of slacktivism. *Foreign Policy*. Retrieved from http://neteffect.foreignpolicy.com/posts/2009/05/19/the_brave_new_world_of_slacktivism.

Morozov, E.. (2011). *The net delusion: The dark side of internet freedom*. Philadelphia: Perseus Books Group.

Nuccio, L. (2014). The Ice Bucket Challenge & the value of slacktivism. [Web log post]. Retrieved from http://www.meltwater.com/blog/ice-bucket-challenge-slacktivism/.

Obar, J. A., Zube, P., & Lampe, C. (2012). Advocacy 2.0: An analysis of how advocacy groups in the United States perceive and use social media as tools for facilitating civic engagement and collective action. *Journal of Information Policy*, 2, 1–25.

Owyang, J. (2014, September 22). The cold hard facts about the Ice Bucket Challenge. [Web log post]. Retrieved from http://www.slideshare.net/jeremiah_owyang/icebucket-challenge-cold-facts-and-stats-icebucketchallenge.

Perez, S. (2014, September 3). The Ice Bucket Challenge, by the numbers. *Tech Crunch*. Retrieved from http://techcrunch.com/2014/09/03/the-ice-bucket-challenge-by-the-numbers/.

Polman, E., & Emich, K. (2011). Decisions for others are more creative than decisions for the self. *Personality and Social Psychology Bulletin*, 37. Retrieved from http://psp.sagepub.com/content/early/2011/02/11/0146167211398362.abstract?rss=1&patientinform-links=yes&legid=sppsp;0146167211398362v1.

Rheingold, H. (2008). Using participatory media and public voice to encourage civic engagement. In W. Lance Bennett (Ed.), *Civic life online: Learning how digital media can engage youth* (pp. 97–118). The John D. and Catherine T. MacArthur Foundation Series on Digital Media and Learning. Cambridge, MA: The MIT Press.

Rotman, D., Vieweg, S., Yardi, S., Chi, E., Preece, J., Shneiderman, B., Pirolli, P., & Glaisyer, T. (2011). From slacktivism to activism: Participatory culture in the age of social media. CHI '11 *Extended Abstracts on Human Factors in Computing Systems* (CHI EA '11). ACM, New York, 819–822. doi: 10.1145/1979742.1979543.

Scheufele, D., & Nisbet, M. (2002). Being a citizen online: New opportunities and dead ends. *Harvard International Journal of Press/Politics*, 7(3), 55–75. doi: 10.1177/1081180X0200700304.

Shirky, C. (2008). *Here comes everybody: The power of organizing without organizations*. New York: Penguin.

Sifferlin, A. (2014, August 18). Here's how the ALS Ice Bucket Challenge actually started. *TIME Magazine*. Retrieved from http://time.com/3136507/als-ice-bucket-challenge-started/.

Solis, B., & Breakenridge, D. (2009). *Putting the public back in public relations: How social media is reinventing the aging business of PR*. Upper Saddle River, NJ: Pearson Education.

Streight, S. (2013, April, 27). UNICEF doesn't understand social media interactions. [Web log post]. Retrieved from http://pluperfecter.blogspot.com/2013/04/unicef-doesnt-understand-social-media.html.

White, M. (2010, August 3). Clicktivism is ruining leftist activism. *The Guardian*. Retrieved from http://www.theguardian.com/commentisfree/2010/aug/12/clicktivism-ruining-leftist-activism.

16 Facilitating the "charged public" through social media

A conversation with Disney Cruise Line's Castaway Club members

Richard D. Waters

Introduction

Whether it be a free sandwich after 10 visits or a free coffee mug after donating 20 pints of blood, organizations from the nonprofit and for-profit sectors frequently launch loyalty programs to engage their external stakeholders. Marketing research has found many organizational benefits stem from these loyalty programs, including increased sales and revenue (Liu, 2007) and higher levels of involvement with the organization's programs and services (Melnick, & Wann, 2011). Increased involvement whether online or offline results in individuals feeling more emotionally invested in an organization.

That emotional investment leads to the development of fans and brand advocates (Coppa, 2014). Lacey and Morgan (2008) concluded that one of the best approaches to developing loyalty with consumers was through the creation of programs that reward continued purchases from a company. After the initial purchase, individuals who have signed up for a loyalty program are drawn into the relationship even more by their subconscious desire to achieve whatever the loyalty program's reward is (McCall, & Vorhees, 2010). This may be a free product, such as Which Wich's buy 10 sandwiches, get one free card; a discount, such as Safeway's 10 cent discount on gasoline for every $100 spent at their grocery store; or an earned status among the company's stakeholders, such as becoming a platinum, gold, or silver medallion passenger with Delta Air Lines. Regardless of the end reward, the psychological desire to achieve drives many into pursuing that goal, which ultimately exposes them more to the offering organization's programs and services (Uncles, Dowling, & Hammond, 2003). Through positive interactions while working to achieve the loyalty program's reward, individuals frequently become advocates for the organization and recommend the company's goods or services as well as joining the loyalty program (Lacey & Morgan, 2008).

The relationship management paradigm of public relations has largely ignored the concept of loyalty as an emotional outcome of organization–public relationships. However, recent literature in public relations has highlighted the importance of loyalty in the management of relationships with stakeholders and found that loyalty is a stronger predictor of behavioral intentions than trust, satisfaction, commitment, and the balance of power in the relationship (Pressgrove, 2013). As such, loyalty should be examined more in the public relations context whether it is examined through the use of loyalty programs or through levels of connectivity an individual may have to an organization or an issue.

Public relations scholarship has proposed levels of connectivity to organizations and issues conceptually though it has not been linked to loyalty. Specifically, the situational theory of publics proposes that there are four distinct types of publics that can be identified for any organization or issue based on their levels of awareness, ability to increase participation, and their level of involvement (Aldoory, & Sha, 2007). However, the increased importance of loyalty in strategic communications programming provides evidence that there may be a fifth public that exists in an organization's environment, the charged public. This chapter proposes that a fourth variable should be introduced into the situational theory of publics that can be used to identify the charged public, whose emotional connections to an organization or issue often drive their participation.

Literature review

Organizational Fandom. Marketing literature draws distinct lines between brand ambassadors, those who are paid to represent the organization's image and consumable offerings to the public, and brand fans, those who are not paid to represent an organization but do so because of their own involvement and connection to the products, services, or company philosophy (Hatch & Shultz, 2010). While brand ambassadors are often provided with key messaging to use as talking points and are coached in how to best represent the organization, fans are everyday citizens who most often reach out to their interpersonal network to share information and their excitement about the organization's latest news and offering. While they may be more evident for some industries, such as entertainment, sports, and tourism, research has shown that brand fans exist for almost all consumer goods and services categories listed in the Fortune 500, including telecommunications, oil/petroleum, and financial services (Barnes, & Jacobsen, 2013).

For organizations, having customers become vocal advocates is the ultimate in marketing. Research continues to document that individuals are most trusting when they hear information about nonprofit, for-profit, and government agencies from people they know. Conducted annually, the Edelman Trust Barometer highlights the power of word-of-mouth marketing among interpersonal networks (Edelman, 2015). For organizations, tapping into the networks of their fans has the potential to not only boost interest in their products and services but also to boost the organizations' reputation and perception among potential audiences. Research from the Content Marketing Institute's 2015 trend report highlights that the top three goals of business-to-consumer marketers are customer retention/loyalty, brand awareness, and engagement (Pulizzi, 2015).

Creating mechanisms that make it easier for fans to talk about and share information about the organization enhances all three of these marketing goals (Lipsman, Mudd, Rich, & Bruich, 2012). While practitioner literature documents several strategies for developing fans, the general process involves first identifying the targeted audience that is key to the organization's success so that messaging and activities can be created that will be most likely to engage them. Once fans are connecting with the organization's engagement efforts, these efforts should be evaluated to see which are most successful so that variations can be designed for continued, long-term interactions. By providing fresh content over longer periods of time that are regularly scheduled, organizations keep their fans energized and willing to talk to others about the brand. Finally, measurement and evaluation about these brand communities should be done to ensure that the process is heading in the desired direction to support organizational goals (Jahn & Kunz, 2012). These individuals may start out as normal customers, but their interest in the organization and its offerings transforms them into energized, excited customers who are willing to become fans and vocal advocates for the brand.

Situational Theory of Publics. The evolution of the one-time customer to a regular customer to a fan of a brand parallels an individual's connection to an organization or issue as is highlighted by the situational theory of publics from public relations scholarship. Ultimately, organizations have many different stakeholders both internally and externally, which can be grouped around common characteristics and issues of importance. The situational theory of publics argues that when these groups become of sufficient size, they become important ones that the organization needs to engage. Thus, the situational theory of publics provides a framework for examining what factors influence publics' attitudes and behaviors based on their perception of messaging about a situation or issue (Grunig, & Hunt, 1984; Grunig, 1997).

As it is currently conceived, the situational theory of publics argues that one's awareness of an issue or organization, current involvement with that issue or organization, and ability to remove obstacles preventing further involvement can be used to predict whether someone is likely to seek out information and ultimately process the information that is received. Problem recognition is defined as the moment when people recognize that something should be done about an issue or situation, and stop and think about what to do. Constraint recognition happens when people perceive that there may be obstacles in the way of acting related to the problem, and level of involvement is the extent to which people connect with the issue or situation (Grunig, 1989a, 1997).

Information seeking and processing may be passive or active forms of communication. Passive or low levels of information seeking and processing may simply imply that an individual receives or consumes information that is presented to them. Active or higher levels of information seeking and processing, on the other hand, implies that individuals expend effort to locate or consume information about an issue or situation. In this regard, active publics and fans are inextricably linked as they are an organization's stakeholder group that is most connected and engaged. As Grunig (1989b) stated, "people communicating actively develop more organized cognitions, are more likely to have attitudes about a situation, and more often engage in a behavior to do something about the situation" (p. 6). However, it is important to note that the situational theory of publics largely is positioned around how individuals react and respond to organizations not other individuals.

Based on these variables, individuals can be considered latent, aware, or active publics, a classification system that can help organizations determine information dissemination strategies and create communication campaigns (Aldoory, & Sha, 2007). Additionally, those publics who are not impacted by an issue or organization are labeled as nonpublics. Latent publics are frequently considered to be those who may be affected by an issue or organization but are either unaware that it impacts them or have constraints that fully prevent their involvement with the issue or organization. As the label implies, aware publics know about an issue or organization and its impact on themselves, but generally have obstacles that prevent greater involvement. Active publics, on the other hand, not only know about the issue or organization and its effects on themselves, but they also actively work to remove obstacles that get them involved with that issue or organization.

Since its conceptualization, studies have found support for and advanced the situational theory of publics. Aldoory (2001) focused on involvement related to health communication targeting women, while Sha (2006) highlighted the importance of cultural identity among various publics. Weberling, Waters, and Tindall (2012) connected the situational theory of publics to an audience's willingness to use new technology to connect with an organization.

The Charged Public. Despite the successes in different domains where the situational theory of publics has been tested, the theory has largely been tested under the framework of an individual's connection to an issue or organization. Social media has created an environment that challenges the traditional variables discussed in the situational theory of publics. Specifically, individuals do not need communication campaigns and messages from organizations to learn about issues; instead, through the use of the entirety of social web platforms, people are connecting with each other and acting both positively and negatively in response to different situations that arise with issues and organizations. These charged actions occur outside the parameters of the situational theory of publics in that they are mobilizing through social efforts outside organizational communication efforts and messaging.

For example, Chick-fil-A's Chief Operating Officer Dan Cathy spoke out against gay marriage in June, 2012, and media reported that the Cathy family-operated Winshape Foundation made donations to organizations that opposed LGBT civil rights. In response to the media coverage of these revelations, members of the LGBT community protested at many Chick-fil-A locations and even held LGBT kiss-ins at certain locations. To counter this behavior, former Arkansas Governor Mike Huckabee used the media to facilitate a Chick-fil-A appreciation day, which resulted in reports of record-breaking sales

(Bingham, 2012). Social media has enabled individuals to connect with one another, share words of encouragement, and organize behavior in support of and in protest of organizations in a way that was difficult to imagine in a pre-Web 2.0 environment. Unofficial Twitter and Facebook accounts have been created for most Fortune 500 brands to allow individuals to connect and share positive and negative stories about their involvement with an organization. In many situations, these conversational exchanges turn into online and offline behaviors that have potential benefits or consequences for the featured organization.

As the situational theory of publics highlights, individuals are also connected to issues that may not be sponsored or supported by any particular organization. This also happens with charged publics' behaviors. One only has to look to news coverage to see where individuals have used both positive and negative behaviors to rally against questionable police actions in communities across the United States and globally at the annual G8 summits to discuss the status of the world's economy.

Charged publics go beyond the level of an active public as identified in the situational theory of publics. Charged publics are not only aware of an issue but follow it closely so that they are up-to-date on the latest developments about an organization or issue. Charged publics have high levels of involvement with an organization or issue because of their heightened interest in the topic, and charged publics remove obstacles to boost their involvement level just as active publics do. As predicted by the situational theory of publics, charged publics are very likely to seek out and process information about organizations and issues that are important to them. But, the charged public goes beyond seeking out and processing information. They act, and they reach out to other charged individuals to create a group that must be acknowledged and legitimized by the organizations or issues on which the charged public is centered. Charged publics use their connections to mobilize themselves, whether the end behavior is a supportive rally, a protest, or simply to further engage with organizations and issues to learn new information, plan new events, or pursue greater involvement than the organization or issue organizers anticipated.

Because the charged public is a new, emerging public in relation to the situational theory of publics, this chapter seeks to investigate individuals who readily identify themselves as a charged audience for an organization. Specifically, the following research questions were addressed in relation to fans of the Disney Cruise Line company:

RQ1: How do fans view their relationship with the Disney Cruise Line?
RQ2: What are their motivations for engaging in behaviors that are outside of the Disney Cruise Line's communication channels and processes?
RQ3: Do these fans see themselves as being different from other Disney Cruise Line passengers?

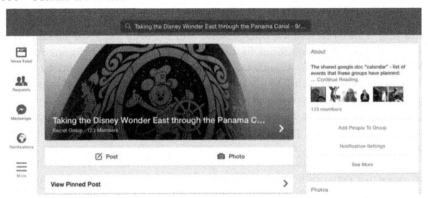

Figure 16.1 Screen shot of private Facebook group created by passengers on Disney Cruise Line 2014 sailing through the Panama Canal.

These questions will help provide additional insights into what defines the newly emerging charged public and what their motivations are for moving beyond simply acting in response to organizational initiatives to being proactive in reaching out to one another and planning events outside of the organization.

Method

Given that this research sought to identify charged publics, it was necessary to find individuals who shared a similar affinity and connection to an organization. The researcher used a planned vacation on a sailing with the Disney Cruise Line to reach out to other vacationers to conduct focus groups on board the 2014 sailing. The researcher joined a private Facebook group, shown in Figure 16.1, created so that passengers on this particular cruise vacation could meet each other before the cruise. Prior to the cruise, the researcher asked if people would be willing to participate in focus groups to talk about their experiences with the Disney Cruise Line, their connection to the Facebook group, and their motivations for becoming involved with others prior to the vacation and outside of the Disney Cruise Line's official communication channels. Individuals representing six different nations agreed to participate in four sessions during the cruise, and ultimately 51 individuals participated in the focus groups.

The 51 individuals had varying levels of connection to the Disney Cruise Line based on the number of cruise vacations they had taken with the company. For four individuals, this was their first vacation with Disney Cruise Line yet it was the thirty-fourth vacation for one couple that participated. On average, this was the sixth vacation with the Disney Cruise Line for the participants. This high number of sailings qualified most participants to be gold members of the company's "Castaway Club," a loyalty program that provides elevated benefits as additional cruises are taken. The participants were assigned to groups based on the number of vacations they had taken with the company so that individuals who had taken few vacations were not grouped together with those who had taken many. Overall, 28 women and 23 men participated in the focus groups, and the average age was 47, with ages ranging from 19 to 72.

Because the focus of the research questions explores new concepts in relation to the situational theory of publics, a qualitative methodology was chosen over quantitative surveys. The focus groups opened with a grand tour question that asked the participants to reflect on their views of the Disney Cruise Line broadly. From there, the researcher allowed the participants to describe positive and negative interactions that they had had with the company in an open manner. Probes were used on occasion to keep the conversation on topic with the research questions (Rubin & Rubin, 1995).

Prior to starting the focus group, the participants were reminded about the goals of the research and signed informed consent documents detailing the purpose of the study. Participants agreed to have the focus group sessions digitally recorded. The focus groups were scheduled for 90 minutes each, and participants were encouraged to speak freely about their experiences and were told that their personal information would be kept confidential and not used in conjunction with any responses.

While on the ship, the researcher transcribed the recordings personally rather than outsourcing the task afterward to someone unfamiliar with these focus groups to allow for more careful thematic analysis of the data (Lindlof, 1995). Validity checks were conducted by asking members to make sure that their words and experiences were accurately transcribed (Lincoln & Guba, 1985). For both projects, member checks were conducted within 15 days of completing the full analysis.

Results

From the introduction period during the focus groups' grand tour question, it was evident that the participants even in the group that had been on the least number of Disney Cruise Line vacations were very loyal and involved with the company. Therefore, it was not a huge surprise to see a range of positive descriptors and stories used to answer the first research question that asked fans to describe their relationship with the Disney Cruise Line. A 57-year-old female from Texas noted, "I've been on cruises with Royal Caribbean, Norwegian, and Princess. Disney is much more expensive, but it's worth it. I'm happiest when sailing with DCL." Even those that were having issues with the current cruise were still loyal to the company. A 39-year-old male from Ohio who had his cabin changed twice during the cruise due to water leaks said, "There are times when I'm mad we've been shuffled from one cabin ... but I've already booked another cruise on board because everything else they do makes it a great experience."

The positive connections to Disney Cruise Lines were not limited to the company, but they also were to specific employees. "We first met [our head waiter] on a cruise three years ago, and we've seen him on a few cruises since then. He remembers us and makes us feel welcome every night when we walk into the dining rooms," said a 52-year-old male from England. The interactions that cruise passengers had with the Disney Cruise Line staff resulted in one female from the Netherlands who was traveling alone saying, "They make me want to come back. They're helpful and so friendly."

Those experiences were not limited to the employees working on the ship. One 70-year-old female from Indiana reflected on her experiences with setting up special meetings and activities with employees at DCL headquarters. "It took some time to get them to respond, but I pestered them til we got our meet-and-greet sessions scheduled," she said. A 63-year-old male passenger with a disability from Massachusetts noted, "I was annoyed that the customer service rep wouldn't answer a simple yes or no question [about boarding policies], so I turned to others on the Facebook group for help."

The Facebook group, which was not sanctioned by the Disney Cruise Lines, wound up being a common point of reference for all of the focus group participants. "I would be lost without everyone's advice. I would have forgotten so many things to pack if you all hadn't mentioned them," said one 46-year-old female from Canada. Turning to the second research question, passengers had their own motivations for bypassing Disney Cruise Line communication channels and activities to ensure the vacation met their needs. A 52-year-old male from New Zealand said, "if it weren't for the Facebook group, I wouldn't have had as much fun as I did. I felt like I knew people before we left San Diego, and I didn't have to wait to make friends on the ship." One 48-year-old male from Illinois added, "Even though I'm traveling with family, I wanted to meet other people on the ship. If I waited til the ship's planned activities to meet people, there wouldn't be much time left. So the (Facebook) group made this a more social group."

The Facebook group also allowed individuals to coordinate special activities that were then forwarded on to Disney Cruise Line employees, who scheduled them on behalf of the passengers. "I could only sign up for one brunch in Palo (an adult-only restaurant) online, but by signing up with the group I broke that DCL rule," said one 39-year-old male from Georgia. Facebook interactions also allowed passengers to plan activities that were not scheduled for the ship. Bartending classes, chocolate and wine tastings, and private tours of the ship were scheduled at the request of the Facebook group. "If I had waited to see what was going to be done on the ship through the normal itineraries, I would have missed out. I'm glad people on Facebook volunteered to organize these events," said one 32-year-old female from Washington.

Other activities that were held included gift exchanges that were set up online through a popular online discussion forum, DISboards.com. At the forum, people signed up to be part of a postcard exchange with other passengers as well as part of fishextender groups, which have individuals dropping off small gifts in baskets that hang outside participating cabins. These small gifts proved to be more valued than the souvenirs sold at many of the shops on the ship. "I know they're small gifts, but the things I got from the people in my fishextender group mean so much to me because they are picked out and hand delivered by people I've grown to know very well on this cruise," said one 46-year-old female from Florida. The DISboards.com discussion forum also allowed people to exchange files of graphics and images that could be printed out as magnets and used to decorate their cabin room doors with Disney-themed magnets rather than buying officially licensed Disney Cruise Line merchandise.

The study's final research question sought to determine whether the members of the Facebook group for this Disney cruise saw themselves as being different from other passengers on the ship. "I felt like I knew more about what to expect and what to do on board than the people I met who weren't in the Facebook group," said one 65-year-old female from Mexico. Another passenger was a bit more blunt; a 29-year-old male from New Jersey said, "Yah, we vacationed the right way. We didn't wait for Disney to give us things to do. We planned what we wanted." This outside planning by the entire Facebook group united them as a public that the Disney Cruise Line had to contend with, but it also resulted in stronger experiences for each passenger. As one 35-year-old female from New Zealand concluded, "I got married on this cruise, so I knew it was going to be great. Facebook let me get to know everyone before the cruise, and having you come to the wedding made a great vacation even better. People that weren't in the Facebook group missed out. I'm sure they had a great cruise, but there's no way they got as much out of the experience as we did."

Discussion

Through the exploration of individuals who describe themselves as fans of the company and highly connected to the company's philosophy and offerings, this project provides evidence that can further be used to refine the notion of a charged public. The passengers on the Disney Cruise Line vacation who established their own communication forums outside of the officially sanctioned Disney communication channels sought to create an experience for themselves that was build around their own needs and wants. The participants all expressed an affinity for Disney Cruise Line, but they did not just want the standard passenger experience. They wanted their vacation to be more meaningful. This motivation resulted in the individuals becoming energized and excited to reach out to one another and mobilize, the key characteristics of a charged public.

In this situation, the charged public used the social web through Facebook and the DISboards.com discussion forum to connect, exchange stories, and create requests for activities to be carried out by Disney Cruise Line. They were not satisfied with having a prepackaged vacation designed by Disney; instead, they wanted to make sure that events they wanted to partake in were actually offered – even if it meant having to pay extra for them and recruiting others to meet a minimum number of participants. Communicating outside of

Disney channels allowed this mobilization to happen. These efforts by the individuals disrupted the typical pattern and processes that the company uses for planning each of its itineraries, but it also provided the company with additional revenue as the private bartending classes, meals and tastings, and tours all were extra activities paid for by the Facebook group members.

The results of the focus group revealed that the Facebook group members knew that they would have a positive experience with Disney Cruise Line as they previously had on other sailings, but they wanted more control of their experiences. Using situational theory of publics terminology, they enacted characteristics of active publics by removing obstacles to participation with their vacation so they could become more involved; however, they also became charged publics in their efforts to move beyond the organization's processes and plans for the cruise by creating their own events and establishing their own communication channels to interact with one another before, during, and after the cruise.

Just as research has shown positive outcomes in terms of revenue and increased engagement as a result of loyalty programs (Liu, 2007; Melnick, & Wann, 2011), organizations also run the risk of creating fans that may disrupt their products and processes because of their high levels of connectivity. Sengupta and Fitzsimons (2000) note that fans of brands can be a double-edged sword for organizations. While fans may have longer relationships with a brand that results in increased revenue and willingness to see the brand through difficult times in an organization's history, they also are more likely to express both positive and negative feelings toward the brand.

The Disney Cruise Line and other companies must devise strategies to tap into charged publics' energies to develop mutually beneficial relationships with these charged individuals. For example, the positively charged actions, such as those expressed by the focus group participants in the current study, can be leveraged to create meaningful experiences for the vacationers while yielding additional revenue streams for the company. Likewise, negatively charged actions by the public must be acknowledged and acted on appropriately so as to not prolong the protests and negative attention by those who do not fall into the charged public.

The situational theory of publics has established a framework that allows organizations to classify their audiences into categories that can predict who is most likely to seek out and process information from the organization. The social web has created an environment where individuals no longer need to go to the organization for information, but can seek it from others and then mobilize to act on that organization or issue. The theory must be further developed to provide for stakeholders' actions that go beyond being reactive to organizational messaging. Charged publics want to be heard and acknowledged by organizations. Charged publics are not simply activists as they can be positively or negatively charged toward an organization or issue. Instead, these charged publics are proactive individuals who want to ensure that their experiences with organizations and issues meet their needs and wants.

In conclusion, this chapter proposes an expansion of the situational theory of publics by introducing the proactive behavior by charged publics. It is important to note that although this study focused on positively charged Disney Cruise Line passengers, the expansion encompasses negatively charged stakeholders who could demand an organization or issue accommodate their perspectives. Research needs to examine the range of emotionally charged individuals and publics in relation to other organizations and issues. Additionally, scales must be created to measure the two new variables that are proposed to be added to the situational theory of publics, the publics' attitudes toward an organization or issue (the emotional charge) as well as the behavioral intentions that cause the disruption to normal processes and programs. These survey measures could then be used alongside the established situational theory of publics scales to determine whether the charged public exists. While the results of these focus groups indicate that the Disney Cruise Line Facebook group members feel they are different from others connected to the company because of their outside interactions and disruption of normal Disney Cruise Line practices, statistical testing should be carried out to test whether there is truly a difference between the theory's current active public and the proposed charged public.

References

Aldoory, L. (2001). Making health communications meaningful for women: Factors that influence involvement. *Journal of Public Relations Research*, 13, 163–185.

Aldoory, L., & Sha, B. (2007). The situational theory of publics: Practical applications, methodological challenges, and theoretical horizons. In E. L. Toth (Ed.), *The future of excellence in public relations and communication management* (pp. 339–355). Mahwah, NJ: Lawrence Erlbaum.

Barnes, N. G., & Jacobsen, S. (2013). Adoption of social media by fast-growing companies: Innovation among the Inc. 500. *Journal of Marketing Development and Competitiveness*, 7(1), 11–17.

Bingham, A. (2012, August 2). Chick-fil-A has "record-setting" sales on appreciation day. *ABC News*. Retrieved online: http://abcnews.go.com/Politics/OTUS/chick-fil-record-setting-sales-appreciationday/story?id=16912978#.UWm30qWTmdI.

Coppa, F. (2014). Fuck yeah, fandom is beautiful. *The Journal of Fandom Studies*, 2(1), 73–82.

Edelman. (2015). 2015 Edelman Trust Barometer. Retrieved online: http://www.edelman.com/2015-edelman-trust-barometer/.

Grunig, J. E. (1989a). Publics, audiences and market segments: Segmentation principles for campaigns. In C. T. Salmon (Ed.), *Information campaigns: Balancing social values and social change* (pp. 199–223). Beverly Hills, CA: Sage.

Grunig, J. E. (1989b). Sierra Club study shows who becomes activists. *Public Relations Review*, 15(3), 3–24.

Grunig, J. E. (1997). A situational theory of publics: Conceptual history, recent challenges and new research. In D. Moss, T. MacManus, & D. Vercic (Eds.), *Public relations research: An international perspective* (pp. 3–38). London: International Thomson Business Press.

Grunig, J. E., & Hunt, T. (1984). *Managing public relations*. New York: Holt, Rinehart, and Winston.

Hatch, M. J., & Schultz, M. (2010). Toward a theory of brand co-creation with implications for brand governance. *Journal of Brand Management*, 17, 590–604.

Jahn, B., & Kunz, W. (2012). How to transform consumers into fans of your brand. *Journal of Service Management*, 23(3), 344–361.

Lacey, R., & Morgan, R. M. (2008). Customer advocacy and the impact of B2B loyalty programs. *Journal of Business & Industrial Marketing*, 24(1), 3–13.

Lincoln, Y. S., & Guba, E. G. (1985). *Naturalistic inquiry*. Beverly Hills, CA: Sage.

Lindlof, T. R. (1995). *Qualitative communication research methods*. Thousand Oaks, CA: Sage.

Lipsman, A., Mudd, G., Rich, M., & Bruich, S. (2012). The power of "like": How brands reach (and influence) fans through social media marketing. *Journal of Advertising Research*, 52(1), 40–52.

Liu, Y. (2007). The long-term impact of loyalty programs on consumer purchase behavior and loyalty. *Journal of Marketing*, 71(4), 19–35.

McCall, M., & Vorhees, C. (2010). The drivers of loyalty program success: An organizing framework and research agenda. *Cornell Hospitality Quarterly*, 51(1), 35–52.

Melnick, M. J., & Wann, D. L. (2011). An examination of sport fandom in Australia: Socialization, team identification, and fan behavior. *International Review for the Sociology of Sport*, 46(4), 456–470.0

Pressgrove, G. (2013). Making stewardship meaningful for nonprofits: Stakeholder motivations, attitudes, loyalty and behaviors (Doctoral dissertation). University of South Carolina, Columbia, SC.

Pulizzi, J. (2015). B2C content marketing: 2015 benchmarks, budgets, and trends – North America. Retrieved online: http://contentmarketinginstitute.com/wp-content/uploads/2014/10/2015_B2C_Research.pdf.

Rubin, H., & Rubin, I. (1995). *Qualitative interviewing: The art of hearing data*. Thousand Oaks, CA: Sage.

Sengupta, J., & Fitzsimons, G. J. (2000). The effects of analyzing reasons for brand preferences: Disruption or reinforcement? *Journal of Marketing Research*, 37(3), 318–330.

Sha, B. (2006). Cultural identity in the segmentation of publics: An emerging theory of intercultural public relations. *Journal of Public Relations Research*, 18, 45–65.

Uncles, M. D., Dowling, G. R., & Hammond, K. (2003). Customer loyalty and customer loyalty programs. *Journal of Consumer Marketing*, 20(4), 294–316.

Weberling, B., Waters, R. D., & Tindall, N. T. J. (2012). The role of text messaging in public relations: Testing the situational theory of publics for mobile giving campaigns. In S. C. Duhé (Ed.), *New media and public relations*, 2nd Edition (pp. 189–197). New York: Peter Lang.

Part IV

Stakeholder engagement and communication in traditional fan spaces

17 The transmedia practices of *Battlestar Galactica*

Studying the industry, stars, and fans

Melanie Bourdaa, Bertha Chin and Nicolle Lamerichs

Introduction

The cult success of the re-imagined *Battlestar Galactica* (2004–2009; hereafter *BSG*) has led to a dedicated fanbase. Even long after the series has finished, additional storylines still flourish in graphic novels and other media products. The series repositioned science fiction and its sub-genre, space opera as major genres in television. Its political and cultural themes, visual aesthetics and serial storytelling gave the series a cult status and a solid fanbase (Bourdaa, 2012). Moreover, the series is built as an entire universe. This sense of worldness is still conveyed on different media platforms.

This chapter will focus on *BSG* as a franchise that adheres to processes of "transmedia storytelling," as discussed by Henry Jenkins in his seminal work *Convergence Culture* (Jenkins, 2006). Transmedia, or augmented storytelling (Bourdaa, 2012) refers to an extensive narrative spread across different media platforms. Ideally, the different parts of the narrative are told in individual media, such as graphic novels, cartoons, or games.

Different media platforms are integral to the storytelling, world-building, and narration of *BSG*. The relationship between fans, media professionals, and the media text, however, is more complex than the idea of transmedia storytelling suggests. We show this complexity by focusing on unique examples that are related to the series, but also move away from official media channels that are exclusive to the television network. Our studies not only focused on how the industry extended *BSG*, but also on the public relationships between actors and fans, as well as the reception by fans themselves.

Our chapter consists of three parts. First, we will start by exploring the different tie-ins of *BSG*. Then we will examine two case studies where consumer and producer relationships are redefined. The first case study explores recent Twitter messages of *BSG* actors. As a large ensemble show, actors who play secondary characters such as Chief Galen Tyrol and Karl "Helo" Agathon have developed their own fan followings. These celebrities can be considered as "subcultural celebrities," "mediated figures who are treated as famous only by and for their fan audience" (Hills, 2003, p. 61). As such, the actors sometimes cater to their social media following interchangeably between being "in character," and through their own "celebrity persona." Through social media, the actors purposefully extend the story of *BSG*, or juxtapose it with their new work, suggesting that its characters and story continue as fans' memories of their characters live on through how they interact with the actors.

The second case study focuses on the board game of *BSG* (Fantasy Flight Games, 2008). The game proved that the translation from a television series to a board game can be a perfect match. This co-operative board game, with three expansion packs, has received many prizes and has been praised by critics and fans alike. By working with the potential in *BSG*, and by focusing on its central themes such as mistrust and betrayal, the game offers new readings of the television series and its latent possibilities. Most strikingly, it puts the player or fan in a position of control and power over the original text. By making choices and by interacting carefully with the game, players can weave their own *BSG* story and are put in the position of producers rather than consumers. Through the game, players can move away from the canon of the television text and explore its latent possibilities.

We argue that transmedia storytelling is not necessarily a coherent process, but a complex dynamic that is constantly developed by fans and the media industry. The extension of a narrative is not only a process of coordinated planning by the industry, but a practice to which fans and professionals, such as actors, actively contribute. *BSG* has gone a long way and its story still continues on venues where we least expect it.

The development of television and transmedia storytelling

The millennial television landscape is defined by changes in the television industries that led to the development of transmedia strategies. *BSG* must be read in light of three developments in television production, writing, and reception.

Firstly, emerging technologies such as the Internet and the development of social media drastically changed the television landscape. Fan interactivity was included in production strategies and television became a medium that relied on the activity of its audiences (Gillan, 2010). NBC's *Heroes* (2006–2010) is an early example of a transmedia production that enriched storylines from television with tie-in websites for the characters, an ongoing collaborative fan fiction, an interactive game and web comics that deepen the background histories of the characters (Hassapopoulou, 2010). Today many American television shows have narrative extensions, which are developed through websites and social media. Examples include the Pawnee website of *Parks and Recreation* (2009–2015), the Massive Dynamic website of *Fringe* (2008–2013), the FBI files of *Dexter* (2006–2013) or the ARG and the Online University of *Lost* (2004–2010).

Secondly, recent television series have been developing what Jason Mittell (2006) calls "narrative complexity." Television shows increasingly include seriality in their writing. They do this on several levels: firstly, production strategies such as cliffhangers at the end of episodes or seasons; secondly, more complex characters; and thirdly, a re-working of existing genres. These techniques rely on active audiences to decode them:

> You cannot simply watch these programs as an unmediated window to a realistic story world into which you might escape; rather, narratively complex television demands you pay attention to the window frames, asking you to reflect on how it provides partial access to the diegesis and how the panes of glass distort your vision of the unfolding action.
>
> (Mittell, 2006, p. 38)

Finally, television has encouraged participation and included fan cultures in their practices. As Henry Jenkins (2006) noted, the current media culture is a participatory culture, in which fans and producers are part of similar spheres of production and reception. This ties in with a renewed appreciation and validation of fan cultures by showrunners and marketers. Fans are an expert audience who perform activities and create transformative works in organized communities of practice or interest groups. These organized forms of fan cultures are also called "fandom." They are willing to interact with their shows and search the multiple media platforms to find clues and information on the shows.

In the context of media and digital convergence, one strategy of production stands out as particularly engaging for audiences, namely "transmedia storytelling." Henry Jenkins was first to coin this term in relation to the franchise of *The Matrix*. He explains that *The Matrix* is "entertainment for the age of media convergence, integrating multiple texts to create a narrative so large that it cannot be contained within a single medium" (Jenkins, 2006, p. 95). The most recent definition that Jenkins has offered of transmedia storytelling is "a process where integral elements of a fiction get dispersed systematically across multiple delivery channels for the purpose of creating a unified and coordinated entertainment experience. Ideally, each medium makes its own unique contribution to the unfolding of the story" (Jenkins, 2011).

Thus, technological and cultural changes paved the way for transmedia storytelling. These changes led to a more participatory culture in which fans consume, share, and spread what they like throughout virtual communities, fan sites or social networks. The active role of fans in this participatory culture implies that power relationships are shifting and becoming more complicated as fans now have more direct interaction with producers and the actors via social media networks. Fans also have more significant power in the creative industries, as our case studies will demonstrate. In particular, they redefine the production of a show, the profession of actors, cast, and crew, and the storytelling process.

Transmedia strategies in *Battlestar Galactica*

In *BSG*, human civilization has migrated from its home world Kobol to a group of planets called the Twelve Colonies. They are engaged in a war against the Cylons, robots created to support them in their daily chores. The Cylons rebel and commit genocide against mankind. In contrast to the original series from the 1970s, the Cylons have evolved to look like humans and have been living on the colonies for a long time to infiltrate key positions for their plan. This re-imagined version is more complex and frames the series in a post-9/11 American society. While the theme is still survival, the series also interrogates what makes us human. During four seasons, showrunner Ronald D. Moore and his team developed storylines and created complex characters: humans and Cylons alike.

The success of the show can largely be contributed to the vast storyworld that the showrunners and the production team developed. They created an extended universe around the show, adding stories and plots on different media platforms. Suzanne Scott (2008) writes about these transmedia strategies:

> BSG has aimed unparalleled wealth of fan-oriented content at its audiences and, whether one chooses to view this as a dialogic departure from the producer/consumer binary or merely a tech-savvy marketing ploy, it is an integrated media model that is rapidly gaining popularity.
>
> (p. 210)

These tie-in extensions pursued three aims: to give more depth to the characters, to fill time lapses in the production of the series, and to focus on different points of view.

To deepen the characters, the tie-ins often explored the past of the humans and the origins of the Cylons. For example, in collaboration with Dynamite Entertainment, Syfy created comics devoted to the past of characters of the shows, specifically Kara and Helo, Adama, Zarek, and Gaius Baltar. To explore the origins of the Cylons, Dynamite Entertainment produced a comic book entitled *The Final Five*. This comic focuses on how the Cylons created the Final Five − five of the twelve humanoid models of the Cylons whose identity was lost to the Cylon collective. The story explores why they wiped their memories from this period. Another example of how transmedia deepens characterization is the web series *The Face of the Enemy* (2008–2009). It focuses on the supporting character Felix Gaeta and explores his homosexuality and the motivations for his future actions in the show.

When one of the authors of this chapter, Melanie Bourdaa, interviewed comic author Brendan Jerwa, he told her that they worked closely with the showrunners to bring coherence to the whole universe. He explained in the interview: "It is my understanding that the comics were passed through Mr. Moore's office, and they were certainly vetted by Syfy and Universal" (Brandon Jerwa, Interview with Melanie Bourdaa, email, 6/3/2014). He emphasized that transmedia strategies are useful to give a new breath to the universe and storylines and to continue to expand the storyworld of the show.

While deepening the characters was one reason to create these tie-ins, the second objective was thus to fill in some time gaps before the very beginning of the show or in between seasons, during the hiatus. During the Hollywood writers' strike, the producers created the previously mentioned web series *The Face of The Enemy* to post on Syfy's official website and to give some complementary materials to the show. Prior to this series, they had already produced the web series *The Resistance* (2006) which offered additional information on what happened on New Caprica that formed the Resistance. We learn how the Resistance organized itself around Saul and Tyrol and how two characters are going to choose their side.

The producers and showrunners also tried to give some new points of view on the stories. The comic book *Battlestar Galactica: Ghosts* (2008), for example, offers a new perspective on the war focusing on brand new characters on a new Battlestar. This strategy, which diverts from a "what if" scenario, explores possibilities and alternative universes: what happened to other survivors? How are they coping with the Cylon attacks? Similarly, the telefilm *The Plan* (2009) re-tells the story from the Cylon perspective. The producers took the plot from the first and second seasons and re-wrote the story from the Cylons' points of view. By doing this, the writers can fill certain plot holes and answer various questions that were raised throughout the series. The telefilm *Razor* (2006) deepens events from the second season by adopting the point of view of the crew of the Pegasus.

Overall, *BSG* can be defined as a series with augmented storytelling potential. Each tie-in offers some add-ons for fans without alienating new potential audiences. The coherence of this narrative universe, maintained through the showrunners as gatekeepers, plays an important part in the development of narrative arcs and characters. We believe, however, that transmedia strategies are also adopted by other participants than these official teams. In our case studies, we focus on actors and fans as agents that contribute to the world-building.

Actors as world-builders

As a first case study, we focus on actors from *BSG* and how they extend the universe beyond the television screen. Specifically, we explore the ways in which they present their public persona to fans on social media, as well as how fans react to their presence on the platform. These interactions play off each other since the actors and the characters they embody, become almost one and the same. This is even the case when the show is not airing on television anymore and the actors have moved to other projects.

Before the proliferation of social media networks, and celebrities' presence on Twitter and Facebook, we often think about celebrity culture in the context of mediation (Turner, 2010). News and information about the celebrity are gathered via paratextual outlets such as entertainment news press, official press releases from studios, networks, and the like. Fans watch interviews with celebrities on talk shows and premieres to get a sense of who they are and what they are like. Now, however, fans can tweet celebrities directly, or leave messages on Facebook profiles to share their love and appreciation (or hate) of the actor's work.

This study specifically extends Bertha Chin's work on social media and celebrity culture (Chin, 2010 and forthcoming). Nick Muntean and Anne Helen Petersen argue that "celebrity tweeting has been equated with the assertion of the authentic celebrity voice; ... [it is] the privileged channel to the star him/herself" (2009, n.p.). Twitter also offers the "possibility of interaction" (2011, p. 144), argue Alice Marwick and danah boyd, so some fans tweet the celebrities they love because there's always the possibility that one's tweets will be acknowledged or responded to, while a celebrity follow raises the profile and status of the fan in fandom. This is not necessarily one-sided, as Marwick and boyd go on to argue that celebrities who have a social media presence also have to present a seemingly authentic and "intimate image of the self" (2011, p. 140). They also have to meet fan expectations in this presentation, as well as using the platform to maintain important relationships with other entertainment industry professionals and fans who help run and maintain their fansites.

These so-called "parasocial" relationships take a unique form in fandom. In 2003, Matt Hills proposed the concept of subcultural celebrity, which he described as "mediated figures who are treated as famous ... by and for their fan audience" (p. 61) to explore cult TV celebrities whom cult TV fans may consistently have personal contact with, through conventions, signings, and other personal appearances. Actors like Leonard Nimoy (*Star Trek*, 1966–1969) and Misha Collins (*Supernatural*, 2005–), for instance, while not considered international stars in the vein of actors like George Clooney, are highly respected in scifi and cult TV media fandoms. Both Nimoy and Collins gain dedicated fan followings from their performances, with Nimoy being re-introduced as Mr. Spock, the iconic character he played in the original *Star Trek* in J.J. Abrams's reboot film in 2009. These cult and scifi TV actors continue to play the iconic roles they are often known for at fan conventions and at times, that performance extends to social media. They are referred to as their characters years after shows end and they have moved on to other roles. But there is also a sense that fans' love for the characters, their "sense of ownership" over them transfers over to the actors as well.

In the context of *BSG*, several actors, namely Aaron Douglas (Tyrol), Edward James Olmos (Adama) and Tahmoh Penikett (Helo), are prolific Twitter users; their interaction with fans or their tweets at times embodying the characters they play on screen. Olmos frequently ends his tweets, particularly on social issues, with the show's mantra, "So Say We All" (2014, 2015). Douglas probably resembles the character that he plays, Chief Tyrol, more than any of the other cast members. He frequently uses the word "frak" (2010) and refers to Tyrol while tweeting (2014). It is almost as if the characters that the actors embody have become extension of themselves, particularly when interacting with fans or presenting themselves on social media.

Fans similarly reciprocate this extension of character to the celebrity-self, as tweets to actors are also replaced with character names. For example, fans lamented the string of villainous and morally ambiguous roles Tahmoh Penikett played post-*Battlestar* in high-profile guest-starring roles for it clashed with the heroic characterization of Helo, who always had an astute sense of right and wrong. Fans will also go on to promote Penikett's current work by referring directly to Helo, using the pronoun "our" (She's All Nerd, 2014), suggesting a sense of ownership fans feel towards these beloved characters.

This recalls a study Matt Hills and Rebecca Williams conducted in 2005, where they suggest that fans' engagement with Spike, a popular character in *Buffy the Vampire Slayer* and *Angel* stimulated "fan adoration, fantasy and interest" (p. 346) for both the actor and the character. Hills and Williams argue that fans are not merely fans of the character or the actor, but of both, made possible by the subcultural celebrity status of James Marsters, who plays Spike. Likewise, fans who identify actors like Penikett and Douglas by their character names exhibit the same affections, borne out of years of familiarity and a sense of intimacy created through the television screen with the characters they play onscreen.

In this sense, we can argue that world-building is collaborative: fans see the actors as their characters just as the actors embody the essence of their characters in their public persona. This suggests that the notion of world-building extends beyond industry-sanctioned texts such as digital games, comics, and web series; that actors' interactions on social media, even for post-show fandoms, help to strengthen the characters' presence for the fans.

Reworking the narrative through the board game

BSG is a show that asks its audiences to participate and think through the plot. The suspicions among the crew, and the Cylon revelations, often led to fan speculation. This kind of behavior has been described as "forensic fandom" (Mittell, 2009). Fans theorize, speculate, and interpret the clues that a series provides them and function as detectives of sorts. This mode of fandom is interpretive, and relies on what Jenkins has often called "collective intelligence" (Jenkins, 2006, pp. 25–59). Such fans operate as a knowledge community that seeks consensus and theorizes media content itself. Fandom in this sense is a type of play, an unrestricted and free activity that relies on puzzle-solving.

While television formats and their audiences are increasingly playful, there is one medium that is particularly outstanding in shaping play through rules and mechanics, namely games. The *BSG* board game (Fantasy Flight Games, 2008) has been met with critical acclaim, having received various prizes and nominations in international awards for board games, and has an average rating of 7.84/10 (February 26, 2015) on the popular site BoardGameGeek.

The game manages to convey similar tensions and themes as the show. Players have to work together to survive, but there is always an element of mistrust, because there are Cylons on board. The rules mediate themes that make the television series exceptional and engaging to watch. Like the show, *BSG* revolves around secrecy, deception, and mistrust. *BSG* is a team game, with the added mystery that who is in which team is kept secret. Each player is put in one of the teams, either Cylon or human, and his or her identity is revealed at the start of the game. Players get a loyalty card which they can never show openly.

Each team has a specific objective. Human players are trying to find the map to earth, and reach Kobol, while Cylon players want to annihilate the human race. Players work together with their team to win, but first they have to find out who is on their side. As the tagline says, this is "a game of survival, politics, and betrayal." The character roles that players can adopt closely resemble those of the show and come with unique abilities and skills. Players re-enact existing characters from the television show, but can mix them up in new ways. For instance, the admiral character can be Adama, Tigh, or even Helo. Players do not have to adhere to the canon or storyline as it enfolds in the series itself.

The goals are fairly straightforward. For humans, the key objective is keeping their resources, which consist of food, morale, and population. There will be many events, like attacks or riots, that will affect these resources. At each turn, a player will struggle to keep the resources afloat. Similar to the show, the crew faces the deplenishment of food and a decrease in population. There are also Cylon agents that can sabotage actions of the crew. A crucial theme in this game is distrust, which will inform how the players resolve certain situations.

Halfway through the game, more sleeper agents awaken. New loyalty cards are distributed and the Cylons can now start their full-on attack on the *Galactica*. The winning conditions are easy: Cylons destroy the survivors by infiltrating the ships, or by destroying their morale. Humans need to make sure that the crew survives by maintaining their resources and morale, as well as reach Kobol.

Theoretically, the game can be understood as an adaptation of the show but it also has medium-specific qualities as a game. This is a game that does not fit the transmedia storytelling model. Though it is a product of the show, which clearly features the same characters and themes, it does not fit into the universe coherently and it has not been coordinated to expand the storyline. Through the game, *BSG* fans can play out different scenarios and alternative universes that relate to the television show. In other words, the game is about envisioning possibilities, rather than about fidelity to the narrative. Depending on the choices of players, a session can be much darker than the television show itself.

The concept that perhaps best fits this game is that of the "transmedial world" (Tosca & Klastrup, 2011). This concept was coined by the Scandinavian scholars Klastrup and Tosca to examine the online game of *Lord of the Rings*, which is similar to the *BSG* game in that it diverges from the source text. It allowed fans primarily to be in that world and contribute to it. In other words, the transmedial world model theorizes world-building across media platforms. Unlike transmedia storytelling, it does not assume that these narrative instances create a coherent storyline but instead argues that they provide a different perspective of a world. As Klastrup and Tosca write: "A distinct characteristic of transmedial worlds is that audience and designers share a mental image of the 'worldness' (distinguished features of its universe)" (2011, p. 48).

The authors describe worldness further through topos, mythos, and ethos, roughly translated as the fictional space and geography, the myths and history of the world, and its ethics that also underline politics and decision making. The game translates these elements clearly by zooming into the storyworld and its themes rather than plot, by exploring the lore of *BSG,* and finally, by focusing on the norms and morale. Especially in this survival story, the stakes are high and the norms differ from what we would find acceptable in everyday life. Ethics in this case is turned into an explicit game play mechanic by emphasizing the importance of morale as a resource. The humans can lose in battle, but they can also lose their morale and then they are doomed as they cannot stick together anymore.

Unlike the television show, the game has multiple outcomes and lots of variety. In each session, there will be different Cylons, humans, and even traitors that have to be faithful to the other side. The possibility of new alliances, crews, and character histories makes each session into a unique story. Through the board game, fans and non-fans can explore alternative scenarios to the television show and play out the plot differently. The game teases out the possibilities of the show. This storytelling process empowers the fans and allows them to envision this storyworld long after the show has finished.

Conclusion

While *BSG* ended several years ago, the story is still re-enacted on different media platforms. We have argued that transmedia storytelling is not only an industrial and coordinated process, but a complex dynamic that is partly facilitated by audiences and continued by media professionals. In our research we found that transmediality is a model that facilitates storytelling but also unique performances and spaces of play. The model enables different actors (e.g. fans, actors) in the current media landscape to rework and perform media content.

In our case studies we saw clear forms of extension and play, which do not clearly divide between professional and audience roles. Firstly, media professionals benefit from transmedia connections and performing on different media channels. Actors, for instance, "stay in character" on Twitter not as a playful way of addressing their fans, but also to call them to action and motivate them to contribute to sociopolitical causes. Secondly, through transmedia strategies, fans can also become active media producers and characters by re-enacting and revisiting the *BSG* narrative. These case studies showed that specific transmedia texts, such as games and social media messages, can reinforce a sense of ownership over the original media text.

BSG has a universe and fandom that extends well beyond its official time and space of production. Actors and fans still perform and rework this story on different media channels. This also means that the creative industries still profit from the franchise, if they preserve interest through consistent public interactions with fans.

Bibliography

BattlestarGalactica, Board Game, BoardGameGeek. (2015, February 26). Retrieved April 25, 2015, from https://boardgamegeek.com/boardgame/37111/battlestar-galactica.

Bourdaa, M. (2012). Transmedia: between augmented storytelling and immersive practices. Retrieved April 25, 2015, from http://www.inaglobal.fr/en/digital-tech/a rticle/transmedia-between-augmented-storytelling-and-immersive-practices?tq=7.

Chin, B. (2010). *From textual poachers to textual gifters: Exploring fan community and celebrity in the field of fan cultural production*. Cardiff: Cardiff University Press.

Chin, B. (forthcoming). When hated characters talk back: Twitter, hate and fan–celebrity interaction. In M. Click (Ed.), *Dislike, hate, and anti-fandom in the digital age*. New York: NYU Press.

Douglas, A. [theaarondouglas]. (2010, June 24). Iron Maiden tonight baby! FRAK yeah! Anyone want a tweeted pic? :-) [Tweet]. Retrieved from https://twitter.com/theaa rondouglas/status/16951913058.

Douglas, A. [theaarondouglas]. (2014, May 11). Tyron sent me a text to share with everyone. Happy Mothers Day from Chief ... who never had one [Tweet]. Retrieved from https://twitter.com/theaarondouglas/status/465554984247894016.

Hills, M. (2003). Recognition in the eyes of the relevant beholder: Representing "subcultural celebrity" and cult TV fan cultures. *Mediactive*, 2, 59–73.

Hills, M. (2006). Not just another powerful elite? When media fans become subcultural celebrities. In S. Holmes & S. Redmond (Eds.), *Framing celebrity* (pp. 101–118). London: Routledge.

Hills, M., & Williams, R. (2005). It's all my interpretation: Reading Spike through the "subcultural celebrity" of James Marsters. *European Journal of Cultural Studies*, 8(3), 345–365.

Gillan, J. (2010). *Television and new media: Must-click TV*. London: Taylor & Francis.

Hassapopoulou, M. (2010). Spoiling heroes, enhancing our viewing pleasure: NBC's Heroes and the re-shaping of the televisual landscape. In H. Urbanski (Ed.), *Writing and the digital generation: Essays on new media rhetoric* (pp. 45–57). Jefferson, NC: McFarland.

Jenkins, H. (2006). *Convergence culture: Where old and new media collide*. New York: New York University Press.

Jenkins, H. (2011). Transmedia 202: Further reflections. Retrieved November 17, 2015 from http://henryjenkins.org/2011/08/defining_transmedia_further_re.html.

Jerwa, B. (2014, June 3). Melanie Bourdaa interviews Brendan Jerwa. Email.

Marwick, A. E., & boyd, danah (2011). To see and be seen: Celebrity practice on Twitter. *Convergence: The International Journal of Research into New Media Technologies*, 17(2), 139–158.

Mittell, J. (2006). Narrative complexity in contemporary American television. *The Velvet Light Trap*, 58, 29–40.

Mittell, J. (2009). Lost in a great story: Evaluation in narrative television (and television studies). In R. Pearson (Ed.), *In reading "Lost": Perspectives on a hit television show* (pp. 119–138). London: I.B. Tauris.

Muntean, N., & Petersen, A. H. (2009). Celebrity Twitter: Strategies of intrusion and disclosure in the age of technoculture. *M/C Journal* 12(5). Available at: http://journal. media-culture.org.au/index.php/mcjournal/article/viewArticle/194

Olmos, E. J. [edwardjolmos]. (2014, 25 November). Their about to announce the grand jury decision on Michael Brown. Remember. Non violent social disobedience is key.

#sosayweall [Tweet]. Retrieved from https://twitter.com/edwardjolmos/status/537064375073247232.

Olmos, E. J. [edwardjolmos]. (2015, January 25). Water & Power is now on Hulu. vudu.com/movies/Movies_ ... hope you like it an original! SoSayWeAll [Tweet]. Retrieved from https://twitter.com/edwardjolmos/status/559417044354232320.

Scott, S. (2008). Authorised resistance: Is fan production frakked? In T. Potter & C. W. Marshall (Eds.), *Cylons in America: Critical studies in Battlestar Galactica* (pp. 210–223). New York: Continuum.

She's All Nerd [ShesAllNerd]. (2014, March 5). Hey BSG fans: Check out our lovely Helo (Tahmoh Penikett) in this trailer for a short film that he's done. It's...fb.me/2GKxp3fQR [Tweet]. Retrieved from https://twitter.com/ShesAllNerd/status/441011853515182080.

Tosca, S., & Klastrup, L. (2011). When fans become players: LOTRO in a transmedial world. In T. Krzywinska, E. MacCallum-Stewart, & J. Parsler (Eds.), *Ring bearers: The Lord of the Rings online as intertextual narrative* (pp. 46–69). Manchester: Manchester University Press.

Turner, G. (2010). Approaching celebrity studies. *Celebrity Studies* 1(1), 11–20.

18 Structuration and fan communities in sport

A public relations perspective

Justin A. Walden

In 2015, revenue relating to the global sport industry was expected to reach $145 billion (PWC, 2011). Although the United States is the largest sport market in the world, Latin America, Europe, and Asia have all experienced varying rates of expansion in sport-related revenue (PWC, 2011). Even after the global economic downturn of several years ago, the market for sport goods, activities, and services appears strong. Several important factors are driving this growth, including corporate sponsorship of events, attendance at events, merchandise sales, lucrative television contracts, and consumer participation in sports and related recreational activities. From the consumer's perspective, research indicates that sport fandom is a time-intensive endeavor. This is particularly true when it comes to fans' time spent per week consuming sport content in the United States (average of 7.7 hours per week); Great Britain (7.5 hours per week); Spain (10.1 hours per week); and Indonesia (12.3 hours per week), according to research from Kantar Media Sport. At the start of this discussion, two intertwined observations must be offered, even if they are perhaps obvious: sport is a big business across the globe and many fans make sport spectatorship an important part of their lives.

Scholars from multiple areas (including sports management, psychology, marketing, and linguistics) have explored the various dimensions of sport fandom and consumers' recreation and leisure activities. The communication discipline has also joined in this discussion, notably with the launch of a new journal, *Communication & Sport* in 2013. Yet public relations scholarship has largely overlooked this area (L'Etang, 2006, 2013). However, several recent developments suggest this is changing. L'Etang's *Sports Public Relations* and Hopwood, Kitchin, and Skinner's *Sport Public Relations and Communication* are two recent books on this topic, while Hutchins and Tindall (this book and a special issue of *PRism*) have edited volumes on fandom in which sport and public relations are explored in-depth.

As scholarly interest in sport grows, a deeper understanding is needed with respect to organizations' management of stakeholders and how public relations practitioners contribute to the development of the sport industry as a set of culturally situated phenomena. In particular, scholars should investigate how sport is communicated, the centrality of sport to public culture, and the strategic intent involved in managing sport spectacles, organizations, and celebrity involvement in sport (L'Etang, 2006, 2013). Theories and research that emerge from the public relations discipline may capture the complexities involved in organizational communication and stakeholder outreach. Sport also offers a lens to understand public relations professionals' roles as organizational relationship builders and cultural intermediaries. A similar point was addressed in a foundational article on sport by Jacquie L'Etang in 2006: "Since sport is a rapidly expanding world business embedded in cultures as social practice and as a form of communication, it provides a domain to explore PR's cultural and symbolic role in the commodification of lifestyles, values and relationships" (p. 388). There have been recent calls to examine the social construction of public relations practice (Edwards & Hodges, 2011) and the social construction of individual identities within public relations (Vardeman-Winter, Tindall, & Jiang, 2013). Studies of sport organizations, sport public relations, and sport fandom can advance these discussions.

The goals of this chapter are twofold. I want to briefly review the extant literature on sport fandom, online communities, and public relations. There are common threads between public relations and fan studies that have not yet been explored. Since sport fandom is a relatively new subject of academic study and since public relations research in this area is likewise emerging, it is helpful to consider where public relations theory intersects with the literature on sport and fandom. This chapter also advocates for a holistic treatment of fan culture and fan behavior from the organization's perspective with respect to *where* fandom is cultivated. Along with physical spaces (Kraszewski, 2008), sport fandom is increasingly situated within digitally mediated spheres and online communities. Scholars, particularly those with an expertise in public relations and organizational communication, should examine the relationship between online community participation and the development of fan identities. We need rich and multi-faceted considerations of the ways in which fans participate in multiple online and offline sport networks and how organizations contribute to the development of sport culture. A literature review suggests that there are unexplored tensions at the intersection of organizational behavior and strategic communication and fan-driven participatory culture in sport. To help push this discussion forward, this chapter concludes with suggestions to guide future scholarship.

Situating fandom studies

A number of trade and scholarly commentaries highlight the intense and lasting relationships that fans develop with teams. Sponsor-generated content in *Adweek* glowingly talked about the "passion of the fan" and noted that sport enthusiasts "want to talk about sports and be part of the active fan community" (Feil, 2013). Indeed, sport fandom has quasi-religious properties given sport's ability to foster individual commitment to greater social units (Serazio, 2012). Fans become connected to certain teams and players, and with this sense of connection and the routine of fandom, sport becomes embedded in the fabric of communities. Extending this beyond a particular team or city, sport can also unify nations, promote social change and affect the national psyche (Curtin, & Gaither, 2007). Given its reach, the industry of sport is intertwined with commerce and culture, politics and religion, education and entertainment, morality and ethics, science and technology (Gantz, 2012). To put it simply: "Sports matters because it is a multibillion dollar industry driven by tens of millions of fans who open their hearts – and wallets – to follow their favorite players and teams" (Gantz, 2012, p. 177). Yet it is not simply about opening up one's wallet to purchase shirts, posters, and subscriptions to sport or league-focused cable television channels.

Sport is patterned into peoples' lives on a consistent basis and as people participate in various sport fandom processes, they can develop and maintain interpersonal relationships in a variety of venues. As Sifferlin (2014) argued, teams provide a sense of community and connectedness in our increasingly isolated world. Sport fandom is habitually enacted and performed in fans' lives, from checking event scores on a daily basis to participating as spectators in annual (Super Bowl) or quadrennial (Olympics, FIFA World Cup) spectacles. As sport follows seasons, so too do fans' consuming and participating behaviors. There is always *something* on television, and another event to look forward to. Sport, for many fans, is a comfortable place of routine and a constant source of entertainment and social interaction.

Despite the prevalence of sport in society and the prominent role that sport has in individuals' lives, the scholarly literature still has not fully explored how fan affiliations with sport teams (and other sport organizations) develop (Dixon, 2011). There is, however, a broad umbrella of fan studies that helps us understand the ways in which people relate to each other and how we interact with mediated texts in our digitized world (Gray, Sandvoss, & Harrington, 2007). Fandom is typically defined by a person's engagement with media texts such as a sporting blog or a film/television series. This engagement features regular interactions with (and readings of) popular culture material and involves varying degrees of content co-creation and appropriation and information sharing by fans. An important component of these discussions is fans' involvement in participatory culture, which features low barriers to artistic expression and civic engagement, support for creating and sharing fan-created content, and informal mentorship whereby experienced participants share knowledge with novices (Jenkins, Ford, & Green, 2009).

Much of the seminal fan studies research followed the advent and popularization of fan communities on the Internet in the early 1990s (Reagin & Rubenstein, 2011). The first wave of fan studies focused on cultural power struggles and how fans appropriated popular media content (Gray, et al., 2007). Building upon this, a significant body of early fandom research examined agency and fans' appropriation and refashioning of media texts in resistance to corporate ownership of intellectual property (Murray, 2004; Scodari, 2003). The second wave of fan studies considered the development of social and cultural hierarchies within fan communities; rather than countering existing social hierarchies, fans in this next set of studies were seen as agents to maintain economic, social, and cultural norms. As fan studies have evolved, "fans have become an ever more integral part of life in modern societies ... and fandom has grown into a truly global phenomenon" (Gray, et al., 2007, p. 9). The literature has also seen a shift that builds on the two initial stages of fan studies to a third stage that considers the relationships between fans' selves and their fan objects (Gray, et al., 2007).

Scholarly definitions of fandom tend to emphasize the process of being a fan. For example, fandom develops when groups of individuals form collective or subcultural identities around shared tastes (Brough, & Shresthova, 2012). Another way to view fandom is to consider it the regular and emotionally involved consumption of a popular narrative or text (Sandvoss, 2005). Stated another way, fans are active participants in popular culture (Reagin & Rubenstein, 2011). Implicit in these definitions is that fandom is actively maintained via social interaction and consumption of cultural content. Developed and encouraged through one-on-one or group interactions, fandom can be viewed as a social process that one experiences through their engagement with a particular media text. Yet fans are not passive consumers of content. Fans participate in shared meaning making and share collective intelligence (Jenkins, 2007). Put another way, fans are "individuals who engage deeply with, and often assert their identity through, popular culture content" (Brough & Shresthova, 2012, para. 3).

The introduction of organizational interests into the fandom realm is viewed as problematic by some scholars. This concern is seen in commentary from pioneering fan studies scholar Henry Jenkins in 2007: "We should certainly avoid celebrating a process that commodifies fan cultural production and sells it back to us with a considerable markup" (p. 362). Even as they accommodate consumer demands, companies seek to train them to behave in ways that benefit their own interests (Jenkins, 2007; Morrissey, 2013). Jenkins et al. (2013, p. 36) further highlight the inherent tension that exists in the cultural industries with respect to fandom: "Corporate interests will never fully align with those of participatory culture, and frictions will frequently emerge." For example, this conflict is highlighted in the area of copyright ownership. Murray (2004) asked a question that still has not been answered when it comes to fan-organization interaction: whether (fan-centered) viral marketing generates complementary publicity for a product/good or whether this publicity dilutes a company's valuable intellectual property assets. Companies struggle to retain control over their copyrighted works as they actively cultivate fan (content-creating) interest through targeted marketing and publicity efforts.

There are also important questions about the commodification of audience/ fan labor and transparency of corporate communications efforts in the area of publicity build-up for cultural products (Jenkins, et al., 2013). Regarding the state of sport fandom, PricewaterhouseCoopers's 2011 projections for the industry noted a key change that builds on these scholarly questions and a shifting of power: "Sports organisations are finding it increasingly difficult to balance the needs of all their stakeholders – it used to be all about the fan who would simply vote with their feet, but now the fan has a louder voice via social media" (p. 5). In many ways, this statement from an industry research firm reifies a key aspect of fandom. Fans have increased ability to co-opt official sport messages and texts. Fans also have louder platforms to voice their displeasure with their favorite teams.

One example that comes to mind from my personal experiences as a fan is the website www.icethetics.co. The site has a blog with news about hockey jerseys and logos. The site proprietor has posted information directly from teams about changes to team brands and images and they have attended at least one formal press event for a team's rebranding. Thus the site is a clearinghouse for news about hockey jerseys and an argument can be made that, on some level, it is sanctioned by teams and the industry. The site is also home to dozens of fan-submitted concepts in which hockey team jerseys are re-imagined and re-designed. Another example of a site that blends team news with participatory fan culture is sportslogos.net, which features news about multiple sports in North America and a vibrant discussion forum about these issues.

On the surface of it, it would seem that sport clubs should welcome this fan interest. This behavior could enhance a fan's relationship with their favorite team. Yet we have little empirical proof of how *both* parties view the creation and modification of team logos and color schemes and comments about new designs. One would surmise that at a certain point, if fans started taking their own images and making their own collectible items without a team's permission that the organization would seek to stop this behavior. Several questions come to mind. At what point does the appropriation of these sport texts become problematic from the organization's point of view? To what degree would fans question their affiliation with a team if the organization sought to curb this co-creating behavior? These uses of sport imagery extend beyond rooting for a particular team and repurposing logos for fun. Sport logos have been re-appropriated in acts of political and social protest. For example, user-created logos have surfaced for the Cleveland Indians (Major League Baseball) and Washington Redskins (National Football League) as a means of countering the offensive portrayals of Native Americans in the teams' current designs. These are statements of resistance to official team images.

These tensions present fertile ground for public relations-focused research with respect to fandom. The media studies and rhetoric literatures have done a splendid job of analyzing media texts, and exploring the experience of fans and the factors that shape one's involvement in participatory culture. Yet the cultivation of fandom – particularly in sport – remains underexplored from the organization's point of view. The circuit of culture model is relevant to this discussion as it helps explain the role that strategic communicators have in shaping shared meaning among different groups (Curtin & Gaither, 2007). The model, according to Curtin and Gaither, includes regulation (which is the controls on cultural activities); production (the processes by which creators of cultural products give them meaning); representation (the form an object takes and the meaning encoded in that form); consumption (audience decoding of messages); and identities (meanings that cross to social networks). My argument is that we should look more closely at sport organizations' role in these activities. Scholars need to consider how sport organizations maintain control over their content and brand identities, how fans participate in the co-creation of sport culture, and how fans move from online community to online community. To address the latter point, I review some of the work from the media studies discipline on network composition.

Exploring the composition of sport communities

Driven by both global media spectacle and the proliferation of access points from which to engage popular culture content, fans' social interactions have increasingly become a part of everyday life in modern societies (Gray, et al., 2007). These interactions must be understood in terms of the means by which consumers enact their fandom. Sport has followed a broader consumer technology usage trend with sport fans increasingly engaging with social media as they watch events on television (Broughton, 2013). One industry estimate suggested that more than half of sports fans use social media while watching games (Broughton, 2013). Certainly there are multiple opportunities for a sport organization to reach its fans during a single sporting event. Related to this, a mutually reinforcing cycle exists when it comes to social media and sports organizations. Teams and leagues have become content providers and reach audiences directly with social media content. As fan interest in social content increases, content-providing organizations are forced to come up with new ways to entertain their content-hungry and passionate fans (Barris, 2014; Burns, 2014). Today's sport fans engage with multiple platforms at multiple points during the day. They shift from social network to social network, dropping in to watch a live television while live tweeting and participating in online discussions. As we consider fan engagement with social networking sites, a logical step is to look at this behavior at a holistic level and to understand fans as multi-platform content consumers and producers.

Additionally, scholars should look at social network engagement from both the fan's perspective and the organization's point of view. This resonates with Morrissey (2013), who issued a strong and appropriate call to study fan networks. "Fan studies must … attend to the ways that fandom emerges as a negotiation between various cultural stakeholders at the individual and the group level" (para. 14). This push is important because of the growth of social networks and availability of multiple information streams. The "passion of the fan" is fueled by the sheer abundance of communication channels and online communities. The negotiation of meaning at the individual and group levels in these communities warrants consideration in the public relations literature.

The sport industry consists of a series of interlocking organizations (teams, governing bodies, and media outlets) that all play a role in shaping fan experiences. Although one might have a favorite team, their fan behaviors extend well beyond that particular team's social media platforms and website. For example, companies such as ESPN and Sky Sports have websites that feature fan-generated comments and intense discussions about sport-related news stories. Elsewhere, an array of web sites and blogs has arisen for the primary purpose of discussing updates to team logos (e.g., SportsLogos.net and uni-watch. net) and sharing fan art such as re-designed team and organization logos. Meanwhile, fans trade and sell sport memorabilia in numerous vibrant Internet forums. Thus sport fans, as with fans of other areas, engage with content from a variety of sources and platforms. The literature in this area needs a more complete accounting of these various network-to-network, community-to-community behaviors.

As several media studies scholars have indicated (Deuze, 2007; Raine, & Wellman, 2012; Vitak, 2012), the lines between online and offline and personal and private spaces have blurred. The term "context collapse" describes the flattening out of multiple distinct audiences in one's social network (Vitak, 2012). This means that rather than treating each audience as distinct, the technical features of social networking sites erase the lines between temporal, social, and spatial boundaries to the point where one's audiences are treated as one large homogenous group (Vitak, 2012). The technical structure of these sites encourages one-to-many communication over individualized interactions, according to this perspective. In this context, those who engage with these sites have new power to create media and to communicate with extended audiences online; these audiences thus become part of the user's social world (Raine, & Wellman, 2012). Online communities are seen as new neighborhoods where people meet to discuss common issues and develop strong social bonds with each other. My argument is that sport fandom, for many, is a driver of this community interaction in many online spaces. That is, sport fandom is the means by which a large number of spectators from across the globe share their common interests online and as a cultural phenomenon, it warrants additional study.

It remains to be seen how sport fans perceive their own audiences and who they are communicating with. How do fans construct their audiences when they engage with mediated (online) team content and sport media content? What is the relationship between online fan behavior and face-to-face interactions? Within the realm of sport behavior some work has begun to address these questions. Dixon (2011) found that the expression of fandom on a regular basis may strengthen interpersonal relationships as online interactions through Facebook and fan message boards extend into real-life encounters. Research on live-tweeting of television programs concluded that Twitter is both a tool for the long-term cultivation of fandom and a venue for audience members to show that they are actively participating (or "audiencing") in a shared media event such as a television show (Highfield, Harrington, & Bruns, 2013). As sport fans continue to engage in split-screen behavior, there are more opportunities to understand these audiencing behaviors.

Public relations scholars should consider how sport organizations view and how they encourage various audiencing behaviors. Within the fandom literature generally and within the sport fandom literature specifically, little research has been conducted to understand the origins of fandom, the incorporation of fan-related behaviors with other interpersonal communication activities in physical and mediated spaces, and how online communities are developed, maintained, and commodified through organizations' strategic communication efforts. At a high level, the cultivation of sport fandom by organizations presents an ideal means to explore these questions. In summary, it would be beneficial to understand the ways in which organizations encourage the development and maintenance of sport fan behavior across multiple communication channels.

Understanding sport fan behavior

A review of several literature areas indicates that the nexus of organizational behavior and sport fandom is a promising area for research. However, over-emphasizing fans' resistance to corporate texts is potentially problematic and limited as a scholarly narrative (Scodari, 2003). Fan researchers and theorists should examine relevant textual and institutional factors that shape fan experiences. The co-development of fandom-related participatory culture by both fans and organizations needs to be more fully explored. The larger point of this chapter is to suggest that fan culture and organizational attempts to reach fans are ultimately wedded. Sport fandom research in public relations should better account for this linkage, and should also consider fan behaviors and audiencing in a multitude of situations.

One perspective that scholars may find informative for answering these questions, particularly when it comes to the study of online communities in fandom and the development of new publics in public relations, is structuration theory. In structuration, a social system's interactions are both the medium and the outcome of recursively organized practices (Giddens, 1984). A central concept in structuration is the duality of structure, which suggests that structure is both the medium and the outcome of social interaction (Giddens, 1979). Structure both enables and constrains human behavior, and knowledge-imbued agents harness aspects of these structures for their own ends. Undergirding this perspective is the idea that reflexive agents make sense of their environments by drawing on various rules and resources, and this helps them act. In placing emphasis on the duality of macro-level social structure and the routine and habitual processes of micro-level everyday life, structuration analyses address a "meso" or middle ground (Dixon, 2011). Such an approach pays attention to both high-level social forces *and* individual agents' routine-based communication practices.

This approach is suited to understanding the development of contemporary sport fandom. Although they did not write from a structuration perspective, Gray et al. (2007, p. 9) implicate a broader sociological theme in their description of fan culture: "fandom has emerged as ... an important interface between the dominant micro and macro forces of our time." This point is relevant to public relations if we are to examine how organizations engage with fans, and the balance that organizations and fans maintain when it comes to meaning making and authority in online communities.

According to Cozier and Witmer (2001), structuration offers the public relations theorist two levels of analysis: the strategic conduct and constitution of social systems *and* an institutional analysis on how these social systems are reproduced. Structuration analysis also allows researchers to determine a public's level of openness, how members of a public perceive interdependent organizations, the organization's ideological meaning systems, the motivations that influence the production and re-enactment of communication by both the organization and a public, and the organization's possibility for recreating other publics online and offline (Cozier, & Witmer, 2001). This analysis enables the researcher to explicate the development of new publics and the effects of a social system's members' communication with the organization. In structuration, publics emerge through the creation and re-creation of shared meaning and experiences, which are embedded in various discursive and institutional practices (Cozier, & Witmer, 2001).

Structuration scholars look at the processes that occur when organizational members mutually co-construct social reality (Falkheimer, 2007). Structuration "enhances the holistic understanding of how public relations communication may be used both as a reproductive and a transforming social instrument" (Falkheimer, 2007, p. 292). We can apply this idea to studies of fan and organization behavior online. Indeed, structuration considers the interconnection between human actors (strategic communicators and organizational publics) and institutional efforts to manage these communities (Witmer, 2006). A particular benefit of structuration is that it captures the complexities of modern public relations practice, and it views organizations as dynamic and subject to transformation. We know that organizations evolve, and structuration can be a lens to understand how this evolution occurs.

Assuming that fans' co-creation of content and engagement with social media content has an effect on organizations, the processes by which organizational priorities are influenced by fan behavior should be better understood in the sport realm. Are certain events, certain groups of fans, or certain patterns of behavior more likely to elicit a response and therefore change sport organizational behavior? According to Giddens (1979), there are three primary structures that are the outcome and medium of social systems: domination (or the allocation of resources); legitimation (normative behavior); and signification (symbolic action and language). These structures may shed light on the patterning of interactions between sport fans and organizations. With the domination structure, one would surmise that within individual communities, various groups of fans would begin to assert their authority and expertise over others. These group behaviors need to be investigated since they may influence a person's willingness to visit a community and it could, potentially, impact their relationship with the team or organization. It would be relevant, for example to understand how sport organizations allocate and control resources online at their social media sites. With the legitimation structure, it will be worthwhile to understand the degree to which group behavioral norms among sport fans are shared in different contexts and venues. In other words what patterns of knowledge sharing are apparent at team-sponsored sites or on news sites? How do knowledge-sharing and culture-building behaviors differ from online to offline contexts? With the signification structure, it is relevant to consider the negotiation of language and meaning in fan communities. How do fans and organizations jointly develop rules for communication in these communities? As fans appropriate sport texts and develop their own acceptable terms, to what degree do sport organizations respond and react to this behavior? These are just some of the questions that come to mind when we think about the intersection of fans and sport organizations online and how meaning is co-created in various digital and in-person spheres.

The next steps for research in sport fandom and public relations

Sport offers a wonderful vantage point to continue theory development in public relations given its overall prominence in everyday life and the strength of the relationship that consumers have with sport brands. As argued, scholars have yet to fully consider how organizations cultivate fandom. The literature in this area can, and should, be advanced to more explicitly account for the development of sport culture and meaning construction by both consumers and public relations practitioners and organizations. The interest in audiences *and* organizational behavior affords public relations scholars with opportunities to explore these issues. As a cultural good, sport has its own unique patterns involved in the creation, shaping, modification, and re-creation of meaning (Curtin, & Gaither, 2007). It is thus important to investigate how individual- and collective-level sport identities and meanings are formed, understood, and navigated.

In conducting this research, qualitative methodologies can help with exploring the shifting contexts of content production and content consumption, the socio-technical contexts of sport fandom, and how people shift between online and offline realms. Scholars may need an open approach to data collection that is facilitated through online/digital ethnographies. To frame this research, this chapter also encourages a structuration approach to public relations and sport fandom. Structuration affords us a micro-level consideration of communication within social systems and how social rules are developed and maintained. Structuration also allows for an understanding of macro-level (organizational) forces that shape production and consumption of cultural goods. These types of analyses consider questions of power, sensemaking, and rule setting in social systems, which are important but heretofore-overlooked aspects of sport fandom and sport fan network behavior.

In summary, we know that fans invest considerable amounts of time and financial resources in supporting teams, following sport news, and participating in the overall spectacle of sport. Yet beyond just hours and dollars spent in support of one's team, this investment is about fan/fan interactions and fan/organization interactions. It is not simply enough to examine how sport fans read and interpret texts. It is necessary to understand how fans move from network to network and to understand the interplay and exchanges between sport fans and organizations. Exploring these issues in the context of sport will facilitate a more complete understanding of the development of new publics and public relations work as a socially embedded and socially transforming practice.

References

Barris, M. (2014, October 14). MSN leverages real-time sports video to boost fan engagement. *Mobile Marketer*. Retrieved from: http://www.mobilemarketer.com/cms/news/media/18917.html.

Brough, M. M., & Shresthova, S. (2012). Fandom meets activism: Rethinking civic and political participation. *Transformative Works and Cultures*, 10. doi: 10.3983.twc.2012.303.

Broughton, D. (2013, September 30). Fan social media use passes a threshold. *Sports Business Daily*. Retrieved from: http://www.sportsbusinessdaily.com/Journal/Issues/2013/09/30/Research-and-Ratings/Catalyst-social-media.aspx.

Burns, M. J. (2014, December 18). 85+ sports business professionals discuss biggest emerging trends, hot topics for 2015. *Forbes.Com*. Retrieved from: http://www.forbes.com/sites/markjburns/2014/12/18/85-sports-business-professionals-discuss-biggest-emerging-trends-hot-topics-for-2015/.

Cozier, Z., & Witmer, D. (2001). The development of a structuration analysis of new publics in an electronic environment. In R. L. Heath (Ed.), *Handbook of public relations* (pp. 615–623). Thousand Oaks, CA: Sage.

Curtin, P., & Gaither, T. K. (2007). *International public relations – negotiating culture, identity, and power*. Thousand Oaks, CA: Sage.

Deuze, M. (2007). *Media work*. Malden, MA: Polity Press.

Dixon, K. (2011). A "third way" for football fandom research: Anthony Giddens and structuration theory. *Soccer & Society*, 12(2), 279–298. doi: 10.1080/14660970.2011.548363.

Edwards, L., & Hodges, C. E. M. (2011). *Public relations, society, & culture: Theoretical and empirical explorations*. London: Routledge.

Falkheimer, J. (2007). Anthony Giddens and public relations: A third way perspective. *Public Relations Review*, 33(3), 287–293.

Feil, S. (2013, January 28). The passion of the fan. *Adweek*. Retrieved from: http://www.adweek.com/sa-article/passion-fan-146722.

Gantz, W. (2012). Reflections on communication and sport: On fanship and social relationships. *Communication & Sport*, 1(1/2) 176–187.

Giddens, A. (1979). *Central problems in social theory: Action, structure, and contradiction in social analysis*. Berkeley, CA: University of California Press.

Giddens, A. (1984). *The constitution of society*. Berkeley, CA: University of California Press.

Gray, J., Sandvoss, C., & Harrington, C. L. (2007). Introduction: Why study fans? In J. Gray, C. Sandvoss, & C. L. Harrington (Eds.), *Fandom: Identities and communities in a mediated world* (pp. 1–16). New York and London: New York University Press.

Highfield, T., Harrington, S., & Bruns, A. (2013). Twitter as a technology for audiencing and fandom: The #Eurovision phenomenon. *Information, Communication & Society*, 16(3), 315–339.

Hopwood, M. (2011). Public relations and communication in sport. In M. Hopwood, P. Kitchin, & J. Skinner (Eds.), *Sport public relations and communication* (pp. 13–32). Oxford: Butterworth-Heinemann.

Jenkins, H. (2007). Afterword: The future of fandom. In J. Gray, C. Sandvoss, & C. L. Harrington (Eds.), *Fandom. Identities and communities in a mediated world* (pp. 357–364). New York and London: New York University Press.

Jenkins, H., Ford, S., & Green, J. (2013). *Spreadable media: Creating value and meaning in a networked culture.* New York and London: New York University Press.

Kantar Media Sport. (2014). The global sports media consumption report 2014. Retrieved from: http://www.knowthefan.com/.

Kraszewski, J. (2008). Pittsburg in Fort Worth: Football bars, sports television, sports fandom, and the management of home. *Journal of Sport & Social Issues*, 32(2), 139–157.

L'Etang, J. (2006). Public relations and sport in promotional culture. *Public Relations Review*, 32, 386–394.

L'Etang, J. (2013). *Sports public relations: Concepts, issues and practice.* London: Sage.

Morrissey, K. E. (2013). Fan/dom: People, practices, and networks. *Transformative Works and Cultures*, 14. doi: 10.3983/twc.2013.0532.

Murray, S. (2004). "Celebrating the story the way it is": Cultural studies, corporate media and the contested utility of fandom. *Continuum: Journal of Media & Cultural Studies*, 18(1), 7–25

PricewaterhouseCoopers. (2011). Changing the game – Outlook for the global sports market to 2015. Retrieved from: http://www.pwc.com/gx/en/industries/hospitality-leisure/changing-the-game-outlook-for-the-global-sports-market-to-2015.html.

PWC (2011, December). Changing the game: Outlook for the global sports market to 2015. Retrieved from www.pwc.com.

Raine, L. & Wellman, B. (2012). *Networked: The new social operating system.* Cambridge, MA: The MIT Press.

Reagin, N., & Rubenstein, R. (2011). "I'm Buffy, and you're history": Putting fan studies into history. *Transformative Works and Cultures*, 6. doi: 10.3983/twc.2011.0272.

Sandvoss, C. (2005). *Fans: The mirror of consumption.* Cambridge: Polity Press.

Scodari, C. (2003). Resistance re-examined: Gender, fan practices, and science fiction television. *Popular Communication: The International Journal of Media and Culture*, 1(2), 111–130. doi: 10.1207/S15405710PC0102_3.

Serazio, M. (2012). The elementary forms of sports fandom: A Durkheimian exploration of team myths, kinship, and totemic rituals. *Communication & Sport*, 1(4) 303–325.

Sifferlin, A. (2014, January 31). Super Bowl and super fans: Why we care so much. *Time.com*. Retrieved from: http://healthland.time.com/2014/01/31/super-bowl-and-super-fans-why-we-care-so-much/.

Vardeman-Winter, J., Tindall, N., & Jiang, H. (2013). Intersectionality and publics: How exploring publics' multiple identities questions basic public relations concepts. *Public Relations Inquiry*, 2(3), 279–304.

Vitak, J. (2012). The impact of context collapse and privacy on social network site disclosures. *Journal of Broadcasting & Electronic Media*, 56(4) 451–470.

Witmer, D. (2006). Overcoming system and cultural boundaries: Public relations from a structuration perspective. In C. H. Botan & V. Hazleton (Eds.), *Public relations theory II* (pp. 361–374). Mahwah, NJ: Lawrence Erlbaum Associates.

19 Entertainment–education and online fan engagement

The power of narrative to spark health discussions/action

Heidi Hatfield Edwards

Entertainment media often use health-related storylines in character narratives. While the health issue may be merely a tool to further a plot, more often health communication professionals are seeking ways to extend campaigns outside traditional tactics and work with program producers to introduce specific health-related content. Research in entertainment-education (E-E) has long shown fan involvement in a narrative can have significant impact on the persuasiveness of pro-social messages.

This chapter explores an audience analysis of discussion about *Sex and the City*'s breast cancer storyline on HBO's online message board. The issue sparked considerable discussion and debate about breast cancer and other health topics and provoked some fans to do breast self exams, get mammograms, and encourage friends and family to take action for their health. Consistent with entertainment-education and fan involvement research, discussions indicated that fans who exhibited high character and narrative involvement had strong responses to the breast-cancer story.

Studies analyzing fans' response to and engagement with entertainment-education storylines can help communicators gauge how the health message is perceived and where messages should be modified, improved, and reinforced. Advances in technology and social networking provide outlets to extend discussions among fans who interact with each other to discuss plotlines. Social media provide a distinctive view of how fans are using and spreading information. When fans discuss health-related content, health campaign planners have a unique opportunity to address public concerns, perceptions, and misconceptions.

Entertainment–education and fan involvement

Research shows people tend to use the social cues media provide to guide their actions when faced with situations similar to those they see in media (Lindlof, & Meyer, 1987; Janis, 1980). Entertainment-education (E-E) capitalizes on fan engagement with media to disseminate prosocial messages, especially regarding public health issues (see Singhal, Cody, Rogers, & Sabido, 2004). Health-related stories embedded in entertainment media reinforce messages in more traditional informational campaigns and can reach wider audiences. These embedded messages can have an impact on fan knowledge and behaviors (Brodie, et al., 2001; Collins, et al., 2003; Howe, Owen-Smith, & Richardson, 2002). For example, researchers found that cervical cancer screening increased in the United Kingdom after a soap opera character was diagnosed and then died from the disease (Howe, et al., 2002). Viewers exposed to messages about genetic-based breast cancer on *ER* and *Grey's Anatomy* had greater knowledge about the breast cancer gene and treatment options, and changes in intended or actual behavior than those who had not viewed the shows embedded with the health message (Hether, Huang, Beck, Murphy, & Valente, 2008).

Social Cognitive Theory (SCT) is often used to explain the impact of television narratives on people's attitudes and behaviors (Bandura, 1986, 2004). According to SCT, people model what they see on television, but the effects are not direct. Other factors, including level of viewer involvement and perceived consequences of character behaviors impact viewer motivation to model that behavior (Bandura, 2004). Recently, E-E researchers have begun to explore mediating factors to determine whether viewers are likely to adopt healthy behaviors seen on entertainment programming. In particular, researchers have investigated how viewer involvement with characters and/or the narrative impacts E-E persuasiveness (see, e.g., Moyer-Gusé, Chung, & Jain, 2011; Murphy, Frank, Moran, & Patnoe-Woodley, 2011).

In addition to SCT, the Extended-Elaboration Likelihood Model (E-ELM) offers insight into how involvement may work to heighten viewers' acceptance of embedded messages. Moyer-Gusé (2008) argues "SCT highlights the importance of motivation in modeling behaviors, whereas the E-ELM addresses how these programs may reduce counterarguing" (p. 414).

Involvement is multi-faceted. Moyer-Gusé (2008) differentiates between narrative involvement (audience engagement with the storyline) and character involvement (how viewers interact with characters). Narrative involvement is the degree to which viewers feel they have been "transported" into and through the story. Character involvement is a continuum upon which viewers may experience the narrative as the character (identification); "wish" they were the character (wishful identification); see themselves as similar to the character (similarity); perceive the character as part of their social world (parasocial interaction); or evaluate the character positively (liking) (Moyer-Gusé, 2008).

Research shows the relationships among involvement factors are difficult to isolate and use to predict viewer response (Murphy, et al., 2011). In an experiment, Moyer-Gusé & Nabi (2010) tested whether character and/or narrative involvement might reduce counterarguing. Using a non-narrative news story about teen pregnancy and a teen pregnancy storyline from *The OC*, the researchers found character identification decreased counterarguments, but transportation into the narrative did not. Yet, when Murphy et al. (2011) examined viewers' character and narrative involvement with a lymphoma storyline in the drama *Desperate Housewives*, they found viewers who were transported into the story (high narrative involvement) were more likely to have increased knowledge, attitude, and behavior change. Like Moyer-Gusé, Murphy et al. (2011) suggest transportation reduces counterarguing, leading to greater persuasive effects, but transportation alone may not be sufficient given the complex relationship among involvement factors. According to the researchers, viewers experience the story in such varied ways that isolating the concepts may be less important than understanding the "nuanced" outcomes of E-E efforts (Murphy, et al., 2011, p. 426).

Audiences, fans, and socially constructed meaning

Audience-centric studies based in a cultural studies perspective can help better understand those nuanced outcomes. Much media effects research, including investigations about E-E effects, approach the topic from a message transmission model in which media disseminate information and people gain knowledge or change attitudes or behaviors based on that information (Carey, 1975). However, the complex relationships among the narratives, characters, and audience necessitate inquiry based on communication as a social process. The messages are best understood by studying audience interpretations (see, e.g., Fiske, 1986; Hall, 1980). While message creators may have carefully crafted the narrative, how the audience interprets the meaning and makes use of the narrative provide invaluable insights for communicators who look at the complex social structure in which audiences negotiate meaning (see, e.g., Acosta-Alzuru, 1999; Radway, 1984).

Online fan communities provide rich context to the fan experience and negotiations about the meanings of the stories they consume. Viewers gather electronically to discuss the programs, characters, stories, and related concerns that resonate within the fan community (Baym, 2000; see also Scodari, 1998; Scodari & Felder, 2000; Wakefield, 2001). Cultural studies scholars uncover meaning fans derive from programs (see, e.g. Gray, Sandvoss, & Harrington, 2007). Participants in these communities are no longer ordinary viewers who merely consume the stories, but fans who take action by joining the fan group (Costello, & Moore, 2007). Level of fandom varies, from lurkers who merely read the online forums, to superfans who may go so far as to use the original text to create their own fan fiction. While involvement may vary, fans who engage in fan communities and discussion boards have gone beyond the casual viewer to a higher level of character and narrative involvement.

The popularity of social network sites like Facebook and Twitter has led to a decline in online forums (Whiteman, & Metivier, 2013), however, fan communities are still popular among viewers looking for information or interaction with others who share their interests (Andrejevic, 2008). The communal nature of fan forums has the potential to increase the persuasive power of narrative messages (Condit, 1989). Collectively, fans discuss individual interpretations, "perusing the sentiments of others and, perhaps, considering those views in light of their own negotiations" (Scodari, 1998, p. 170). Fans are negotiating the primary texts and creating meaning together.

Let's talk about *Sex and the City* and breast cancer

In the last season of HBO's original series *Sex and the City*, one of the show's four main characters, Samantha, was diagnosed with breast cancer. For the length of the season, viewers watched Samantha go from the diagnosis to treatment and recovery, and fans discussed the storyline on HBO's online message board. The show was a hit among women aged 18 to 49 (Battaglio, 2004).

Because the storyline continued through the season, the show broached multiple aspects of breast cancer. Samantha was diagnosed after a consultation about possible breast augmentation. From diagnosis, the story turned to treatment options, then chemotherapy and its side effects. The series also delved into personal relationships and the impact of Samantha's diagnosis on the other characters. Characters even discussed causes of the disease, including the potential effects of lifestyle choices that may have increased risk.

This study analyzed posts to HBO's fan forums to answer the following research questions:

RQ1: How did fans discuss and interpret the breast cancer storyline?
RQ2: What impact did the storyline have on fans' attitudes and behaviors regarding breast cancer?

Uncovering the rich nuances

Scholars researching audience interpretation are increasingly using qualitative techniques to collect and analyze the complex data generated by audience discussion. For example, Sharf, Freimuth, Greenspon, and Plotnik (1996) interviewed viewers and originally intended to do a quantitative content analysis of the interviews. However, they found the method masked "the nuances and richness of viewer responses and did not uncover the richer meaning imbedded in the interview text" (p. 161). Instead, using qualitative techniques they found a "constellation of contextual factors, social interactions, and intrapersonal responses that belie the seemingly simple act of 'turning on the tube' at night and shape how program content is interpreted by individuals" (Sharf, et al., 1996, p. 170).

Unlike studies that captured viewer interpretations through interviews (Sharf et al., 1996) or viewer letters (Collins, 1997), this project captured asynchronous conversations among the show's fans. Similar to analyzing letters, however, analysis of the online conversations made it possible to observe the interactions without participating in or influencing them. Discussions were observed during *Sex and the City*'s final season, the timeframe of the breast cancer storyline (January–March 2004).

High narrative or character involvement is likely among forum participants. While not onerous, one requisite to posting to HBO's discussion boards is to "join" the forum, providing HBO.com an email address and user name that identifies the posts. (Email addresses are not publicly available.) Casual observers do not need to register.

Multiple discussion groups existed within the show's main forum including a general conversation, one for each character, and music and fashion. These groups varied through the run of the show as participants added groups and threads and older groups were archived. Within each group, multiple threads addressed a wide variety of topics, many of which overlapped among the discussion groups. Data analysis concentrated on discussions about the breast cancer narrative and related comments.

Discussion participants self-identified as viewers with varying involvement with the show. Many appeared to be highly involved based on the number of posts they made to the forum. New viewers occasionally identified themselves in questions to the veteran fans. Demographic data was unavailable unless revealed in forum posts. Most appeared to be women based on self-identification and names, however, some men were evident in the discussions.

Analysis of the discussion data was interpretive and iterative. This study adapted Kasper's (1994) five-stage approach to interview data analysis for use on the bulletin board discussions. The five-stage technique moves from an individual interpretation to a larger theoretical framework (Kasper, 1994). First, discussants chose the discussion topics and patterns, revealed through the different discussion thread headings and topics. Second, a careful reading of each thread clarified the topics and identified those related to the breast cancer storyline. After the initial reading, the text of the conversations was imported into a qualitative data analysis program (QSR N-Vivo). Third, relationships between the facts and meanings identified in stage two emerged. For example, individuals posted their concerns about what would happen to Sam, why she had the disease. Having identified these ideas in stage two, these individual concerns were put together to identify, for example, relationships between concerns about the plot, the character, and how it affected the viewers' perceptions of the disease. Fourth, individual relationships were put into perspective as collective data. Links among the different postings revealed areas within which ideas converged or diverged with other postings. Finally, the collective meanings became patterns and themes that formed the basis of the findings (Kasper, 1994).

How did fans discuss and interpret the breast cancer storyline?

Fans revealed different levels of character and narrative involvement through their discussions (Moyer-Gusé, 2008). "Why Sam?" they asked, sometimes blurring the lines between fiction and reality. Some fans seemed to answer the question from the narrative perspective while other responses focused on the character. Many of the posts blended statements of narrative and character involvement.

Narrative Involvement. Contributors to the threads indicating strong narrative involvement offered possible reasons for breast cancer entering the series, justifying or vilifying the producers' decisions. Fans had mixed reactions to the series' inclusion of the disease, especially as it touched a main character. They were offended, their sense of escape through the show violated. One breast cancer survivor rebuked HBO, writing, "[T]his show helped me escape reality for 30 minutes a week and now the BREAST CANCER is shoved right back in my face." Another viewer announced to the board:

> To me, SATC is like candy … Each week I live for ½ hr. with the characters. Sunday's show was a little upsetting for me. I have known many people with breast cancer and it kind of just destroyed the fun time I have with the show … I don't see how they can make humor out of cancer. It will put a cloud on all the remaining episodes.

Nevertheless, others posted hopeful messages that the writers would use the narrative to show women ways to deal with cancer. One person wrote, "I just think that the show wants to send a message out there that breast cancer is real and it can happen to anyone." Though anxious about the story arc, this group was optimistic the show would offer beneficial coping strategies. Still others were enthusiastic about the story:

> I think it was a brilliant move to introduce a serious storyline like Sam's breast cancer in the finale of the series. It gives the writers a chance to present different character arcs as the girls deal with Sam and the effects of her disease … It is also a great way to increase awareness about breast cancer and to show inspiration and hope to those and their loved ones who are stricken.

Character Involvement. Participants in the threads revealed character involvement by focusing on Samantha and her individual characteristics. Fans described Sam as promiscuous, strong, independent, beautiful, sexy, fun, free-spirited, older, and stoic (when she didn't cry when she was diagnosed). However, at least one discussion thread blurred the distinction between narrative and character involvement when a post queried the writers' motivations for choosing Sam for this particular story. The initial post reflects character involvement:

> The one thing that bothers me about Sam's cancer is the reason the writers chose her. It almost smacks of some ridiculous far, right wing hardliner saying "See … the 'bad' girl is getting punished for her promiscuity."

However, a response in this thread focused on the narrative:

> Sam isn't being punished for promiscuity, she's being jostled by fate because she's the most confident and proud, and tragedy occurs when a king falls from a great height, not when a peasant stumbles on the curb.

Further, focusing on the character and narrative and blending it with reality, fans talked about the logic of Sam's diagnosis given her age relative to the other main characters, or the irony that the character is extremely body conscious. Some were concerned that Sam may die, but others countered with statistically based arguments about the survivability of breast cancer. For example, one forum member wrote:

> I sincerely hope they don't kill her off ... It would be okay with me as a story line ... but I think it would be really hopeful and even more realistic to show her beating [cancer]. Survival rates for breast cancer when caught in its early stages are quite good ... and treatments have come a long way. This is true ESPECIALLY for women who don't smoke and live healthy lifestyles. Add her natural-born fighter attitude (which is also ... proven to increase survival rates) and Sam's character is tailor-made to be a breast cancer survivor.

Discussion ultimately revealed that for many fans, involvement with the character and narrative was intertwined with their personal experiences with cancer or other life-changing illnesses. Fans identified themselves as breast cancer survivors, and friends, family, and caregivers of cancer patients. Others who did not have such close ties with the disease often identified as women who *could, someday* be touched by it. While some praised the portrayal of Sam with the disease, others criticized it as insensitive or ill-conceived. For many, the breast cancer narrative pushed them into the online forum, shifting their involvement with the show to a new level as they engaged with other fans.

Support for the story increased as the season progressed and the story gained traction through what some fans described as realism. After Sam gave a fundraiser speech in one of the last episodes, survivors cheered that the episode "struck a chord." One breast cancer patient, now in her third recurrence, stated:

> I was becoming afraid they were going to just gloss over this part of Sam ... glad to see they gave this ... story line some meat ... I'm glad to see the issue addressed in a less "proper" manner. There are so many things about the disease that just are plain improper, and insane. Let's talk about it.

And, in one very poignant commentary, a man confided to the board in what was his first post:

> Sunday before last ... I had my wife die in my arms of metastatic breast cancer. Obviously, I did not see the episode where Samantha removed her wig until it was rebroadcast later in the week. The impact was truly dramatic to all in my house. My daughter, who had been with her mother for [a year and a half] of treatments rose and cheered. I, frankly, sobbed out loud.

Similar statements consistently showed the catharsis fans felt by experiencing Sam's crisis through the show. The man quoted above went on to encourage fans to take action: "My wife only missed ONE yearly mammogram. Please be sure your loved ones and friends remember theirs."

What impact did the storyline have on fans' attitudes and behaviors regarding breast cancer?

The most powerful indication of the show's ability to impact its audience was when two forum participants revealed that the show motivated them to do a breast self-exam and they found lumps. The first post told her story and thanked the show for prompting her to action:

> Thanks to the episode with Samantha detecting a lump in her breast it reminded me to do my self-exam and found a lump. My doctor has confirmed the lump and also found out I am pregnant and because of the pregnancy I am not able to go any further in finding out if the lump is cancer ... I thank the show and its cast for reminding me of what I as a 30 year old woman am supposed to do to keep safe. Thanks, ladies.

She only posted once, despite supportive notes from others on the board who encouraged her to seek a second opinion and shared similar stories with positive endings. The second woman seemed to be reaching out to the community:

> Thursday night, for whatever reason, while watching my newly purchased SATC Season 5 on DVD, I started probing around and I found a lump on my left side. Actually, there may be two or more going up into my arm ... I suspected something (small) was there [two months ago] but I let it go. Now it's about the size of a nickel. I'm not sure why I posted this. I've told my boyfriend ... and today a friend via email. I haven't had the heart to tell my mother yet ... I guess I just needed to tell someone else.

Forum participants supported these women in their responses. Though optimistic, they were also realistic, acknowledging that both these women could have cancer. They gave statistics and facts about breast cancer and treatment options. They offered advice. They told their own stories. And they vehemently advocated for assertive action. When the second woman posted on a Friday, noting her doctor didn't have Friday office hours, one person wrote: "Call your doctor's office [Monday] and INSIST upon speaking to your doctor ... not his staff ... [I]f your doctor is worth anything he will have you in IMMEDIATELY!" In an update to the board, the woman reported the good news that it was likely not cancer, but she was having some more tests.

While perhaps less dramatic, other forum posts clearly indicated the narrative had an impact on fan attitudes and behavior regarding breast cancer. Fans posted examples of how they and their friends had learned from Sam's experiences and the implications for their own lives. Rarely were posts about the breast cancer storyline limited to comments about the show. Most often they included observations or anecdotes about real-life experiences. And sometimes they conceded the effect the series can have:

> I can name a dozen women friends who were spurred by the storyline to get their first mammograms and who shook their heads in amazement that it took something like a TV show to reach them. Hey ... if the medium can be used to entertain and provoke action and discussion, so much the better.

Discussion

Interpretive communities like the HBO forum provide fans a space in which to share opinions and negotiate understanding of the media texts, creating a multi-dimensional viewing experience (Lindlof, 1987; Scodari & Felder, 2000). By bringing their relationship with the media text into their personal and social lives, fans become "connected" (Russell, & Puto, 1999). This connectedness depends upon viewers' commitment to the show and identification (and parasocial interaction) with characters in the show.

Most fans who engage in online discussion boards have strong character and/or narrative involvement (Moyer-Gusé, 2008). They are connected. The HBO *Sex and the City* forum was full of veteran fans who made thousands of posts on a multitude of topics throughout the run of the show.

The data in this case indicate many of the breast cancer discussion participants were prompted to join the forum after Sam was diagnosed. Their posts were almost exclusively about the storyline, and they seemed to become more connected to the show because the story resonated with them. Some were frustrated with the choice to introduce breast cancer, disrupting their involvement with the narrative and instigating some counterarguing (Moyer-Gusé, & Nabi, 2010). Nevertheless, even these fans took action, even if it was to join the discussion to voice their discontent and then stop watching the show.

Some of the discontent focused on how the story may have glossed over the realities of the disease. However valid this critique, these findings suggest the show sparked considerable discussion and debate and prompted some fans to take action for their own health. This kind of counterarguing within the community may be helpful as fans discuss the health issue with each other, citing information, correcting misinformation, encouraging one another, and having frank discussions that might not otherwise be likely to occur outside the community.

Research repeatedly shows people do not have uniform interpretations or understanding of health-related content (Sharf, et al., 1996). Even knowledge gain and accuracy of that knowledge varies (see, e.g. Collins, et al., 2003). Audience interpretations are "filtered through their own experiences and interactions with one another" (Sharf et al., 1996, p. 170). The filtering process is clearly illustrated in the online discussion boards.

Social media tools offer health communicators and program producers a valuable resource to observe audience/fan negotiation of health-related topics and see how those stories are interpreted. When narratives develop over time, producers can adjust the story in ways to better reach the audience if interpretations are skewed away from the intended health message.

At a more basic level, medical professionals who scan social media discussions may be better able to talk to their patients, addressing common questions and concerns and correcting misinformation. Local health communicators may want to use popular media narratives as starting points for conversations in their own campaigns, including through social media outlets like Facebook and Twitter, and online discussion groups like the HBO forum. While online forums are not as popular as they once were compared to other social media outlets, people seeking information or social support will use online communities that offer quality information and are easily accessed (Lin & Lee, 2006).

This study was limited to those fans who posted to the HBO discussion forums. Most were likely superfans (Costello & Moore, 2007), highly involved in the program, though some entered the group to specifically discuss the breast cancer story. Less involved audience members may have different interpretations. Further, other types of social networks may have offered a different audience perspective than those gleaned from the HBO discussion board. Future studies may want to incorporate focus groups, interviews, and broader social network scanning to develop a fuller picture of the impact of health-related entertainment-education programs.

References

Acosta-Alzuru, M. C. (1999). The American girl dolls: Constructing American girlhood through representation, identity, and consumption. Unpublished dissertation. University of Georgia.

Andrejevic, M. (2008). Watching television without pity: The productivity of online fans. *Television & New Media*, 9(1), 24–46.

Bandura, A. (1986). *Social foundations of thought and action: A social cognitive theory.* Englewood Cliffs, NJ: Prentice-Hall.

Bandura, A. (2004). Social cognitive theory for personal and social change by enabling media. In A. Singhal, M. J. Cody, E. M. Rogers, & M. Sabido (Eds.), *Entertainment-education and social change: History, research, and practice* (pp. 75–96). Mahwah, NJ: Erlbaum.

Battaglio, S. (2004). It's a Big finish: Last edition of "Sex" scores series' best ratings ever. *Daily News (New York)*, February 25, 2004, p. 75.

Baym, N. K. (2000). *Tune in, log on: Soaps, fandom, and online community.* Thousand Oaks, CA: Sage Publications.

Brodie, M., Foehr, U., Rideout, V., Baer, N., *et al.* (2001). Communicating health information through the entertainment media. *Health Affairs*, 20(1), 192–200.

Carey, J. W. (1975). A cultural approach to communication. *Communication*, 2, 1–22.

Collins, C. (1997). Viewer letters as audience research: The case of Murphy Brown. *Journal of Broadcasting & Electronic Media*, 41(1), 109–131.

Collins, R. L., *et al.* (2003). Entertainment television as a healthy sex educator: The impact of condom-efficacy information in an episode of Friends. *Pediatrics*, 112(5), 1115–1121.

Condit, C. M. (1989). The rhetorical limits of polysemy. *Critical Studies in Mass Communication*, 6(2), 103–122.

Costello, V., & Moore, B. (2007). Cultural outlaws: An examination of audience activity and online television fandom. *Television & New Media*, 8(2), 124.

Fiske, J. (1986). Television: Polysemy and popularity. *Critical Studies in Mass Communication*, 3(4), 391–408.

Gray, J., Sandvoss, C., & Harrington, C. L. (2007). Introduction: Why study fans? In J. Gray, C. Sandvoss, & C. L. Harrington (Eds.). *Fandom: Identities and communities in a mediated world* (pp. 1–16). New York and London: New York University Press.

Hall, S. (1980). Encoding/decoding. In S. Hall, D. Hobson, A. Low, & P. Willis (Eds.), *Culture, media, language: Working papers in cultural studies, 1972–1979* (pp. 128–138). London: Hutchinson.

HBO Community Forums. Sex and the City bulletin board discussions. Available at: http://boards.hbo.com/index.jspa?categoryID=1

Hether, H. J., Huang, G. C., Beck, V., Murphy, S. T., & Valente, T. W. (2008). Entertainment-education in a media-saturated environment: Examining the impact of single and multiple exposures to breast cancer storylines on two popular medical dramas. *Journal of Health Communication*, 13(8), 808–823. doi: http://dx.doi.org/10.1080/10810730802487471.

Howe, A., Owen-Smith, V., & Richardson, J. (2002). The impact of a television soap opera on the NHS cervical screening programme in the North West of England. *Journal of Public Health Medicine*, 24(4), 299–304.

Janis, I. (1980). The influence of television on personal decision-making. In S. B. Withey & R. P. Abeles (Eds.), *Television and social behavior: Beyond violence and children* (pp. 161–189). Hillsdale, NJ: Lawrence Erlbaum.

Kasper, A. S. (1994). A feminist, qualitative methodology: A study of women with breast cancer. *Qualitative Sociology*, 17(3), p. 263–281.

Lin, H. F., & Lee, G. G. (2006). Determinants of success for online communities: An empirical study. *Behaviour & Information Technology*, 25(6), p. 479–488.

Lindlof, T. R. (1987). Media audiences as interpretive communities. In J. A. Anderson (Ed.), *Communication yearbook, 11* (pp. 81–87). Newbury Park, CA: Sage.

Lindlof, T. R., & Meyer, T. P. (1987). Mediated communication as ways of seeing, acting and constructing culture: The tools and foundations of qualitative research. In T. R. Lindlof (Ed.), *Natural audiences: Qualitative research of media uses and effects* (pp. 1–30). Norwood, NJ: Ablex.

Moyer-Gusé, E. (2008). Toward a theory of entertainment persuasion: Explaining the persuasive effects of entertainment-education messages. *Communication Theory*, 18, 407–425.

Moyer-Gusé, E., Chung, A. H., & Jain, P. (2011). Identification with characters and discussion of taboo topics after exposure to an entertainment narrative about sexual health. *Journal of Communication*, 61(3), 387–406.

Moyer-Gusé, E., & Nabi, R. L. (2010). Explaining the effects of narrative in an entertainment television program: Overcoming resistance to persuasion. *Human Communication Research*, 36(1), 26–52.

Murphy, S. T., Frank, L. B., Moran, M. B., & Patnoe-Woodley, P. (2011). Involved, transported, or emotional? Exploring the determinants of change in knowledge, attitudes, and behavior in entertainment-education. *Journal of Communication*, 61(3), 407–431.

Radway, J. A. (1984). *Reading the romance: Women, patriarchy, and popular literature.* Chapel Hill: University of North Carolina Press.

Russell, C. A., & Puto, C. P. (1999). Rethinking television audience measures: An exploration into the construct of connectedness. *Marketing Letters*, 10(4), 393–407.

Scodari, C. (1998). "No politics here": Age and gender in soap opera "cyberfandom". *Women's Studies in Communication*, 21(2), 168.

Scodari, C., & Felder, J. L. (2000). Creating a pocket universe: "Shippers", fan fiction, and The X-Files online. *Communication Studies*, 51(3), 238–257.

Sharf, B. F., Freimuth, V. S., Greenspon, P., & Plotnick, C. (1996). Confronting cancer on thirtysomething: Audience response to health content on entertainment TV. *Journal of Health Communication*, 1(2), 157–172.

Singhal, A., Cody, M. J., Rogers, E. M., & Sabido, M. (Eds.) (2004). *Entertainment-education and social change: History, research, and practice.* Mahwah, NJ: Erlbaum.

Wakefield, S. R. (2001). "Your sister in St. Scully": An electronic community of female fans of *The X-Files. Journal of Popular Film & Television*, 29(3), 130–137.

Whiteman, N., & Metivier, J. (2013). From post-object to "Zombie" fandoms: The "deaths" of online fan communities and what they say about us. *Participations: International Journal of Audience and Reception Studies*, 10(1). Available at: http://www.participations.org/Volume%2010/Issue%201/contents.htm.

20 When going silent may be more productive

Exploring fan resistance on Twitter to the Baltimore Ravens live-tweeting the Ray Rice press conference

Jimmy Sanderson and Karen Freberg

With advances in social media, public relations have become a multi-faceted practice involving diverse stakeholder groups who can actively contribute to public relations narratives (Chewning, 2015; DiStaso, Vafeiadis, & Amaral, in press). While using social media for public relations opens up viable dialogic opportunities with stakeholders, it also brings risks. This chapter explores the risk emanating from a participatory culture stemming from the intersection of public relations and social media, through an examination of the Baltimore Ravens organization live-tweeting a press conference involving player Ray Rice. On May 23, 2014, Rice and his wife Janay Rice held a press conference to address Rice's arrest charges for simple assault in February 2014. Although details at the time of the arrest were scarce, the situation was exacerbated when video was leaked after Rice's release that depicted him dragging Janay Rice out of an elevator (Bien, 2014). During the press conference, Ray Rice made several unfortunate statements including, "Failure is not getting knocked down. It's not getting up." Additionally, Janay Rice also apologized for her role in the incident (Burke, 2014).

While the efficacy of the press conference itself was debatable, the Ravens Twitter account live-tweeted the press conference, tweeting some of Ray and Janay Rice's statements verbatim. Not surprisingly, this resulted in significant backlash from media outlets (Yoder, 2014), leading to headlines such as "Ray Rice is an asshole and the Ravens couldn't care less" (Van Bibber, 2014). The Ravens decision to live-tweet the press conference also generated considerable backlash from audience members. Through the participatory nature of Twitter, audience members took control of the Ravens public relations narrative and dramatically changed its course, providing an illustrative example of how participatory cultures affect public relations efforts.

Presence of social media within sports

Social media provides the ultimate personalized, networked hub of information, dialogue, and relationship management. Social media is sometimes referred to as "emerging media" or "new media" to capture the association of the advanced integration, strategy, and application of new communication technologies (Duhe, in press). According to the Pew Research Center's 2014 social media update report, Facebook is the most popular social media site (Pew Research Center, 2015). Yet, this same study also noted a rise in multiplatform use. This suggests that one social media platform is not universally dominant, as users have different purposes, uses, and needs associated with each platform community (Pew Research Center, 2015).

Social media platforms serve as gateways where content and conversations are created among individuals, brands, organizations, and nations. In addition, social media platforms provide initial impression management tools for corporations and individuals to showcase individualized brands and reputations. These virtual platforms allow user-generated content to be shared in highly dynamic and interactive communities in real time, which allows for co-creating of content and extending of conversations and ideas. Additionally, social media has enabled audience participation to an extent not seen previously in traditional media. Increased empowerment of individual stakeholders leads to greater feelings of control over the situation and a willingness to help others in the community, which could potentially be leveraged by brands and sports teams to engage with audiences, formulate message strategies, and disrupt narratives being disseminated by others online (Sanderson, 2011).

Essentially, the relationship between organizations and their community (or in this case sports teams and their fans) helps to establish a relationship identity (Coombs & Holladay, in press). A relationship identity focuses on how individuals define themselves based on the correspondence and exchange of information, emotions, and tasks, that fluctuate over time and can shift from positive to negative depending on the circumstances. One of the key points for a positive and proactive relationship between a brand and its audiences is to have dialogue (Kent, & Taylor, 1998). Without the exchange of information and discussion in a community, relationships may be at a standstill and not evolve. There are cases where these relationships are based on real exchanges, but there are occasions where individuals (and fans) create illusions of these relationships with athletes, celebrities, and even with sports teams. In some cases, fans may have a parasocial relationship (Horton, & Wohl, 1956) with athletes and teams based on how they identify themselves. Baek, Bae, and Jang (2013) defined a parasocial relationship as a "simulacrum of conversational give and take" between mass media performers and the audience (p. 513). With the rise in social media, fans feel more attached to players and teams through technology and formulate these parasocial relationships.

Social media, sports, and crisis communications

Social media have added additional challenges and situations for sport teams that have caused both reputation and financial consequences for sport organizations and athletes. In addition, compared to having a designated spokesperson

conveying key points about a crisis, as traditional crisis communications practices have promoted, social media allows anyone the power and influence to
generate their own messages and interpretations about the crisis situation to
others who are actively engaged online. As Gruber, Smerek, Thomas-Hunt,
and James (2015) stated:

> social media has accelerated the speed at which information is shared,
> amplified the reach of messages, and solidified the ability of disparate
> individuals to organize. Some crises originate on social media, while others
> start offline and are brought to social media only if they are otherwise not
> resolved.
>
> (p. 2)

Twitter is arguably one of the most power social media tools for real-time
communication and updates in crisis situations (Cameron, & Geidner, 2014;
Sanderson, & Hambrick, 2012).

Many scholars have studied crisis communication, and most have observed
that the "apology strategy had the strongest positive effect on perceptions of an
organization's reputation" (Coombs & Holladay, 2008, p. 253). Benoit's (1995,
1997) image restoration theory (IRT) classifies the apology message strategy as
mortification. Some scholars make a distinction between the conceptual definitions of apology and apologia. Hearit (1994) states that "an 'apologia' is not
an apology (although it may contain one), but rather a defense that seeks to
present a compelling, counter description of organizational actions" (p. 115).

There have been several cases exploring crises involving professional athletes
using image restoration theory. Hambrick, Frederick, and Sanderson (in press)
explored how Lance Armstrong used image repair across both traditional and
social media. They observed that while Armstrong used similar strategies on
both platforms, he failed to engage fans on social media after admitting to using
performance-enhancing drugs (PEDs). The authors observed that many fans
conveyed support for Armstrong after this admission, and posited that Armstrong missed an opportunity to strengthen their fandom through dialogue.
Holdener and Kauffman (2014) explored Michael Vick's use of image repair
after a dog-fighting conviction and evaluated how he used specific strategies to
help improve his reputation. They found that Vick used the correct message
strategies, but did not optimize them (Holdener, & Kauffman, 2014). One
strategy however that did work was the relationship Vick created after the dog
fighting incident with the Humane Society.

Bentley (2014) discussed the rise of pseudo-apologies first discussed by Lazare
(2004), which focuses on the incomplete and vague acknowledgement of
the situation, questioning whether the victim was damaged, minimizing the
offense, and using the empathic "I'm sorry." Apologies allow users to implement
these measures to gain forgiveness and to repair their images to try to get their
reputation back into good standing with key audiences. If apologies are committed in public or in a public forum, these specific situations have

consequences to those involved and could bring forth new issues and challenges (Bentley, 2014). Effective apologies are timed carefully and tailored to the crisis situation and relevant audiences. By issuing an apology to the media, stakeholders, and other groups, an organization can focus attention on the crisis as a public relations issue rather than a systemic organizational flaw (Hearit, 2005). Whereas apology can be an effective message strategy for sport teams, with the advent of social media, regardless of the messages that are disseminated to manage crisis, fans and other audience members have a mechanism to intervene in these narratives.

Social media and crises: issues and challenges

There are particular issues and challenges that arise when implementing social media in crisis situations. This is exemplified through using social media (e.g., Twitter) as an official media source for information. In its lifetime, Twitter has been the primary platform for sharing real-time updates regarding news events (e.g., 2012 and 2014 U.S. Elections), entertainment and sports events (e.g., Super Bowl and Academy Awards), crises (e.g., Boston Bombing and 2015 Paris Attacks), as well as press conferences, statements from key spokespeople, and conversations. Users also can participate in chat sessions surrounding particular common interests and topics by following a hashtag.

Many organizations attempt to control their message by stating publicly that employee messages do not reflect the organizations' values and mission statements (Myers, 2014). However, making these statements and exerting such controls have complex legal implications. Media users like journalists, bloggers, and others use social media as resources for stories rather than taking statements from an official spokesperson in a crisis response (Wigley, & Fontenot, 2011). Reputations (brands and individuals) are at risk with regards to engagement during crises on social media as well (Ott, & Theunissen, 2015). Social media has transformed how messages are being sent and the overall pace of updates and dialogue has increased not only in scope, but also in impact (Ott, & Theunissen, 2015).

The second challenge facing brands and sports teams when it comes to social media use in a crisis is when users take over the conversation and disrupt the narrative. Brown and Billings (2014) explored how University of Miami fans utilized Twitter in response to news of National Collegiate Athletic Association (NCAA) violations against the school. Twitter essentially allows one user's post to start a dialogue and for brands to directly engage with audiences about topics related to the brand community (Kim, Sung, & Kang, 2014). People follow certain brands based on relationship norms and when there are violations against those norms, this impacts their overall perception and view of the brand (Li, & Li, 2014). Via social media, critics and individuals who are part of a community can fuel the crisis to become bigger than originally projected, which in some cases, can elevate the crisis (Ott, & Theunissen, 2015).

Method

Data collection

Data consisted of tweets mentioning the Ravens Twitter account (@Ravens). The Radian6 software program was utilized to cull tweets. Radian6 is social media tracking software that enables users to search publicly available social media posts within defined time parameters for user-defined search terms. Given that the Ravens made the decision to live-tweet Rice's press conference, selecting their Twitter account as the search term was deemed appropriate for this study. This decision was also informed by the high presence of sport consumption that occurs on Twitter (Hull & Lewis, 2014; Sanderson & Truax, 2014). Utilizing the Radian6 software, we searched for "@Ravens" for a 48-hour period beginning with the date of the press conference – May 23, 2014 – and ending on May 25, 2014. This resulted in 4,070 tweets. We then elected to remove "as is" re-tweets from the data (e.g., when a Twitter user disseminates another Twitter user's message to his/her followers without any commentary). "As-is" re-tweets are a complex social signal (Freelon, 2014) and their meaning can range from simple information dissemination (Highfield, Harrington, & Bruns, 2013; Meraz & Papacharissi, 2013) to serving as an indicator that one is "listening" to a social conversation (boyd, Golder, & Lotan, 2010). The ambiguity surrounding "as-is" re-tweets coupled with the interpretive design of our study informed this decision. However, if the re-tweet included user commentary, we included it in the sample. There were a total of 2,842 re-tweets, leaving a final sample of 1,228 tweets.

Data analysis

To understand how people were participating in the Ravens public relations narrative, a thematic analysis of the tweets was conducted using constant comparative methodology (Glaser, & Strauss, 1967). Each tweet served as the unit of analysis. First, both authors independently immersed themselves in the data. Braun and Clarke (2006) observed that this process allows researchers to identify meanings and patterns that emerge, to make notes about what is interesting and compelling in the data, and to generate initial categories, rather than just casually reading through the data. Braun and Clarke (2006) noted that this process can be driven by theory or data and we took a data-driven approach, allowing categories to emerge as data analysis unfolded rather than *a priori* (Kassing & Sanderson, 2009). Next, each researcher independently coded 25% of the tweets ($n = 307$) developing themes by micro-analyzing them and classifying them into emergent categories (Sanderson & Emmons, 2014; Strauss & Corbin, 1998) based on the ways that audience members were co-constructing and responding to the Ravens public relations narrative. Tweets that appeared to involve more than one type of response were placed into the category that was thought to identify the most dominant theme. Development, clarification, and refinement of categories continued until new observations did not add substantively to existing categories (Suter, Bergen, Daas, & Durham, 2006).

Both authors then met and reviewed the categories and differences were resolved until they reached consensus. After reaching agreement on the categories, both authors used these themes as a template for the remaining tweets, which were divided equally and analyzed. After completing this analysis, both authors again reviewed the themes and agreed that the remaining tweets could be categorized into one of the previously established themes. During coding it was discovered that 95 tweets were not relevant to the study (e.g., spam, conversing with another Twitter user on a subject not related to the Ravens). These were removed leaving a final sample of 1,133 tweets.

Results and interpretation

Through the data analytic procedure described above, four categories emerged: (a) criticizing the Ravens organization / disrupting the Ravens narrative; (b) criticizing the Ravens PR team; (c) voicing empowered advocacy; and (d) supporting the Ravens organization. Tweets are reported verbatim from the data and spelling and grammatical errors are left intact. For ease of reading, for tweets that contained URL's within them we use the notation [link].

Criticizing the Ravens organization / disrupting the Ravens narrative

The most prominent theme in the data was critiques leveled at the Ravens organization ($n = 959$). This consisted of expressions of general contempt, "@Ravens Disgusted with the Ravens and Ray Rice!"; "From a team with ZERO CLASS RT @Ravens: Ray Rice apologizes, says he failed. Full Story [Link]"; and "Weren't quite disgusted with Ray Rice beating his wife? How about his wife apologizing for it? Good job, @Ravens!" Some audience members used sarcasm to lambaste the Ravens, "@Ravens what is Ray Rice's 40 yard 'drag an unconscious woman out of an elevator time?"; "Rice sub-tweeting his wife RT @Ravens: Ray Rice: 'I won't call myself a failure. Failure is not getting knocked down. It's not getting up"; "Congrats to the @Ravens and Ray Rice for setting back women's rights 50+ years. Only thing missing was a stabbing joke. [link]"; and "Sometimes jokes write themselves. MT @ Ravens: Ray Rice: I won't call myself a failure. Failure is not getting knocked down. It's not getting up."

Although these general critiques were problematic, they paled in comparison to statements from audience members that insinuated that the Ravens were endorsing domestic violence. For example, "@Ravens you and this post is EVERYTHING that's wrong with the NFL. This woman was beaten and knocked out. FUCK YOU RAY RICE FUCK YOU RAVENS"; "@nflcommish you may want to talk to the @Ravens their handling of Ray Rice abuse might lead some to think they condone domestic violence"; "@Ravens please stop talking about Ray Rice and him beating up his wife.

Move on already. You guys have done a disservice to women"; and "Janay Rice gets one-punched by Ravens RB Ray Rice and she regrets her role? Welcome to the 16th century @Ravens." Still others contended Janay Rice's comments about being apologetic for her role in the incident were evidence of the Ravens perpetuating problematic ideology about victim-blaming. Examples here included, "Fuck Ray Rice and fuck the @Ravens for taking part in his victim blaming horseshit"; "@Ravens, stop victim blaming and hold Ray Rice accountable. He is a disgrace to sports because of his actions"; and "@nfl @Ravens Ray Rice blames the female that he knocked out. NFL and ravens silent again on domestic violence." One individual summed up these perceptions by suggesting the Ravens sole interest was profit, "@Ravens Shorter Ravens: Just forget about this beating thing and go buy a Ray Rice jersey already."

Audience members essentially used Rice's words against him to counter the PR narrative that Rice and the Ravens were remorseful about the incident. Specifically, people interjected commentary that positioned Rice's remarks in the press conference as disingenuous. For some, this involved expressing shock and disbelief at Rice's statements. For instance, "@Ravens: Ray Rice: 'I won't call myself a failure. Failure is not getting knocked down. It's not getting up. RT For the love of god"; "Ravens: Ray Rice: 'I won't call myself a failure. Failure is not getting knocked down. It's not getting up. RT Nice choice of words there"; and "Ravens: Ray Rice: 'I won't call myself a failure. Failure is not getting knocked down. It's not getting up'. RT Word choice... ***cringe***." Others played on the circumstances of the incident to counter Rice's assertions that he was contrite. These sentiments were typified by tweets such as, "@Ravens: Ray Rice says 'no relationship is perfect' and says counseling has helped he and his wife' RT When in doubt uppercut her ass"; "@Ravens: Ray Rice: 'I won't call myself a failure. Failure is getting knocked down and not getting up.' RT So his wife is a failure"; "It's the dragging afterward and the surveillance. MT @Ravens: 'Ray Rice: 'I won't call myself a failure. Failure is not getting knocked down'"; and "By being a punching bag? RT @Ravens: Ray Rice said he is working to become a better role model. Thanks his wife for helping him." Finally, some individuals altered the narrative of Rice's rehabilitation by asserting that his transgression was indicative of larger character flaws. For example, "You are a failure "RT @Ravens: Ray Rice: 'I won't call myself a failure. Failure is not getting knocked down. It's not getting up'"; "You're a woman beater sir @RayRice27 RT @Ravens: Ray Rice: 'I won't call myself a failure. Failure is not...'"; "To dudes who punch tiny women real hard RT @Ravens: Ray Rice said he is working everyday to become a better role model"; and "To the penthouse to beat up more women RT @Ravens: Ray Rice: 'I m working my way back up."

Criticizing the Ravens PR team

Some people directed scorn towards the Ravens public relations team and social media personnel, questioning the decision-making process that accompanied the decision to live-tweet Rice's press conference (n = 134). In some instances this involved sarcasm, "Maybe the stupidest tweet ever? @Ravens Ray Rice: 'I won't call myself a failure. Failure is getting knocked down. It's not getting up'"; "So I guess Ray Rice runs this account? RT @Ravens: Janay Rice deeply regrets the role she played the night of the incident"; as well as shock and contempt, "@Ravens OMG you actually tweeted this Baltimore? Your team and Ray Rice are rightly being crucified in the media. Your franchise is dogshit"; and "@Ravens who's running your twitter account today? You got to be kidding us with the ray rice quotes. Any self-awareness?!?!" In other cases, audience members offered scathing critiques such as, "Oh man @Ravens you live tweeting the ray rice conference was horrible. You're making ray look like the victim WHEN HE TKO'D HIS FIANCE."

Given these condemnations, it was not surprising that individuals contended that from a public relations perspective, the Ravens should have known better than to tweet the press conference: "This week's PR fail goes to the folks @Ravens who are live tweeting the Ray Rice press conference. What are you thinking?"; "There are a lot of dumb people out there, but the PR disaster that is Ray Rice and the @Ravens is pretty spectacular. #Clowns"; and "I am a couple of days behind, but looking back, I have seen few PR disasters as bad as the @Ravens live-tweeting Ray Rice's presser. Wow..." Accordingly, people concluded (perhaps sarcastically) that there were tangible action steps that needed to be taken, "Honestly not sure who the @Ravens should fire first: Ray Rice or their social media coordinator"; "@Ravens haven't tweeted anything in half a hour. Probably scrambling to hire a new PR guy. The Ray Rice conference was a disaster"; and "@Ravens who did you fire first? The moron who runs @Ravens twitter feed or the idiot who thought Ray Rice press conf was a good idea?"

Voicing empowered advocacy

Although smaller in frequency (n = 25) some participants communicated empowered advocacy. These expressions served to let the Ravens know that there would be tangible fallout from their public relations efforts. Participants conveyed sentiments such as, "i was gonna root for the @Ravens after drafting Timmy & Brooks but now im too disgusted. yall gonna let Ray Rice play after all that? Srsly?"; "@Ravens Completely appalled at your tweets today dealing with Ray Rice. Will boycott all Ravens games and merch. Domestic violence no joke"; "As a @Ravens fan, I say that Ray Rice conference was damn near unwatchable. If they had any guts, they would cut him from the team"; and "I stopped buying @Ravens gear last season after we gave @AnquanBoldin away. If what I just heard re: Ray Rice mess is true, im glad #done." Still other messages sought to expand the reach of the Ravens public relations missteps by notifying others (including prominent sport media personalities). For instance, "If you didn't hate the @Ravens already, go read their TL recap of the press conference sugar-coating Ray Rice's beating of his fiancé"; "Please read the

@Ravens tweet coverage of today's Ray Rice press conference and try not to be enraged. @RealMichaekKay @DonLagreca"; and "@mikefreemanNFL what is your opinion of the @Ravens extensive coverage on Twitter of Ray Rice's press conference?"

Supporting the Ravens

Although the vast majority of audience comments were negative and implicated the Ravens in being complicit in condoning domestic violence, there were some individuals who expressed support for the Ravens and Ray Rice (*n* = 15). These included comments such as. "Happy Friday to you Ray Rice and your Loving Family. Thank you for Keeping the Faith. We Still Love You! GO @Ravens! Peace Out!"; "I know he messed up…but he is still the ray rice I've grown to love @RayRice27 @Ravens [link]"; and "Pray for Ray Rice #baltimorestrong @Ravens." Yet these also involved admonitions for fans to support the team and move on from the incident, "@Ravens instead of judging Ray Rice and his wife, fans should try maybe SUPPORTING their recovery. You know, just a thought"; and "@Ravens Ray Rice, don't let this incident define u r, u apologized, move 4ward & do what you're gifted 2 do, play football #StandTall."

Discussion

Several research and applied practices for sports and public relations communicators arose with this particular case. The press conference was not only public, but with the PR and social media team live-tweeting some of the Rice statements verbatim, it ignited the crisis to another level on social media. While the PR team had good intentions to create transparency by live-tweeting the press conference, this may not have been the best strategy for this incident. The audience members felt they had a strong relationship and connection with the Ravens on this situation, evident in the "give and take" exchange of information on Twitter during the press conference. There were several fans who advocated for organizational consequences and disrupted the narrative, which is another point of consideration for social media community managers and PR professionals for brands and sports teams in the future. Proper education and training and simulation exercises to prepare for listening and monitoring these conversations and formulating identities for sport communities may be another strategy for sports teams to consider in preparing for crises emerging on social media in the future.

Moreover, the audience reaction indicates that public relations personnel need to be mindful of the larger public perception on social issues when determining how the organization will respond to crisis. In this case, the National Football League has come under criticism for appearing "soft" on domestic violence issues (Pennington & Eder, 2014; Ryman, 2014), and while it is unclear to what extent the Ravens accounted for this sentiment, the overwhelming criticism towards the Ravens generally and the public relations team specifically, suggest that this outcome was not altogether surprising. The large volume of criticism and pushback also suggest that perhaps there should have been no press conference at all, and perhaps, a written statement could have more closely vetted the unfortunate vocabulary used by Rice (although admittedly, he could have been speaking from a prepared statement). At a minimum, when Rice did use words such as "getting knocked down" and "getting back up," discretion in not tweeting these statements verbatim may have helped stem the negativity and criticism the Ravens experienced. Instead, by live-tweeting such remarks, the crisis became more pronounced and enflamed, particularly as individuals expressed that the Ravens were condoning domestic violence.

This case also illustrates the rise in fan resistance to actions and behaviors taken by a sports team and how they use social media to take control of the narrative. Accordingly, fans and in fact, other members of the public, are no longer passive bystanders who idly sit by and accept the narrative distributed by a sports team. Certainly these individuals had mechanisms in the past to voice dissent (e.g., letters to the editor of a sports section, sports-talk radio); however, via Twitter audience members can actively disrupt organizational narratives and promulgate critiques of the organization. This becomes particularly problematic when the organizational Twitter account serves as the initiator for this behavior. Given the high following that many sport organizations possess on Twitter, when an attempt to manage crisis via this venue occurs, fan resistance can quickly develop as participation is available to all audience members, which conveniently mobilizes fan resistance.

Thus, for organizations, particularly those who employ high-profile individuals such as sports organizations, the proverbial statement "discretion is the better part of valor" may be a necessary public relations practice. In this case, while the Ravens were arguably trying to be transparent by disseminating Rice's apology directly to the public without filter, the results of these efforts shifted the narrative in an entirely different, and undesirable direction. Chewning (2015) observed that via online media, there are a polyvocality of voices that collectively shape the narrative of crisis. In this case, the Twitter audience was severely displeased with the Ravens and not only expressed censure, but counter-acted the narrative by interjecting their sarcastic commentary into the Ravens reporting of Rice's comments.

The action of audience members in this case is similar to what Wan, Koh, Ong, and Pang (in press) found with social media parody accounts. Specifically, they observed that parody accounts enforced negative perceptions of the organization and hindered their public relations efforts. The results here illustrate that negative perceptions also can manifest as audience members "hijack" organizational tweets and disseminate views that counteract the organization's efforts. Interestingly, in September 2014, video footage surfaced that showed Ray Rice hitting Janay Rice and the Ravens subsequently released Rice and NFL commissioner Roger Goodell suspended him indefinitely. Rice appealed this suspension and is currently cleared to play although as of this writing, has not signed with an NFL team. Rice's current unemployment may be indicative of NFL teams learning from the public reaction the Ravens experienced. This also demonstrates that when audiences perceive a team has violated shared values, it decreases the sports team's reputation and its relationship with communities and fans.

References

Baek, Y. M., Bae, Y., & Jang, H. J. (2013). Social and parasocial relationships on social network sites and their differential relationships with users' psychological well-being. *Cyberpsychology, Behavior and Social Networking*, 16, 512–517.

Benoit, W. L. (1995). *Accounts, excuses, and apologies: A theory of image restoration*. Albany, NY: State University of New York Press.

Benoit, W. L. (1997). Image repair discourse and crisis communication. *Public Relations Review*, 23, 177–186.

Bentley, J. M. (2014) Shifting identification: A theory of apologies and pseudo-apologies. *Public Relations Review*, 41, 22–29.

Bien, L. (2014, November 28). A complete timeline of the Ray Rice assault case. Retrieved from http://www.sbnation.com/nfl/2014/5/23/5744964/ray-rice-arrest-assault-statement-apology-ravens.

boyd, d., Golder, S., & Lotan, G. (2010, January). Tweet, tweet, retweet: Conversational aspects of retweeting on Twitter. Paper presented at the meeting of Hawaii International Conference on System Sciences, Kauai, HI.

Braun, V., & Clarke, V. (2006). Using thematic analysis in psychology. *Qualitative Research in Psychology*, 3, 77–101.

Brown, N. A., & Billings, A. C. (2014). Sports fans as crisis communicators on social media websites. *Public Relations Review*, 39, 74–81.

Burke, C. (2014, May 23). Ray Rice apologizes for altercation with wife in controversial press conference. Retrieved from http://www.si.com/nfl/audibles/2014/05/23/ray-rice-apology-aggravated-assault-wife-janay-palmer.

Cameron, J., & Geidner, N. (2014). Something old, something new, something borrowed from something blue: Experiments on dual viewing TV and Twitter. *Journal of Broadcasting & Electronic Media*, 58, 400–419.

Chewning, L. V. (2015). Multiple voices and multiple media: Co-construction BP's crisis response. *Public Relations Review*, 41, 72–79.

Coombs, W. T., & Holladay, S. J. (2008). Comparing apology to equivalent crisis response strategies: Clarifying apology's role and value in crisis communication. *Public Relations Review*, 34, 252–257.

Coombs, W. T., & Holladay, S. J. (in press). Public relations' "relationship identity" in research: Enlightenment or illusion. *Public Relations Review*.

DiStaso, M. W., Vafeiadis, M., & Amaral, C. (in press). Managing a health crisis on Facebook: How the response strategies of apology, sympathy, and information influence public relations. *Public Relations Review*.

Duhe, S. (in press). An overview of new media research in public relations journals from 1981 to 2014. *Public Relations Review*.

Freelon, D. (2014). On the interpretation of digital trace data in communication and social computing research. *Journal of Broadcasting & Electronic Media*, 58, 59–75.

Glaser, B., & Strauss, A. (1967). *The discovery of grounded theory.* Hawthorne, NY: Aldine.

Gruber, D. A., Smerek, R. E., Thomas-Hunt, M. C., & James, E. H. (2015). The real-time power of Twitter: Crisis management and leadership in an age of social media. *Business Horizons,* 58, 163–172.

Hambrick, M. E., Frederick, E., & Sanderson, J. (in press). From yellow to blue: Exploring Lance Armstrong's image repair strategies across traditional and social media. *Communication and Sport.*

Hearit, K. M. (1994). Apologies and public relations crises at Chrysler, Toshiba, and Volvo. *Public Relations Review,* 20, 113–125.

Hearit, K. (2005). *Crisis management by apology: Corporate response to allegations of wrongdoing.* New York: Routledge.

Highfield, T., Harrington, S., & Bruns, A. (2013). Twitter as a technology for audiencing and fandom. The #Eurovision phenomenon. *Information, Communication & Society,* 16, 315–339.

Holdener, M., & Kauffman, J. (2014). Getting out of the doghouse: The image repair strategies of Michael Vick. *Public Relations Review,* 40, 92–99.

Horton, D., & Wohl, R. R. (1956). Mass communication and para-social interaction. *Psychiatry,* 19, 215–229.

Hull, K., & Lewis, N. P. (2014). Why Twitter displaces broadcast sports media: A model. *International Journal of Sport Communication,* 7, 16–33.

Kassing, J. W., & Sanderson, J. (2009). "You are the kind of guy that we all want for a drinking buddy": Expressions of parasocial interaction on Floydlandis.com. *Western Journal of Communication,* 73, 182–203.

Kent, M. L., & Taylor, M. (1998). Building dialogic relationships through the world wide web. *Public Relations Review,* 24, 321–334.

Kim, E., Sung, Y., & Kang, H. (2014). Brand followers' retweeting behavior on Twitter: How brand relationships influence brand electronic word-of-mouth. *Computers in Human Behavior,* 37, 18–25.

Lazare, A. (2004). *On apology.* New York: Oxford University Press.

Li, Z., & Li. C. (2014). Twitter as a social actor: How consumers evaluate brands differently on Twitter based on relationship norms. *Computers in Human Behavior,* 39, 187–196.

Meraz, S., & Papacharissi, Z. (2013). Networked gatekeeping and networked framing on #Egypt. *The International Journal of Press/Politics,* 18, 138–166.

Myers, C. (2014). The new water cooler: Implications for practitioners concerning the NLRB's stance on social media and workers' rights. *Public Relations Review,* 40, 547–555.

Ott, L., & Theunissen, P. (2015). Reputations at risk: Engagement during social media crises. *Public Relations Review,* 41, 97–102.

Pennington, B., & Eder, S. (2014, September 19). In domestic violence cases, N.F.L. has history of lenience. Retrieved from http://www.nytimes.com/2014/09/20/sports/football/in-domestic-violence-cases-nfl-has-a-history-of-lenience.html?_r=0.

Pew Research Center. (2015, January 9). Social media update 2014. Retrieved from http://www.pewinternet.org/2015/01/09/social-media-update-2014/.

Ryman, N. (2014, August 28). NFL cracks down on domestic violence after criticism. Retrieved from http://time.com/3210313/nfl-domestic-violence-ray-rice/.

Sanderson, J. (2011). *It's a whole new ballgame: How social media is changing sports.* New York: Hampton Press.

Sanderson, J., & Emmons, B. (2014). Extending and withholding forgiveness to Josh Hamilton: Exploring forgiveness within parasocial interaction. *Communication and Sport,* 2, 24–47.

Sanderson, J., & Hambrick, M. E. (2012). Covering the scandal in 140 characters: A case study of Twitter's role in coverage of the Penn State saga. *International Journal of Sport Communication, 5,* 384–402.

Sanderson, J., & Truax, C. (2014). "I hate you man!": Exploring maladaptive parasocial interaction expressions to college athletes via Twitter. *Journal of Issues in Intercollegiate Athletics, 7,* 333–351.

Strauss, A., & Corbin, J. (1998). *Basics of qualitative research: Techniques and procedures for developing grounded theory* (2nd ed.). Thousand Oaks, CA: Sage.

Suter, E. A., Bergen, K. M., Daas, K. L., & Durham, W. T. (2006). Lesbian couples management of public–private dialectical contradictions. *Journal of Social and Personal Relationships, 23,* 349–365.

Van Bibber, R. (2014, May 23). Ray Rice is an asshole and the Ravens couldn't care less. Retrieved from http://www.sbnation.com/nfl/2014/5/23/5745888/ray-rice-wife-apology-assault-domestic-violence-ravens.

Wan, S., Koh, R., Ong, A., & Pang, A. (in press). Parody social media accounts: Influence and impact on organizations during crisis. *Public Relations Review.*

Wigley, S., & Fontenot, M. (2011). The Giffords shootings in Tucson: Exploring citizen-generated versus news media content in crisis management. *Public Relations Review, 37,* 337–344.

Yoder, M. (2014, May 23). It was not a good idea for the Ravens to live tweet Ray Rice's press conference. Retrieved from http://awfulannouncing.com/2014/it-was-not-a-good-idea-for-the-ravens-to-live-tweet-ray-rices-press-conference.html.

Index

Printed in the United States
by Baker & Taylor Publisher Services